Canadian Securities EXAM

FAST-TRACK STUDY GUIDE

Fourth Edition

Sean Cleary Ph.D., CFA

WILEY

For general information about our other products and services, please contact our Customer Care Department within the United States at (800) 762–2974, outside the United States at (317) 572–3993 or fax (317) 572–4002.

Wiley publishes in a variety of print and electronic formats and by print-on-demand. Some material included with standard print versions of this book may not be included in e-books or in print-on-demand. If this book refers to media such as a CD or DVD that is not included in the version you purchased, you may download this material at http://booksupport.wiley.com. For more information about Wiley products, visit www.wiley.com.

Library and Archives Canada Cataloguing in Publication Data

Cleary, W. Sean (William Sean), 1962–, author
Canadian securities exam fast-track study guide / W. Sean Cleary. — 4th edition.
ISBN 978-1-118-60568-4 (pbk); 978-1-118-62958-1 (ebk); 978-1-118-62964-2 (ebk); 978-1-118-62967-3 (ebk)
1. Securities—Canada—Examinations—Study guides. 2. Investments—Canada—Examinations—Study guides. I. Title.
HG4514.C54 2013 332.63'20971 C2013-902329-1

Production Credits
Acquiring Editor: Karen Milner
Managing Editor: Alison Maclean
Production Editor: Lindsay Humphreys
Cover design: David Riedy
Composition: Laserwords
Printer: Courier Printing Corporation

John Wiley & Sons Canada, Ltd.
6045 Freemont Blvd.
Mississauga, Ontario
L5R 4J3

Printed in the United States

1 2 3 4 5 CR 17 16 15 14 13

TABLE OF CONTENTS

Withdrawn from Collection

ACKNOWLEDGEMENTS

I would like to thank my wife, Grace, my children, Jason, Brennan, Brigid, and Siobhan, and my parents, Bill and Beryl, for their support. I would also like to acknowledge the support and direction provided by the Wiley editorial team, with special acknowledgement to Karen Milner and Lindsay Humphreys.

INTRODUCTION

HOW TO USE THIS BOOK

This text is designed primarily for students who are enrolled in the Canadian Securities Course (CSC)™ through CSI Global Education Inc. and who are in their final stages of preparing to write either of their two CSC exams. CSI Global Education Inc. does not in any way endorse this product.

One of the most common concerns expressed by my past CSC students has been the abundance of material they need to know (and understand) for the day of the examination. This concern has been alleviated to a certain extent by the reorganization of the CSC, which has resulted in two exams covering approximately half of the course material each. However, there is still a lot of material covered in each of the exams, and it is a daunting task to assimilate such a wide body of knowledge. In fact, many students have been overwhelmed by this task and have performed below their capabilities as a result of the stress.

This study guide has been conceived and designed in order to help students avoid this problem, and focus on doing their best on the exam. It should be treated as a companion to the CSI materials, not a substitute. It is designed to help students review, digest, and prioritize the vast amount of material they should know. In other words, it provides "quick hits" of the information that's deemed to be need-to-know in order to do well on the CSC exams.

The focus of this study guide is the review, in abbreviated format, of material that has already been covered previously by students, and to provide them with the essential materials required to **pass the exams.**[1]

With this focus in mind, the text includes the following features:

1. The main body of the text provides a clear, succinct summary of the most important topics covered in the CSC textbooks.
2. Within the chapter summaries, high-priority topics will be noted for students, as indicated by a shaded vertical rule with an exclamation mark.
3. Each chapter includes a number of multiple-choice questions relating to the material in the chapter. The amount of core questions corresponds to the suggested guidelines by CSI Global Education Inc. regarding the number of questions per chapter to be included on CSC exams. These guidelines are listed below, and students should keep them in mind as they devote their time and energies to covering the materials included in the course. In other words, **spend the greatest percentage of your study time reviewing the chapters that will cover materials relating to the largest number of exam questions.** To further help you prepare, and for additional practice, I've included a second set of questions (bonus questions) for each chapter.

[1]This study guide does not serve as a substitute for reading all of the materials covered in the CSC textbooks, but it does provide an excellent summary of the most important concepts covered therein.

4. Two practice examinations that cover similar materials to those included on each of the CSC exams, along with detailed solutions, have been included. Just like the actual CSC exams, these sample exams consist of 100 multiple-choice questions each. In addition, the questions per chapter fall within the CSI-recommended guidelines. Each practice exam should be completed after the students have reviewed all the relevant materials and feel they are *almost* ready to write that particular exam. The exams serve two purposes:
   - They provide feedback regarding areas of strength or weakness.
   - They help students become more comfortable with the format of the actual CSC exams.

   However, students should be aware that the actual exams may vary substantially from these practice exams, since the CSI makes a conscious effort to change the actual CSC exams on a regular basis.

CSI GLOBAL EDUCATION INC. EXAM QUESTION GUIDELINES

CSI Global Education Inc. has provided the following guidelines to students regarding the approximate number of questions that will be included on the exams. While these guidelines are useful in assessing the relative importance of topics, the actual number of questions relating to a particular chapter may vary slightly from one exam to the next.

EXAM # 1 (CHAPTERS 1–12)

Chapter	Number of Questions
1–3	15
4–5	14
6	12
7	11
8	13
9	10
10	10
11	7
12	8
Total	**100**

EXAM # 2 (CHAPTERS 13–27)

Chapter	Number of Questions
13	12
14	11
15	12
16	12
17, 22–24	14
18 and 19	15
20 and 21	9
25	7
26	5
27	3
Total	**100**

STUDY SUGGESTIONS

- The CSC exams are 2 hours in length each and consist of **100 multiple-choice questions (1.2 minutes per question)**. They have no essay questions and are designed to test general understanding of a variety of concepts, as well as knowledge of various specific points. It is recommended that students read over the end-of-chapter questions and practice exams included in this study guide in order to get a flavour for the types of questions and concepts that are normally tested. CSI also provides various options to obtain practice questions on their website at www.csi.ca.
- You need to get **60% or better** to pass each of the exams. This means you have to get 60 questions correct. This also means you can afford to get 40 questions wrong. The message is clear—do not get discouraged when you don't know the answer to one question or even a few questions. Remain positive and continue to work your way through the exam with a positive attitude even if you hit a few trouble spots. Maintaining this attitude is also important for your studying schedule. In other words, don't get discouraged if you don't feel comfortable with all of the material. Do your best and devote your greatest effort to those topics that have the highest likelihood of being on the exam.
- You are not penalized for incorrect answers, so even if you don't know the answer or are not 100% certain, **never leave a question blank!** Often, even if you don't know the answer, you may be able to eliminate one or more answers, thus increasing your odds of making an educated guess.

- Cover the relevant material in the CSC textbooks prior to reviewing the material in this study guide. The glossary in the CSC textbook provides a good summary of the major definitions and terms you should know for the exams.
- During the week prior to your scheduled writing of one of the actual CSC exams, allow yourself sufficient time for a general **review** of all the material. You should not be seeing any materials for the first time during this week. Past experience indicates that leaving yourself adequate time to prepare during the last week is **essential** for passing the exam, since you are required to know a lot of material by the exam date.
- When you have completed reviewing the material, simulate actual exam conditions and try the appropriate sample examination. This will give you a feeling of how well prepared you are, where your strengths and weaknesses are, and how well you must manage your time during the actual exam. Writing practice exams and reviewing the correct answers is a great way of reviewing essential topics and simulating actual exam conditions.
- Get a good night's rest and try not to study complex materials the night before your exam, so that your mind will be fresh. Being well rested is especially important for multiple-choice questions, which generally require a great deal of clarity in thought.
- **GOOD LUCK! BE POSITIVE!**

chapter 1

THE CAPITAL MARKET

CSC EXAM SUGGESTED GUIDELINES:
15 questions combined for Chapters 1–3

INTRODUCTION

The vital function served by financial markets is the transfer of wealth from those who have extra wealth to those who need capital. In other words, *financial markets drive economic growth by transforming savings into investments.*

- The three components of this process of wealth transfer are
  1. financial instruments;
  2. financial markets; and
  3. financial intermediaries.

SUPPLIERS AND USERS OF INVESTMENT CAPITAL

Investment Capital

Capital incorporates the savings of individuals, corporations, governments, and other entities. It is scarce and valuable; however, it is only economically significant when it is properly utilized.

! Capital can be utilized through

1. **direct investment** in real assets that generate wealth directly (e.g., land, buildings, equipment, human capital); or
2. **indirect investment** in financial assets (e.g., stocks, bonds, treasury bills), which allows issuers of these securities to invest funds directly in wealth generating assets.

! Capital is **mobile**, **scarce**, and **sensitive**—efficient allocation promotes economic growth, while inefficient allocation can constrain economic growth. As a result of these characteristics, capital is selective and tends to flow toward attractive economic environments.

- Capital tends to flow into and out of countries in response to several variables, such as
  - the political environment;
  - economic trends;
  - fiscal policy;
  - monetary policy;
  - investment opportunities and risk-return opportunities; and
  - labour force characteristics.
- The availability of capital is critical to any nation. It is necessary to promote economic output, improve productivity, encourage innovations, and improve the competitive position of a nation in general.

Sources of Capital

! **Investors**, both retail and institutional, provide investment capital. Retail refers to investors who invest for their own account, while institutional investors are organizations such as pension funds or mutual funds that buy and sell securities on behalf of the underlying entity—which in turn is set up to serve its plan members, unit holders, etc.

- Individuals represent a significant source of investment capital in Canada.
- Corporations tend to retain a large portion of their earnings to finance operations and growth and are not an important source of capital.
- Canadian governments have generally been net borrowers in recent years to fund their deficits.
- Foreign investment has grown in importance in Canada and has been necessary to fund deficits and growth. The benefit of this fact is that it helps to expand our international trading relationships, while the cost is that this may take long-term cash flows out of the country. It is an issue that will be debated for some time to come.

- Nonresidents can invest in Canada through Canadian firms (which may be located at home or abroad), or through bonds or stocks that are listed on foreign exchanges or over-the-counter markets (such as the NASDAQ stock market in the United States).
- The two main categories of international bond issues are
  1. **foreign bonds:** which are offered and denominated in the currency of a country other than the borrower; and
  2. **Eurobonds:** which may be denominated in one of several currencies and are sold in countries other than the currency in which they are denominated.

Users of Capital

- Individuals use capital primarily for consumption purposes, with the funds usually being obtained through personal loans, mortgage loans, or charge accounts.
- Businesses use capital to finance day-to-day operations, to maintain and upgrade plant and equipment, and to finance growth. A large proportion of funds are financed internally (through reinvested earnings), with the remainder coming from bank loans and through the issue of securities such as money market, bond, and equity instruments.
- Canadian governments have a long history of deficits, a situation that requires them to borrow to finance their expenditures.
- The federal government finances its debt using
  1. treasury bills (T-bills);
  2. marketable short- and long-term bonds (debentures); and
  3. Canada Savings Bonds and Canada Premium Bonds (which can be sold only to Canadian residents).

  T-bills and marketable bonds may be purchased by foreign investors.
- Prior to 1995, the yields on the Government of Canada's debt were generally higher than on U.S. government debt. Since then, our yields have been lower than those in the United States. This change reflects the improved financial position of the federal government in recent years, as the government reduced, then eliminated, its federal budget deficit.
- Provincial governments may issue non-marketable bonds to the federal government or borrow funds from the Canada Pension Plan (CPP) assets (or QPP for Quebec firms). They may also issue marketable bonds, T-bills, or provincial versions of savings bonds.
- Municipal governments borrow to provide local services such as streets, sewers, waterworks, and police and fire protection. They often do so in the form of serial or installment debentures (which will be discussed in Chapter 6).

THE ROLE OF FINANCIAL INSTRUMENTS

- The broad categories of financial instruments available are discussed below, and they are elaborated upon in subsequent chapters. The role of these instruments is to enable the transfer of capital from suppliers to users. The financial markets provide the environment that allows this transfer to take place, as discussed in the section below.

Financial Instruments

These are legal, formal documents that set out the rights and obligations of the parties involved. The major categories are described below.

DEBT

- Represents a legal obligation to repay borrowed funds at a specified maturity date and provide interim interest payments as specified in the agreement.
- Examples include bank loans, commercial paper, treasury bills, mortgages, bonds, debentures, as well as many other instruments.

EQUITY

- Represents part-ownership of a company.
- Common shares usually provide holders with voting privileges, and holders may receive dividends (however, they are not obligatory).
- Preferred shareholders typically receive a fixed dividend amount that must be paid before any dividends are paid to common shareholders.

INVESTMENT FUNDS

- An investment fund is a company that manages investments for its clients. The most common form is the open-end fund, which is known as a mutual fund.

DERIVATIVE PRODUCTS

- Derivatives are so called because they derive their value from the price of another underlying asset, such as a stock, stock or bond index, commodity price, etc.
- They are suitable for hedging or speculative purposes by more sophisticated investors.

OTHER INVESTMENT PRODUCTS

- Income trusts and exchange-traded funds are recent innovations that have become very popular investments. Both trade on stock exchanges, and both will be discussed in later chapters.

PRIVATE EQUITY

- Financing can be equity or debt, or a combination of the two.

- Several types include
  1. leveraged buyouts;
  2. growth capital;
  3. early stage venture capital (VC);
  4. late stage VC; and
  5. distressed debt.
- Higher risks/higher returns for providers—also lower liquidity than typical investments.
- Typical providers include
  - pension plans;
  - endowments;
  - foundations;
  - wealthy individuals/families.

FINANCIAL MARKETS

- The benefits of investment products depend on the existence of efficient markets for buying and selling these instruments. An efficient market should allow for fast and low-cost transactions, and maintain a high degree of liquidity. Obviously, proper regulation of these markets is essential.
- **Primary markets** involve the sale of securities by the issuer to the market for the first time, and money flows to the issuer. They may be in the form of seasoned offerings or initial public offerings (IPOs). **Secondary markets** involve the sale of previously issued securities. No funds go the issuer. Secondary markets facilitate the primary markets by making securities transferable. !
- Financial intermediaries improve the efficiency of markets by facilitating the trading or movement of the financial instruments that transfer capital between suppliers and users (including corporate, government, private, and global entities).
- Examples of financial intermediaries include the Bank of Canada, chartered banks, trust and mortgage companies, credit unions, insurance companies, pension funds, investment dealers/bankers, venture capital firms, mutual funds, leasing companies, sales finance companies, and factors.

Auction Markets (Stock Exchanges)

Auction markets are those where all transactions converge to one location. !

- Canadian stock exchanges have undergone significant changes in recent years. At the start of 1999, there were five stock exchanges in Canada: the Toronto Stock Exchange (TSX—formerly called the TSE), the Montreal Exchange (ME), the Vancouver Stock Exchange (VSE), the Winnipeg Stock Exchange (WSE), and the Alberta Stock Exchange (ASE). A complete overhaul of that structure occurred during 1999 and 2000, and as a result of this restructuring, there are three remaining stock exchanges in Canada—the TSX, the newly created TSX Venture Exchange (which replaced the Canadian Venture Exchange in 2001), and the Canadian National Stock Exchange (CNSX) which gained recognition as a stock exchange in 2004 (as an alternative for emerging companies to the TSX Venture Exchange). The first two exchanges are owned by the TMX Group Inc., which became the first North American exchange (under its previous name the TSX Group Inc.) to become publicly listed, in November 2002. Trading operations for both the TSX and the TSX Venture Exchange are conducted by TSX Markets, also a member of the TMX Group.

- In May 2008, the TSX Group and the ME merged to form the TMX Group.
- Today, the TSX is the official exchange for trading of Canadian senior stocks—big companies with solid histories of profits. The TSX accounts for the majority of both the volume of shares traded in Canada and the dollar value of share trades.
- There are over 80 exchanges in 60 countries, and the TSX was the 8th largest exchange in the world in 2009, based on market capitalization. The New York Stock Exchange is the largest in the world, followed in order by Tokyo, NASDAQ, NYSE Euronext, and London.[1]
- Since March 2000, the Montreal Exchange (or Bourse de Montreal) assumed its role as the Canadian national derivatives market, and now carries on all trading in financial futures and options that previously occurred on the TSX, the ME, and the now-defunct Toronto Futures Exchange.
- The only other Canadian exchange is ICE Futures Canada (formerly the Winnipeg Commodity Exchange), which handles futures trading in commodities and is discussed in Chapter 10 along with the ME.
- Traditionally, exchanges were not-for-profit organizations. Under this arrangement, stock exchange memberships (in the form of stock exchange "seats") are sold to individuals, which permits them to trade on the exchange. These seats are valuable assets that may be sold, subject to certain exchange conditions. However, today most exchanges are "for-profit," and are owned by the shareholders, and firms (called Participating Organizations or Approved Participants) do not have to be owners to have access to exchange trading.
- Member firms must be publicly owned, they must maintain capital adequacy requirements, and key personnel must complete required courses of study.
- Exchanges are governed by bodies that consist of at least one permanent exchange official (e.g., the president), plus members of the board of directors who are selected from member firms, as well as two to six highly qualified public governors appointed or elected from outside the brokerage community.
- Exchanges are financed by transaction fees, initial listing fees, sustaining listing fees, fees paid by companies with respect to capital structure changes, and through the sale of historic and market information.

[1]Source: World Federation of Exchanges (www.world-exchanges.org).

- Over the past decade, several trends have emerged in response to increased global trading and the resulting competition, as well as to the availability of enhanced technology. These include the dominance of electronic trading systems over physical locations, increasing mergers and alliances (the number of exchanges has decreased from over 200 to fewer than 100), and the move to the for-profit corporate structure.
- Future trends expected to continue are the move to for-profit structures, additional mergers, increased focus on niche markets, and easier trading between exchanges.
- Exchanges have the power to suspend the trading or listing privileges of an individual security, either temporarily or permanently.

Dealer Markets: The Unlisted Market

Dealer markets or Over-the-counter (OTC) markets comprise a network of dealers that trade directly with each other over the phone or through a computer network. They are negotiated networks, which maintain bid and ask quotations received from the dealers acting as market makers in given securities. Market makers execute trades from their inventories. !

Almost all bonds and debentures are sold through dealer markets (about 14 times the volume that is conducted for unlisted equities); however, the volume of unlisted equity trading is much smaller than the volume of exchange-traded equity transactions. !

- It is important to note that this market does not set listing requirements.
- Unlisted trades need not be reported except in Ontario, where the Ontario Securities Commission (OSC) requires such trades to be reported on the Canadian Unlisted Board Inc. (CUB) automated system.
- The first Canadian quotation and reporting system, the Canadian Trading and Quotation System Inc. (CNQ), was launched in July 2003. These Quotation and Trade Reporting Systems (QTRS) are stock markets that operate similarly to exchanges—by providing users with the means to post quotations and report trades. They provide an alternative market for small-cap emerging companies, since the requirements to trade on these markets are less stringent than those required to trade on organized exchanges, such as the TSX Venture Exchange. In Canada, it is regulated by the **Investment Industry Regulatory Organization of Canada (IIROC)**.

Alternative Trading Systems

- **Alternative Trading Systems (ATS)** are computerized systems that execute orders outside traditional exchange facilities by matching orders from their own inventory or by matching buy and sell orders from outside parties. Sometimes, they permit buyers and sellers to contact each other directly to negotiate trades. These systems are privately owned, often by individual brokerage firms or groups of firms. Most of their customers are institutional investors, who are able to reduce their transactions costs through the use of such a system. In addition, since these systems can operate when exchanges are closed, they are ideal for the trading of securities on a global basis.

- Concern has mounted over the growth of ATS trading because the details of such trades are not available to the general public, there is the ever-present threat of technological problems, and potential issues can arise from trading across country borders. In response to such concerns, both Canada and the United States have recently introduced legislation to regulate ATS trading activities. Trading activity of Canadian ATS is governed by IIROC.
- Three recently launched **electronic trading systems** handle much of the bond and money market OTC trades in Canada. They are
  1. **CanDeal**: A joint venture among Canada's six largest investment dealers, and a member of IIROC. Handles federal government bonds and plans to expand to provincials, corporate debt, and commercial paper. Handles over 80% of market transactions.
  2. **CBID**: IIROC member and ATS. Maintains retail and institutional market places, dealing with more than 2,500 debt instruments.
  3. **CanPX**: Joint venture of Investment Industry Association of Canada (IIAC) and IIROC member firms. Deals in government bonds and T-bills, and some corporate bonds.

Chapter I Review Questions

( ) 1. Private equity is characterized by:

a) low returns

b) low liquidity

c) low risk

d) many small investors

( ) 2. Which of the following represent a source of capital?

a) individuals

b) businesses

c) governments

d) all of the above

( ) 3. All of the following represent an indirect investment EXCEPT for:

a) the purchase of common shares

b) the purchase of T-bills

c) the purchase of new land
d) all of the above are indirect investments

4. Which of the following exchanges trades all financial and equity futures and options? ( )
a) Toronto Stock Exchange
b) TSX Venture Exchange
c) Bourse de Montreal
d) ICE Futures Canada

5. All of the following are characteristics of a liquid market EXCEPT: ( )
a) frequent sales
b) big price fluctuations from sale to sale
c) narrow price spread between bid and offering prices
d) thousands of orders from all parts of the country and overseas

6. Which of the following are privately owned computerized networks that match orders for securities outside of recognized exchanges? ( )
a) CNQ
b) ATS
c) RS
d) UMIR

Bonus Questions

7. Retail investors: ( )
a) generally trade in large volumes of securities
b) buy and sell securities for another company or organization
c) buy and sell securities for their own personal account
d) are an insignificant source of investment capital in the marketplace

8. Which of the following statements concerning foreign investment is FALSE? ( )
a) Foreign investment generally leads to long-term outflows of interest and dividend payments.
b) Foreign investors only supply capital to the Canadian market, and are not consumers of capital.

c) Over the past 20 years, government policy in Canada has tended to favour the protection of Canadian businesses from foreign investment.

d) Foreign investment is an important source of investment capital.

( ) 9. Canada's stock exchanges are ____________ ____________ markets.

a) physical dealer

b) electronic dealer

c) electronic auction

d) physical auction

( ) 10. If the government estimates its revenue to be $100 and its expenses to be $80 for a given year, then:

a) the budget deficit is $20

b) the national debt is $20

c) the budget surplus is $20

d) the national surplus is $20

( ) 11. Which of the following statements concerning financial markets is true?

a) The ask is the lowest price a seller will accept for a security.

b) The bid is the highest price that a buyer will pay for a security.

c) A liquid market is characterized by a narrow bid-ask spread, frequent sales, and small price changes from sale to sale.

d) All of the above statements are true.

( ) 12. Institutional investors:

a) are organizations that buy and sell securities

b) are government owned and operated on behalf taxpayers

c) are high-risk investment vehicles

d) All of the above are true.

THE CANADIAN SECURITIES INDUSTRY

chapter

2

CSC EXAM SUGGESTED GUIDELINES:

15 questions combined for Chapters 1–3

AN OVERVIEW OF THE CANADIAN SECURITIES INDUSTRY

The Canadian securities industry is regulated provincially through laws and securities commissions. Securities commissions delegate some of their powers to self-regulatory organizations (SROs) that establish and enforce industry regulations. SROs include the TSX, the TSX Venture Exchange, the ME, ICE Futures Canada, IIROC, and the Mutual Fund Dealers Association (MFDA), and are discussed in detail in Chapter 3.

Trades are cleared through organizations such as CDS Clearing and Depository Services Inc., while organizations such as the Canadian Investor Protection Fund (CIPF) provide insurance against member insolvency. Finally, organizations such as CSI Global Education Inc. provide education for industry participants. (All of these organizations will be discussed in greater detail later in this chapter and/or in Chapter 3.)

THE ROLE OF FINANCIAL INTERMEDIARIES

- "**Intermediaries**" facilitate the transfer of capital from suppliers to users. There are several categories of intermediaries, and they tend to focus on different aspects of this process. For example, banks and trust companies accept deposits from their customers (capital suppliers) and lend to capital users. Investment funds, pension funds, and insurance companies use the funds collected from their customers to invest in the financial securities (e.g., bonds, equities) of various users of capital.

Investment dealers serve a number of functions in the capital transformation process, sometimes acting as agents for their clients, and sometimes acting as principals on their own behalf.

THE CANADIAN SECURITIES INDUSTRY

The Securities Industry Today

- Some basic characteristics of the Canadian securities industry include the following:
    1. The dollar value of new issues brought to market exceeded $300 billion in 2009 ($186 billion in government debt, $64 billion in corporate debt, and $52 billion in corporate equity).
    2. The combined trading activity in money, bond, and stock markets exceeded $35 trillion in 2009.
- There were 200 securities firms in Canada as of 2009, employing approximately 39,000 people. While this seems large, it pales in comparison to other sectors of the financial services industry such as banking and insurance. For example, the Royal Bank of Canada alone employed over 70,000 people in 2009. The larger securities firms that are national in scope account for the majority of total industry revenue. Many of the smaller firms are referred to as "investment boutiques," which reflects the fact that they tend to concentrate on one particular segment of the market.
- In addition to traditional full-service brokers, there are currently a large number of discount brokerage firms in Canada that execute trades over the phone or via the Internet. They provide fewer services but offer investors much lower fees, and they are ideal for more knowledgeable investors.
- One might expect a typical large securities firm to be organized into several departments dealing with sales, underwriting/financing, trading, research and portfolio services, and administration. A number of the smaller dealers specialize in areas such as unlisted stock trading, tax-shelter sales, etc. In addition, the major banks have opened discount brokerage services.
- The industry is highly leveraged, and short-term funding is obtained through a variety of arrangements, including
    1. day-to-day loans by chartered banks that are secured by the dealer's inventory of T-bills and short-term Canada bonds;
    2. call loans by banks that are secured by a wide range of securities and must be liquidated within 24 hours after notice has been given;
    3. purchase and resale agreements with the Bank of Canada; and
    4. free credit balances from customer accounts, which represent another source of borrowed funds on which interest must be paid.

- Competition in the securities industry has become fierce as a result of the growth of electronic communications and computerized trading, as well as the increased globalization of world financial markets. This increased globalization of markets is evidenced by several developments, including the following:
    1. The increase in the number of "interlisted" securities, which refers to those that are listed on exchanges in more than one country (e.g., Royal Bank is listed on the TSX and the NYSE).
    2. The linking of most major stock exchanges around the world electronically through exchange trading links.
    3. The extension of trading hours that many exchanges around the world offer, in order to allow responses to global events.
    4. The growth of unregulated markets, such as the Eurobond market.
    5. The large increase in investment mobility, with investors shifting their funds across borders much more often and with fewer difficulties than in the past.

Primary Markets

An important role for investment dealers (IDs) is to bring together those with surplus capital with entities that require investment capital. This function is performed in the **primary** or **new issue market**, where the *IDs may act as principals or agents.*

Underwriting or financing refers to the purchase of new securities from the issuer on a given date at a specified price, which is then to be sold to others. IDs serve as *principals* under this arrangement, and their compensation is the "spread" between the purchase price and the resale price. Under this arrangement, *dealers assume the risk* of the security not selling at adequate prices; however, they take a number of precautions to minimize this risk. Typically, they work closely with the issuers regarding the pricing, timing, and design of the issue so that it will be well received by the market. In addition, *underwriting syndicates* are often formed to spread the financing risk and enhance marketability of the issue. The issue may also include special clauses that may terminate the agreement under exceptional circumstances.

IDs may also perform this function by assuming the role of *agents* who market the newly issued securities on a **"best efforts"** basis. They receive compensation in the form of a commission, and it is *the issuer that assumes the risk* of the issue not selling. This arrangement is more typical for issues of smaller or more speculative companies, or for "private placements" for large companies with good credit ratings (where the risk of the issue not selling is negligible).

Secondary Markets

IDs also serve an important role in **secondary markets**, which facilitate the transfer of existing securities among investors. Secondary markets enhance the effectiveness of the primary market. This function may also be achieved by having **IDs act as principals or agents**.

! IDs serve as *principals* by trading securities with clients from their own inventory, and also when they trade for their own account. They earn income in the form of a "spread" and *assume the majority of the risk.*

! IDs act as "brokers" (or *agents*) when they execute transactions for customers and charge them commissions. Minimum commission rates are no longer prescribed by the exchanges, and commissions may be negotiated between clients and their brokers. This has led to the development of several discount brokerage houses in Canada, which eliminate many traditional services offered by full brokerage firms and pass the savings on to investors in the form of reduced commission fees. They are tailored toward knowledgeable, "do-it-yourself" investors.

- A typical "agency transaction" involves clients instructing their IDs to get the best possible price (i.e., a "market order," to be discussed in Chapter 9). Once the transaction is completed on the floor (or electronically), the details of the trade are reported over the exchange's ticker, and the buying and selling firms are provided specific details of the trade (e.g., price, time, identity of the other party). The firms phone their clients to confirm the transaction, and then mail written confirmation to them that day or the next business day.
- Once the transaction has occurred, the parties must "settle" the transaction. If the buying firm has sufficient funds available in its cash or margin account, these funds will be used to execute the transaction. Otherwise, the buyer must provide sufficient funds by the **settlement date** (three business days after the trade for most securities).

! If the certificate is in registered form, the seller must properly endorse and deliver it. In Canada today, most stock and bond certificates are held by the **Canadian Depository for Securities (CDS)** clearing corporation, which electronically settles all transactions between members on a daily basis without physically moving the certificates. This system is used by the TSX, the Bourse, the TSX Venture Exchange, as well as by participating banks and trust companies.

When an ID trades from its own account, the trade occurs at current market value as determined by the exchange. There are detailed regulations that member firms must observe to avoid potential conflicts of interest.

CHARTERED BANKS

- **Banks** concentrate on gathering funds through savings deposits and/or certificates of deposit (CDs) and transferring them to users in the form of mortgages and other forms of loans. Their primary source of income is the "spread," which is the difference between the rate they pay to depositors and the rate charged to lenders (although service charges have grown as an important source of income in recent years).
- They are governed by the *Bank Act*, which is revised periodically (every 10 years or so).

Schedule I banks must be widely held, with no investor holding more than 20%. While there are currently over 70 banks in Canada, the Schedule I banks dominate Canada's capital market, with the "Big Six" accounting for more than 90% of the $2.9 trillion in bank assets. The Big Six are Royal Bank, Canadian Imperial Bank of Commerce, Bank of Montreal, Scotiabank, TD Canada Trust Bank, and National Bank. They maintain a network of more than 9,000 retail branches and 50,000 automated banking machines and are becoming major international participants.

- Banks are generally funded by savings deposits, retained earnings, periodic rights offerings to existing shareholders, debentures (since the 1967 *Bank Act* revision), and preferred share issues (since the 1980 *Bank Act* revision).
- Since most of their liabilities (i.e., savings deposits) are due on "demand," it is important that they maintain an adequate reserve of liquid assets. This used to be a legal requirement, but it has been removed in recent years.
- Canadian banks generally maintain about 10% to 15% of total assets in liquid assets, 40% in personal and business loans, and 30% in residential mortgages.

Schedule II banks are incorporated and operate in Canada but are subsidiaries of foreign banks or other financial institutions. They may accept deposits, which may be eligible to be insured by the Canada Deposit and Insurance Corporation (CDIC). There were 26 of these operating in Canada in 2010.

Schedule III banks are branches of foreign banks that are permitted to accept deposits and provide loans. They differ from Schedule II banks in that they are not subsidiaries, but merely "branches." There were 29 of these operating in Canada in 2010.

The voting shares of "large" Schedule I banks (equity base greater than $5 billion) must be widely held with control restricted to a maximum of 20% for any individual or group and non-NAFTA shareholders. "Medium-sized" banks ($1–$5 billion) are permitted to have a single owner hold up to 65%, provided the remaining 35% of voting shares is traded publicly. "Small" banks (less than $1 billion) face no ownership restrictions other than the "fit and proper" tests.

- Some of the more significant developments in recent years include the following:
  1. The movement by banks into the securities business (i.e., all of the Big Six have acquired investment dealers in the past few years).
  2. Banks are permitted to offer non-banking financial services such as trust and insurance activities through subsidiaries only.
  3. Banks can directly provide investment counselling and portfolio management services.

"Chinese walls" refer to controls put in place to restrict the flow of information between the various bank business segments.

Recent *Bank Act* revisions permit non-depository institutions such as life insurance companies, securities dealers, and money market mutual funds access to the Payment System, which permits these institutions to offer chequing accounts and debit cards.

OTHER INTERMEDIARIES

Trust and Mortgage Companies

- Many services overlap with those offered by banks, including accepting savings, issuing term deposits, making personal and mortgage loans, and selling RRSPs. They remain distinct in that they are the only type of corporations in Canada permitted to act as trustees in charge of corporate or individual financial assets.

Credit Unions and Caisses Populaires

- These are co-operative, member-owned businesses that provide basic financial services to their members. They must adhere to the "prudent portfolio approach" to investment.

Life Insurance Companies

- Life insurance companies act as trustees for funds they receive from policyholders. Safety of principal is a primary investment objective for these companies. Many of their contracts are long-term, and as a result, insurance companies tend to be active in both mortgage and long-term bond markets.
- Key 1992 federal legislation (the *Insurance Companies Act*) now permits life insurance companies to own trust and loan companies through subsidiaries. It also maintained the practice of allowing only life insurance companies to offer annuities and segregated funds. Life insurance companies are required to follow investment rules based on a "prudent portfolio approach."
- The insurance industry has been undergoing a significant amount of consolidation in recent years, a trend that has been contributed to by **demutualization**. Demutualization refers to the reorganization of the ownership structure of life insurance companies, from being owned by policyholders to being owned by shareholders. This is accomplished by providing the policyholders with the appropriate number of shares to compensate them for the value of their policy holdings. A number of insurance companies are now owned by banks.
- Another significant development for life insurance companies has been the growth in new product offerings, such as segregated funds. These products are similar to mutual funds, and they are discussed in detail in Chapter 20.

Property and Casualty Insurance

- These types of insurance companies provide property, automobile, health, and accident insurance. They are much smaller than life insurance companies; however, their investment decisions are also governed by the "prudent portfolio approach." Liquidity is obviously a primary investment objective, since they must be able to settle claims as they arise.

Investment Funds

- Investment funds may be set up as a corporation or as a trust. The funds then sell their shares (or trust units) to the public and invest the proceeds in portfolios of securities.
- Closed-end funds normally issue shares only at their initial start-up. Occasionally, they may issue shares at other points in time. They invest the proceeds from the issue in a portfolio of securities in order to earn income and capital gains.
- Open-end funds (or mutual funds) issue and redeem shares on a continuous basis, at the fund's net asset value per share (or unit). These funds account for 95% of aggregate funds invested.
- The objectives of investment funds vary significantly, which is reflected in their portfolio composition. (Investment funds are discussed in great detail in Chapters 18 and 19.)

Savings Banks

- Savings banks take deposits but do not offer lending services. Currently, there are two relatively small savings banks operating, one in Ontario and one in Alberta. Their deposits are 100% guaranteed by the province in which they operate.

Pension Plans

- Many employees are members of trusteed company pension plans. Pension contributions are made to a trustee who registers the plan and manages it in accordance with the terms of the plan's trust deed. Typically, the trustee is an independent trust or insurance company.
- The main concerns for these plans focus on safety of principal and income, which results in the plans being large buyers of both government and corporate debt. Since pension benefits typically are paid well into the future, many plans purchase substantial amounts of investment-grade common shares to help protect against inflation. These funds cannot invest more than 20% of their assets in foreign securities.
- Government-operated pension plans (the Canada Pension Plan [CPP] and the Quebec Pension Plan [QPP]) originated in 1965, and membership by employed persons is mandatory. Both funds provide certain disability, death, and widows' and orphans' benefits.

Sales Finance and Consumer Loans

- These companies make direct cash loans to consumers and/or purchase installment sales contracts from retailers and dealers at a discount.

Chapter 2 Review Questions

( ) 1. When investment dealers market a new security offering on a best efforts basis, they are acting as ____________ in the ____________ market.

a) principals; primary

b) agents; primary

c) principals; secondary

d) agents; secondary

( ) 2. What role do insurance companies play for the funds entrusted to them by policyholders?

a) trustees

b) principals

c) agents

d) banks

( ) 3. Which of the following statements about Schedule II banks is FALSE?

a) All deposits are covered by CDIC.

b) Their functionality is not limited compared with Schedule I banks.

c) They are incorporated as provincially regulated foreign bank subsidiaries.

d) They do not derive very much of their revenue from investment banking activity in Canada.

Bonus Questions

( ) 4. Which of the following best describes regulation of the Canadian securities industry?

a) Regulation is undertaken by the federal government.

b) SROs have the power to create and enforce their own laws.

c) Provinces have the power to create and enforce their own laws.

d) The Canadian securities industry is unregulated.

( ) 5. In the underwriting process, who bears the risk of adverse price movements?

a) the issuer

b) the underwriter

c) the end purchaser

d) none of the above

6. Which of the following concerning insurance companies in Canada is FALSE? ( )

   a) Property insurance and life insurance companies are very concerned with safety of principal.
   b) Life insurance companies generally have higher liquidity needs than property insurance companies.
   c) They are governed by the prudent portfolio approach.
   d) Property insurance includes loss of home and automobile.

THE CANADIAN REGULATORY ENVIRONMENT

chapter 3

CSC EXAM SUGGESTED GUIDELINES:
15 questions combined for Chapters 1–3

REGULATORY ORGANIZATIONS

The Office of the Superintendent of Financial Institutions (OSFI)

- The Office of the Superintendent was formed in 1987 by the amalgamation of the Department of Insurance and the Office of the Inspector General of Banks. It regulates and supervises banks; insurance, trust, loan, and pension plans; and co-operative credit associations, which are chartered federally. It also supervises federally regulated pension plans. However, it does not regulate the Canadian securities industry, which is a provincial responsibility.

The Canada Deposit Insurance Corporation (CDIC) is a federal Crown corporation that insures eligible deposits up to $100,000 per depositor in each financial institution (banks, trust companies, and loan companies). Total coverage may exceed $100,000, since this amount applies to "each" of six deposit categories per institution: in one name; jointly in more than one name; in a trust account; in an RRSP; in a RRIF; and in a mortgage tax account.

Insured products include savings and chequing accounts; guaranteed investment certificates (GICs) and other term deposits that mature in less than 5 years; money orders, certified cheques, traveller's cheques, and bank drafts; and accounts that hold realty taxes on mortgaged properties. They do NOT include mutual funds and stocks; GICs and term deposits maturing in more than 5 years; bonds and treasury bills; debentures; and deposits held in foreign currency.

The Provincial Regulators

! Regulation of the securities industry in Canada is a provincial responsibility, which is delegated to securities commissions in most provinces and is handled by appointed securities administrators in others. The provincial regulators work closely with the Canadian Investor Protection Fund and self-regulatory organizations to maintain high standards.

The Canadian Securities Administrators (CSA) was formed recently by Canada's 13 provincial and territory securities regulators. Its mandate is to provide a securities regulatory system that protects investors from unfair, improper, or fraudulent practices and that fosters fair, efficient, and vibrant capital markets.

Quebec created a new provincial regulatory organization, the Autorité des marchés financiers (AMF) in February 2004 to administer the regulatory framework for Quebec's financial sector in areas including insurance, deposit insurance, distribution of financial products, financial services, and securities.

Each province has one or more organizations to insure deposits at credit unions and caisses populaires. For example, the **Credit Union Deposit Insurance Corporation (CUDIC)** provides unlimited coverage for losses on deposits held with credit unions in British Columbia. The coverage limits vary from province to province, being $100,000 in Quebec and Ontario at the time of writing.

The Self-Regulatory Organizations (SROs)

- SROs deal with member regulation, listing requirements, and trading regulation. These include the TSX, the TSX Venture Exchange, the Bourse de Montreal, ICE Futures Canada, as well as the two national SROs—IIROC and the Mutual Fund Dealers Association (MFDA).
- The IIROC oversees all investment dealers and trading activity in Canadian debt and equity markets. It was formed in 2008 by consolidating the Investment Dealers Association of Canada (IDA) and Market Regulation Services Inc. (RS). Its mandate is "to set high-quality regulatory and investment industry standards, protect investors, and strengthen market integrity while maintaining efficient and competitive capital markets."
- IIROC serves as the securities industry regulator. Its responsibilities include monitoring member firms for capital adequacy and business conduct, as well as regulating the qualifying and registration process of these firms. As a national SRO, it has the additional responsibility of ensuring that national policies and rules reflect the various perspectives of people in all parts of the country.

! In its efforts to foster more efficient capital markets, IIROC serves as a market regulator:

1. playing a key role in formulating policies and standards for primary debt and equity markets, and

2. monitoring activities of member firms and developing trading and sales practices for fixed-income markets. !

- IIROC strives to ensure the integrity of the marketplace and protection of investors. This requires that member firms maintain financial standards and conduct their business within appropriate guidelines.

The **Mutual Fund Dealers Association (MFDA)** is committed to establishing a fund similar to the CIPF that is designed to protect mutual fund investors from insolvency of an MFDA member firm. The fund is to be funded by MFDA member firms and provides coverage up to $100,000 per eligible account.

- The MFDA was created in 1997 in response to the need for regulation in this rapidly expanding industry. It is responsible for regulating the distribution of mutual fund securities; however, distributors that were previously members of an SRO, such as the IDA, will continue to be monitored by that SRO. Regulation of the actual funds will remain the responsibility of the securities commissions.

Since 2001, all mutual fund dealers must be MFDA members. As of 2010, the MFDA is recognized as an SRO in all provinces except Newfoundland, Prince Edward Island, and Quebec (where the mutual fund industry is the responsibility of the CSF). However, the regulatory bodies coordinate their efforts to ensure investor protection and avoid duplication of efforts. The **MFDA Investor Protection Corporation (MFDA IPC)** was formed in 2005 and provides coverage for losses of up to $1 million related to losses due to insolvency of one of its members, excluding Quebec.

Canadian Investor Protection Fund (CIPF)

- The CIPF is designed to protect investors from loss due to the insolvency of a member of any of the SROs, which include the IDA and the exchanges. It had $559 million in resources for this purpose in 2009. Since inception in 1969, it has paid out $36 million for 17 member insolvencies.

The role of the CIPF is to anticipate and solve financial difficulties of member firms in order to minimize the risk of insolvency, and to attempt to bring about an orderly wind down of a business if necessary. !

- Fund assets are funded by contributions from the securities industry, as well as an operating line, which is provided by a chartered bank.

From the moment an investor becomes a customer of any of the SROs, the accounts are automatically covered by the Fund. The Fund covers separate accounts for individuals provided they are not held for the same purpose. For example, the accounts of a customer maintaining two personal holding corporation accounts held in the same capacity (e.g., RRSPs, RESPs, Partnerships, or Trusts) would be combined into one. The coverage limit of $1 million applies to losses related to securities holdings and cash balances combined. The Fund does not cover losses that result from changing market values, and rejects claims from parties that are not dealing at arm's length with the insolvent firm, or those whose dealings contributed to the insolvency. !

ARBITRATION

- While SROs are permitted to discipline their members, they cannot award restitution to parties that may have been wronged by a member of an SRO. The injured party would normally be required to go to court to obtain restitution. In response to this, SROs in all provinces have begun offering investors the opportunity to seek compensation through arbitration rather than in court, provided the claim meets certain criteria:
    - Attempts were made to resolve the dispute with the investment dealer.
    - The claim amount does not exceed $100,000.
    - The disputed events must have occurred after certain cut-off dates specific to the province (ranging from January 1, 1992, in B.C.; January 1, 1996, in Quebec; June 30, 1998, in Ontario; June 30, 1999, in the Atlantic provinces; and July 1, 1999, in Alberta, Saskatchewan, and Manitoba).

The **Ombudsman for Banking Services and Investments (OBSI)** provides additional protection for investors. This independent body investigates complaints against financial service providers. Final decisions made by the Ombudsman are not binding on investors or financial services providers; however, no member has failed to follow a recommendation by the OBSI to date.

REGULATION AND INVESTOR PROTECTION

- The securities industry is governed by extensive legislation and regulation that is designed to protect investors and ensure high ethical standards. The details are established by provincial securities regulators, in co-operation with the self-regulatory organizations (SROs) since there is no federal regulatory body in Canada, unlike in the United States, where the **Securities and Exchange Commission (SEC)** regulates the industry on a national basis. However, the **Canadian Securities Administrators (CSA)** continues to issue a number of national policies that are designed to promote consistency in the regulatory environment across Canada. Generally, the provincial securities commissions work closely together to maintain uniform standards. The fundamental principle is to provide potential investors with *full, true, and plain disclosure of all material facts* relating to the securities offered. It must be recognized that no laws are infallible, so investors should follow the general rule: "investigate before you invest, and after."

! The three basic methods used to protect investors are

1. registration of securities dealers and advisors;
2. disclosure of material facts; and
3. enforcement of the laws and policies.

- Sellers of securities or investment advisors (IAs) must be registered. Administrators have the power to grant, suspend, or cancel registration. New investment advisors must pass the CSC course, as well as the Conduct and Practices Handbook for Securities Industry Professionals (CPH) exam. In addition, IAs must
    1. complete a 90-day training course before they can deal with the public;
    2. be subject to a six-month period of supervision by his or her branch manager; and
    3. complete the CSI's Wealth Management Essentials (WME) course within 30 months of becoming a licensed IA (or they may choose to be registered as Investment Representatives, which does not require either of these courses).

Investment representatives (IRs) have similar requirements, except that the training course is 30 days (not 90), and they do not face the 30-month WME requirement.

All investment advisors and securities (member) firms must register in the appropriate jurisdiction(s). This must be done electronically using the National Registration Database (NRD), which replaces the old paper-based system based on the Uniform Application for Registration/Approval. Both parties (individual and member firms) must agree to be bound by the regulations of the governing body. It requires applicants to certify details about their personal and educational background. In addition, members must notify administrators of the termination of an IA (providing reasons if they were dismissed), and applicants must notify administrators of any material changes (including address).

An exception to the registration requirements above for individuals is for Non-Trading Employees, who may be exempt from registration and still be permitted to accept orders, provided they are not primarily involved in sales.

Member firms and IAs are bound by several requirements by the SROs:

1. Know the essential facts about all clients and about every order accepted (i.e., the Know Your Client [KYC] rule).
2. Only accept orders that comply with good business practice.
3. Ensure that recommendations are "suitable" for the client with respect to their objectives, risk tolerance, and personal circumstances.

The first step of complying with these requirements is completion of the New Account Application Form.

IAs and member firms have a **fiduciary obligation** to their clients and must

1. not reveal confidential information;
2. avoid situations where conflicts of interest may arise, and advise clients if any such situations exist;
3. ensure all representations to clients are made honestly and in good faith; and
4. follow the client's instructions.

Failure to comply with these requirements would represent a breach of fiduciary duty.

Every director of a public corporation has a fiduciary duty not to reveal privileged or inside information to outsiders, particularly if it is likely to have an impact in the market price of the corporation's securities.

In addition, IAs have a fiduciary duty when advising clients to advise fully, honestly, and in good faith, and to follow the client's instructions or intentions during investment transactions.

The SROs in Canada include the exchanges, IIROC, and the Mutual Fund Dealers Association (MFDA). They are responsible for ensuring compliance with securities legislation.

Four main areas of member regulation include

1. financial compliance,
2. sales compliance,
3. registration, and
4. enforcement.

Three main areas of market regulation are

1. market surveillance,
2. investigation enforcement, and
3. regulatory/market policy.

IIROC safeguards investor protection by administering, interpreting, and enforcing a common set of trading rules (the Universal Market Integrity Rules) across all markets in Canada. The purpose of these rules is to promote fair and orderly markets.

THE ETHICS OF TRADING

- Ethical trading is critical to the proper functioning of capital markets, since without assurances regarding the behaviour of market participants, it would be hard to attract investors. Unethical practices are punishable by fines, suspensions, expulsion, and/or criminal charges. Unethical conduct includes any omission, conduct, or manner of doing business which, in the opinion of the disciplinary body, is neither in the public interest nor in the interest of the exchange.
- Some examples of unethical practices are
    1. preforming any conduct that deceives the public;
    2. creating false appearances of trades (e.g., fictitious orders);
    3. using price manipulation schemes;
    4. deliberately causing the last sale of the day to be higher than warranted by market conditions (high saling or window dressing);
    5. misleading any board of governors or committee;

6. confirming a transaction that never occurred (bucketing);
7. improperly soliciting orders by phone or otherwise;
8. using high-pressure or other undesirable selling techniques;
9. violating any applicable statutes;
10. attempting to sell a dividend;
11. assuring no risk;
12. taking the opposite side of client trades;
13. rebating commissions; and
14. conducting business that brings the securities business, exchanges, or IDA into disrepute.

- Advisors should know and abide by applicable provincial laws. Regulation prohibits unethical, dishonest, or high-pressure sale tactics such as

  1. calling at residences;
  2. selling to parties in other provinces (or countries) without appropriate authorizations; and
  3. deliberately or recklessly making illegal representations to assist in obtaining a trade (i.e., fraud).

- Securities legislation requires disclosure of periodic financial statements (including management discussion and analysis); insider trading reports; information circulars required in proxy solicitation; an annual information form (AIF); press releases; and material change reports.

!

Security purchasers are provided with the following statutory rights:

1. **Right of Withdrawal**: Within two business days of receipt of prospectus, or if a distribution occurs without the required prospectus;
2. **Right of Rescission**: If the prospectus or other related documents contain a misrepresentation (i.e., an untrue statement or omission of a material fact); and
3. **Right of Action for Damages**: Against the issuer, directors of the issuer, the security seller or underwriter, or any other party (including experts, who are liable only for their statements) who signs a prospectus without exhibiting "due diligence."

Typically there are time limits and maximum liabilities associated with claims for damage. A misrepresentation in a prospectus may also be a criminal offence.

- Senior companies listed on the TSX are required to provide continuous and timely disclosure, including comparative audited annual financial statements within 90 days of fiscal year-end (120 days for companies listed on the TSX Venture Exchange), and comparative unaudited quarterly financial statements within 45 days of the first three fiscal quarters (60 days for TSX Venture Exchange companies).

- Most provinces require management to solicit proxies from shareholders whenever it calls a shareholders' meeting, and to supply such holders with an information circular, including, among other things, whether the proxy is revocable or not; whether the solicitation is made on behalf of management; information on the directors to be elected; remuneration of management; matters to come before the meeting; and any interest of management in such matters. Most shares are registered in "street form," which occurs when they are registered in the name of someone other than the true beneficial holder of the shares (e.g., by a bank or investment dealer) and the nominees must mail the appropriate documentation to the true owners.

TAKEOVERS AND INSIDER TRADING

- Takeover bid legislation is designed to protect the interests of the shareholders of the target company. Provincial legislation requires that takeover bids, which would push the acquiring firm's controlling interest in the target company above 20% of voting securities, must comply with several requirements, including the following:
    1. The bid must be sent to all security holders in that class (or holders of convertibles) within the province.
    2. The offeror shall deliver a takeover bid circular, describing material facts of the takeover, as part of the bid.
    3. A directors' circular, including a recommendation and reasons (or reasons for providing no recommendation), must be sent to security holders within 15 days of the bid.
    4. Any securities taken up must be paid for within three days (if more securities are offered than the offeror was willing or able to purchase, the offers would be settled on a pro rata basis, disregarding fractional shares).
    5. When the bid is for less than all securities subject to the bid, the offeror shall accept securities offered on a pro rata basis.

Shareholders have the right of rescission or right to damages for any misrepresentations.

!

- A takeover bid is exempt from the above requirements in any of the following cases:
    1. It is made through the exchange facilities in accordance with appropriate regulations.
    2. It involves acquisitions, at market prices, which do not aggregate more than 5% of the securities in a class within 12 months.
    3. It is a private agreement with five or fewer security holders at a price not exceeding 115% of market value.
    4. It is an offer to purchase shares in a private company.
    5. In Ontario only, if there are fewer than 50 security holders of that class or the aggregate holdings of the offer, would be less than 2% the aggregate holdings of the offer, would be less than 2% of total outstanding.

Shareholders have the rights of rescission or right to damages for any misrepresentations. In addition, every person or company acquiring more than 10% of voting shares (or equivalent convertibles) of another company must provide early warning disclosure in the form of a press release, which must be filed with the administrator.

Insiders of a reporting issuer are required to file reports of their trading activities in its securities. Insiders are generally defined to include

1. a director or senior officer of the company, or a subsidiary;
2. a person or company, or director or senior officer of a company, which controls more than 10% of the voting;
3. a reporting issuer that has acquired any of its securities; and
4. a director or senior officer of a company that is itself an insider due to ownership or control of more than 10% of the voting shares of the company involved.

- Administrators can undertake investigations and subsequent prosecutions to enforce the appropriate laws. While they do not have the power to refund investments or settle internal disputes among shareholders of a corporation, they can suspend, cancel, or revoke registration; order trading in a security to cease; and deny the right to trade securities in a province.

Chapter 3 Review Questions

1. The _____________ was established to protect investors in the event of insolvency of a securities firm. ( )

    a) CDS
    b) IDA
    c) SSRO
    d) CIPF

2. The CDIC provides coverage for customer deposits up to a limit of _____________ per financial institution. ( )

    a) $60,000
    b) $100,000
    c) $250,000
    d) $1,000,000

3. Which of the following is NOT a basic method used by administrators to protect investors? ( )

    a) registration of securities dealers and advisors
    b) enforcement of the laws and policies
    c) disclosure of material facts
    d) none of the above (i.e., they are all methods used by administrators)

( ) 4. Which of the following types of information must listed companies disclose?

I. insider trading reports
II. block trading activity
III. annual information form
IV. monthly profit statements

a) I and II
b) I and III
c) II and III
d) II and IV

( ) 5. Which of the following would NOT be considered corporate insiders?

I. directors of a company
II. a shareholder owning 5.5% of a company's shares
III. the CEO of a company
IV. the CEO of a subsidiary

a) I and IV
b) II and III
c) II
d) IV

( ) 6. Shareholders have the following rights associated with the purchase of newly issued shares:

a) rescission
b) withdrawal
c) both (a) and (b)
d) neither (a) nor (b)

Bonus Questions

( ) 7. The OSFI regulates and supervises the actions of:

a) deposit taking institutions
b) property and casualty insurance companies
c) federally regulated pension plans
d) all of the above

( ) 8. Which of the following statements concerning self-regulatory organizations is true?

a) If an SRO rule differs from a provincial rule, the provincial rule applies.
b) The IIROC, Toronto Stock Exchange, and MFDA are examples of SROs.

c) SROs are an oversight body that monitors the actions of its members, but enforcement of rules and regulations is carried out by the provincial securities commission.

d) All of the above statements are true.

9. Which of the following is NOT a method by which Canadian securities legislation protects investors? ( )

a) registration of securities dealers and advisors

b) approval of the underlying investment merits of a particular issue of securities

c) enforcement of laws and policies

d) disclosure of the necessary facts to make educated investment decisions

10. In addressing a perceived issue with a financial institution in Canada, an individual can undertake each of the following options, EXCEPT: ( )

a) file a lawsuit

b) request arbitration

c) complain to the exchange on which the financial institution's shares trade

d) seek assistance from OBSI

11. Deliberately causing the price of the last sale of the day for a security to be higher than warranted is referred to as: ( )

a) window dressing

b) front running

c) bucketing

d) liquidity

12. Which of the following is a requirement of a takeover bid that is NOT exempt under the relevant act? ( )

a) A directors' circular must be sent to shareholders of the target firm within 30 days.

b) Any security purchased during the bid must be paid for within five business days.

c) A takeover bid circular must be sent out with or as part of the bid.

d) If the offer is made for less than all of the shares outstanding, the number of securities purchased from individual investors may be determined on a pro rata basis.

ECONOMIC PRINCIPLES

chapter 4

CSC EXAM SUGGESTED GUIDELINES:
14 questions combined for Chapters 4 and 5

OVERVIEW OF ECONOMICS

Economics deals with the allocation of scarce resources to produce goods and services within an economy. The decision makers within an economy fall into three main categories: consumers, firms, and governments.

Factors of production are sold in factor markets and include labour, natural resources, capital, and entrepreneurship. Final output is in the form of goods and services sold in the goods markets.

Microeconomics examines the choices made by individual economic agents and how these choices interact in a market economy.

Economics focuses on examining how **demand** and **supply** interact to determine prices and levels of production of goods and services in an economy. The Law of Demand suggests that as the price for a given product increases, the quantity demanded of that product declines. The Law of Supply suggests that as the price of a product increases, the quantity of that product supplied increases. Finally, **market equilibrium** occurs at prices where the quantity demanded equals the quantity supplied. This price is referred to as the **equilibrium price**.

In contrast to microeconomics, **macroeconomics** deals with economic behaviour at the aggregate level. Macroeconomics focuses on issues such as unemployment, inflation, economic growth, and government policies, and it is the focus of this chapter.

MEASURING THE ECONOMY

! **Gross Domestic Product (GDP)** is the value of all final goods and services produced in a country in a given year. It may be measured in two ways: using the **income approach** or the **expenditure approach**. Both outcomes will be the same since GDP must equal gross domestic income, which will be the same as gross domestic expenditures. Under the income approach, GDP includes income earned by labour (wages and salaries); landowners (rent); business (corporate profits); and lenders (interest). Total expenditure is made up of consumer spending (C); investment in household residences, business investment in inventories, and capital equipment (I); government spending (G); and foreigners' spending on Canadian exports minus Canadians' spending on foreign imports (X – M). Thus, we typically see the following equation used to depict GDP level: **GDP = G + C + I + (X – M)**.

! **Gross National Product (GNP)** is the value of all goods and services produced by Canadians at home or abroad. Some countries use this to measure economic activity rather than GDP. GNP = GDP + Income from Canadian investments abroad – Income paid to foreign holders of Canadian investments.

Nominal GDP (or Current Dollar or Chained Dollar GDP) refers to the level of output in prices prevailing in that year. **Real GDP** (or Constant Dollar GDP) refers to the level of output after adjusting for increases in price levels. Normally, economic growth is measured in terms of growth in real GDP, to prevent the influence of inflation. For example, if nominal GDP grew from 100 to 105 during a given year, then nominal GDP growth was 5% ([105 – 100]/100). If inflation was 2% during the same year, then real GDP growth would have been 3% (5% – 2%).

! **Growth of real GDP** generally results from three factors:

1. increases in population,
2. increases in capital stock, and
3. technological innovation.

The Business Cycle

- Although our economy has grown through the years, it has also displayed periods of negative growth. Normal fluctuations in long-term growth have typically followed a series of patterns referred to as business cycles.

The five major phases of these cycles are

1. expansion,
2. peak,
3. recession (contraction),
4. trough, and
5. recovery.

Expansion: Normal growth stages are typically characterized by stable inflation; rises in corporate profits; increased job start-ups and reduced bankruptcies; increasing inventories and investment by business to deal with increased demand; strong stock market activity; and job creation and falling unemployment.

Peak: Demand has begun to outstrip economic capacity, increasing inflationary pressures, which leads to increasing interest rates and falling bond prices. Investment and sales of "durables" fall, and eventually stock market activity and stock prices decline.

Recession (Contraction): Often defined as two consecutive quarters of negative growth (although this definition is not used by Statistics Canada [StatsCan] or the U.S. National Bureau of Economic Research). StatsCan judges a recession by the depth, duration, and diffusion of the decline in business activity (i.e., the decline must be of significant magnitude, last longer than two months, and be spread throughout the entire economy). The most recent recession lasted from July 2008 to July 2009, which saw GDP decline 3.3% from peak to trough, with unemployment peaking at 8.6% over this period.

Trough: Near the end of a recessionary period, falling demand and excess capacity lead to drops in prices and wages. The resulting decline in inflation leads to falling interest rates, which will begin to rally the economy.

Recovery: This phase refers to the period of time it takes for GDP to return to its previous peak. It is generally initiated with an increase in demand for interest-rate-sensitive items such as houses, cars, and other durable goods, and then spreads throughout the entire economy. Another expansionary phase is said to begin once GDP passes its previous peak.

When economic growth declines substantially, but does not turn negative, and inflation remains in check, it is generally referred to as a "**soft landing**."

Business Cycle Indicators

Leading indicators are those that generally change before changes in overall economic activity. They provide useful tools for predicting the future direction of the economy. Some of the more important leading indicators include

1. housing starts;
2. manufacturers' new orders, especially for durables;
3. spot commodity prices;
4. average hours worked per week;
5. stock prices; and
6. money flows.

Statistics Canada's Composite Leading Indicator is composed of 10 leading indicators, which are

1. the S&P/TSX Composite Index;
2. the Real Money Supply (M1);
3. the United States Composite Leading Index;
4. new orders for durable goods;
5. shipments to inventory ratio-finished goods;
6. average work week;
7. employment in business and services;
8. furniture and appliance sales;
9. sales of other retail durable goods; and
10. housing spending index.

! **Coincident indicators** change in conjunction with changes in overall economic activity and are useful for identifying changing points in the business cycle after they have occurred. These include **GDP**, **industrial production**, **personal income**, and **retail sales.**

! **Lagging indicators** change after changes in overall economic activity have taken place. These include **business investment spending**, the **unemployment rate**, **labour costs**, **business loans** (and **interest**), and **inflation.**

LABOUR MARKETS

! Two key labour market indicators are described below:

1. The **participation rate** measures the percentage of the working age population (15–65) that is in the labour force, either working or looking for work. It has risen steadily since World War II, except for a severe decline since the end of the last recessionary period.
2. The **unemployment rate** is measured as the percentage of the labour force that is looking for but hasn't found employment. It will change in response to changes in the number of people employed and/or the number of people looking for work. There are three general types of unemployment:
   - **cyclical**, which arises due to temporary hirings or layoffs that may be attributable to the business cycle;
   - **frictional unemployment**, which is unemployment caused by people in job "transition" stages; and
   - **structural employment**, which is caused by workers being unable to find work because they do not possess the necessary skills.

- Frictional and structural unemployment are caused by a variety of factors, including regulations such as minimum wage laws, strength of unions in negotiating wages, welfare and employment insurance plans that reduce workers' incentive to work, and technological changes that make new skills necessary.
- A certain amount of frictional and structural unemployment will exist in an economy even if it is healthy. This level of unemployment is sometimes referred to as the **natural** or **full-employment unemployment rate**, or the **Non-Accelerating Inflation Rate of Unemployment (NAIRU)**.

INTEREST RATES

- **Interest rates** have a very profound effect on securities markets since they represent the price of credit—as determined by the forces of supply and demand.

Interest rates will differ for a variety of reasons, including the **duration** of the borrowing, the terms of the loan, and the **creditworthiness** of the borrower. !

High interest rates tend to !

1. **raise the cost of capital** to firms, which reduces business investment;
2. **discourage consumer spending**, particularly for durables; and
3. **reduce disposable income** available for net borrowers due to higher debt servicing charges.

Some key interest rate determinants are: !

1. **Inflation**: Rates rise to compensate lenders for loss in purchasing power as inflation rises.
2. **Foreign Developments** and the **Exchange Rate**: Foreign interest rates and domestic exchange rates affect the demand for Canadian debt instruments.
3. **Demand and Supply of Capital**: Government deficits or increases in investment **spending** cause an increased demand for capital, which increases rates, unless there is a corresponding increase in savings.
4. The **Default Risk** of the Borrower: The greater the risk of default, the greater the rate that must be paid to borrow funds.
5. **Central Bank Credibility Operations**: The Bank of Canada can affect short-term rates directly and may affect long-term rates indirectly through its credibility of commitment to controlling inflation. When governments establish a credible, long-term commitment to maintain low inflation, lower interest rates are possible since there is less need to compensate lenders for the risk of rising inflation.

- Interest rates are determined based on future expectations, particularly with regards to future levels of inflation. This is because the real interest rate equals the nominal interest rate minus expected inflation. Real rates were historically in the 5% to 7% range; however, they have fallen below 1% recently.

MONEY AND INFLATION

- Money includes coins, bank notes, and draws on bank accounts. Money serves as a "medium of exchange" for transactions. It serves as a "unit of account," which establishes the relative values of different goods and services. It also represents a "store of value" since it contains no expiration date.

The Bank of Canada uses several **measures of money supply**.

! The most widely used measure of inflation is the Consumer Price Index (CPI), which tracks the price of a given "typical" basket of goods and services (600 different items included). The cost of this basket is related to a base year cost, which is presently 2002. It may overstate the true level of inflation by failing to capture improved quality of the "basket" and consumers' tendencies to switch to less expensive items.

- The inflation rate can be calculated as the percentage change in the CPI level over a given period. For example, if CPI is 145 today and was 140 last year, the inflation rate over the last year was 3.57% ([145 – 140]/140 x 100%).

- **Inflation** refers to a general decline in the value of money due to a sustained trend of rising prices. It is one of the most important factors affecting securities markets because it erodes the real value of long-term investments.

! Inflation has several associated **costs**, including the following:

1. It erodes the standard of living for those on a fixed income, which may aggravate social inequities.
2. It reduces the real value of investments such as fixed-rate loans, since they are paid back in dollars that are worth less.
3. It distorts signals to economy participants that are normally given through asset prices (since "relative" prices may be harder to establish).
4. Accelerating inflation generally causes increases in interest rates, which may lead to recessionary periods.

- Inflation occurs when demand for goods and services exceeds (or grows faster) than supply. The **output gap** refers to the difference between the potential full-capacity level of output from actual output. When actual output is near full capacity, increased demand will lead to inflation. This is referred to as a **demand-pull inflation**.

- **Cost-push inflation** occurs when prices rise or fall due to changes in the cost of production, such as the increase in production costs that occurs when oil prices rise significantly.

- In addition, it is generally accepted that increases in the money supply fuel inflation. Also, many believe that inflation moves in the opposite direction of unemployment in the short run, which is referred to as the **Phillips Curve** relationship.

! A number of **indicators** are monitored for signs of changes in inflation, including commodity and wholesale prices, wage settlements, bank credit, and exchange-rate movements.

While the costs of inflation are apparent, there may also be costs associated with **disinflation**, which refers to decreases in the rate of inflation. The costs arise because of the Phillips Curve relationship, which suggests that declines in inflation tend to cause an increase in unemployment, as well as a corresponding slowing of economic growth. The sacrifice ratio measures the extent to which GDP must be reduced with increased unemployment to achieve a 1% decrease in the inflation rate, with estimates ranging as high as 5 (which implies that 5% of output must be sacrificed to reduce inflation by 1%). Evidence of the costs of disinflation were evident in Canada over the 1988–1994 period when inflation fell from 4% to 0.2%, while unemployment rose from 7.8% to 10.4%.

Deflation occurs when there is a sustained fall in prices (i.e., when the change in CPI is negative). While falling prices are generally a good thing in the short run, sustained declines may lead to declining corporate profits, which leads to layoffs and increases in unemployment, which in turn leads to overall declines in economic growth. While the monetary authorities can decrease interest rates to offset this occurrence to a certain extent, rates can only be lowered so much. The costs of deflation have been evident in Japan during recent years, where deflation persisted and the government was unable to reduce rates, which were near zero for a long period. The damage to Japan's economy is still being felt.

INTERNATIONAL ECONOMICS

- Canada's financial interactions with other countries are captured in its **balance of payments**, which is composed of the current account and the capital account.

The **current account** records all payments between Canadians and foreigners for goods, services, interest, and dividends (i.e., it is similar to an income statement). The most important item is **merchandise trade**. In 2003, Canada exported $402 billion of goods and services, and imported $341 billion. The United States is our major trading partner and accounted for 85% of our exports and 72% of our imports in 2003. Other components of the current account include **investment income**, **services**, and **transfers of funds** (e.g., through foreign aid and/or wealth brought to Canada by immigrants).

The **capital and financial account** reflects net equity and debt financing by Canada with foreigners (i.e., it is similar to a balance sheet). The major components include **direct investment** in assets or companies, **portfolio investment** in debt (treasury bills or bonds) or equity, and **international reserves transactions** in currency markets.

- In order to finance current account deficits, a country must issue foreigners an IOU such as a bond or treasury bill and/or sell domestic assets such as land or companies to foreign interests. This implies that current account deficits require capital account surpluses, since the two accounts must balance.

The Exchange Rate

! The **exchange rate** affects the economy in several ways, most importantly through trade. All else being equal, a higher exchange rate would tend to lower Canada's trade balance. However, there are several other factors at work in determining the impact of a change in the exchange rate on trade. For example, lower inflation rates may offset the impact on foreign trade of a higher exchange rate, due to the lower associated costs.

The **trade-weighted exchange rate** measures the value of the Canadian dollar against 10 major currencies, based on the proportion of our trade maintained with each of those countries. In practice, people tend to focus on the Canada-U.S. exchange rate due to its importance to us as a trading partner, and also because of its widespread acceptance as a leading global currency.

! Exchange-rate systems or regimes are commonly classified as fixed or floating systems. **Floating systems** allow the exchange rate to be freely determined in foreign exchange markets. Under a **fixed exchange-rate system**, the central bank "pegs" the domestic currency against another currency or composites of other currencies. This can be achieved by forcing all purchases and sales of the domestic currency to be handled only through its own banks, at its price. This can be costly and distortive to the operation of the economy and usually leads to the development of black markets. Typically, more advanced countries avoid this approach and maintain a fixed exchange rate by instructing their central bank to buy and sell the currency in the open market and adjust interest rates as required to maintain a certain exchange-rate range. This approach requires the maintenance of a sizable foreign exchange reserve that must be utilized when the currency faces substantial market pressures. Fixed exchange rates are often used to assist high-inflation countries in "importing" the stability of the country to which it pegs its currency; however, it restricts the local monetary authority's ability to deal with interest rates at the local level.

- The Bretton Woods system was adopted by most major countries from the end of World War II to 1971. It involved pegging currencies to U.S. rates, and the U.S. dollars were freely convertible into gold. Currency devaluations required the approval of the International Monetary Fund (IMF). The United States halted the convertibility of its currency into gold in 1971, which led to the end of this system. Canada did not participate in this system from 1950 to 1962.

! The following factors affect the exchange rate to varying degrees:

1. **Inflation Differentials**: Countries with lower inflation tend to appreciate through time to reflect their increased purchasing power relative to other countries.
2. **Interest Rate Differentials**: Higher interest rates tend to attract more capital and make a currency value increase, provided the difference is not merely a reflection of higher inflation.
3. **Current Account**: Countries that continually run deficits will have excess demand for foreign currencies, which puts downward pressure on the

domestic currency. The current account is influenced by the terms of trade, which is the ratio of export prices to import prices, an increase which suggests increased demand for the local currency.

4. **Economic Performance**: A strong economy attracts investment capital by offering higher returns and thus leads to more favourable exchange rates.
5. **Public Debt and Deficits**: Countries with large debts are less attractive to foreign investors because
   - they have higher incentive to allow inflation to grow (and repay in "cheaper" dollars);
   - they rely more on foreign investment; and
   - debt accumulation affects the country's ability to repay.
6. **Political Stability**: Capital tends to exhibit a "flight to quality," particularly in times of increased uncertainty, which implies that instability exerts downward pressure on exchange rates.

Most countries maintain a **foreign exchange reserve**, including Canada, where it is called the Exchange Fund Account. This is a federal government account that is managed by the Bank of Canada and is made up of foreign currencies (mainly U.S. dollars—almost 43% in 2003), gold, and reserves in the IMF.

Chapter 4 Review Questions

1. The following are all major determinants of interest rates EXCEPT for: ( )
   a) inflation
   b) exchange rate
   c) default risk
   d) none of the above
2. The following are all determinants of exchange rates EXCEPT for: ( )
   a) inflation differentials
   b) current account
   c) political stability
   d) none of the above
3. Which of the following are business cycle leading indicators? ( )
   I. housing starts
   II. business investment spending
   III. GDP
   IV. stock prices
   V. inflation

a) I, IV, and V
b) II and V
c) II and III
d) I and IV

( ) 4. Which of the following are business cycle lagging indicators?

I. retail sales
II. business investment spending
III. GDP
IV. personal income
V. inflation

a) I, IV, and V
b) II and V
c) II and III
d) I and IV

( ) 5. The following are components of the capital account EXCEPT for:

a) direct investment
b) investment income
c) international reserves transaction
d) all of the above are components of the capital account

( ) 6. Which of the following statements concerning inflation is true?

a) The Phillips Curve says that when unemployment is low, inflation tends to be low.
b) The sacrifice ratio describes the extent to which unemployment must be increased to generate a 1% increase in GDP.
c) A positive output gap can result in demand-pull inflation.
d) Disinflation occurs when the annual change in CPI is negative year over year.

( ) 7. ____________ unemployment refers to unemployment caused by people in job transition stages.

a) Cyclical
b) Frictional
c) Structural
d) Natural

( ) 8. From 2002 to 2003, the nominal GDP growth of country X increased by 7.05%, while its real GDP growth was 3.24%. What was the inflation rate?

a) 2.16%
b) 3.81%

c) 4.26%
d) 5.00%

Bonus Questions

9. Which of the following statements about microeconomics and macroeconomics is FALSE? ( )
   a) Microeconomics deals with the behaviour of individual consumers and firms.
   b) Microeconomics deals with how prices impact production and consumptions of goods and services.
   c) Macroeconomics deals with the challenges resulting from limited resources in the economy.
   d) Macroeconomics deals with issues such as minimum wage and its impact on labour supply.

10. Which of the following statements about prices is true? ( )
    a) Prices are determined independent of market participants.
    b) As the price increases, the quantity of goods demanded increases.
    c) As the price increases, the quantity of goods supplied increases.
    d) At a price below the equilibrium price, demand is less than supply.

11. Statistics Canada measures a recession ( )
    a) as two consecutive quarters of declining growth in nominal GDP.
    b) as two consecutive quarters of declining growth in real GDP.
    c) by the depth, duration, and diffusion of a decline in business activity.
    d) between one- and three-quarters before it takes place.

12. If the CPI in 2006 is 114 and in 2007 is 110, then: ( )
    a) the estimated deflation over 2007 is 3.51%
    b) the estimated inflation over 2007 is 3.51%
    c) the estimated deflation over 2007 is 3.64%
    d) the estimated inflation over 2007 is 3.64%

13. Inflation imposes costs on the economy as: ( )
    a) it reduces the real value of investments
    b) it usually brings about rising interest rates
    c) it erodes the standard of living for a large portion of the population
    d) all of the above are costs of inflation

( ) 14. If the nominal interest rate is 8% and the expected inflation rate is 2%, then what is the real interest rate?

a) 6%

b) 10%

c) negative and therefore does not exist

d) none of the above are true

( ) 15. If total exports are \$50, total imports are \$45, net transfer payments are –\$5, and net investment income is \$10, then what is the current account balance is

a) \$0

b) \$5

c) \$10

d) \$15

( ) 16. Which of the following is the LEAST significant factor in Canada's real GDP growth?

a) increase in capital

b) increase in imports

c) increase in population

d) improvements in technology

ECONOMIC POLICY

chapter

5

CSC EXAM SUGGESTED GUIDELINES:

14 questions combined for Chapters 4 and 5

ECONOMIC THEORIES

Governments have historically tried to use monetary and fiscal policy (both discussed later) to influence the long- and short-run performance of economies. Usually, the purpose is to attempt to smooth out the business cycle by adopting countercyclical policies, which try to boost output during times of weak economic activity and to slow down the economy during growth periods.

- **Monetarist Theory** advocates a lack of intervention by the government based on the belief that the economy will gravitate toward stable economic growth, if left to its own devices. It also argues that increases in the money supply are the major causes of inflation and that the best monetary policy is to increase money supply at a stable amount that approximates the economy's long-run growth rate (i.e., 2% to 3% per year).
- **Keynesian Theory** advocates government intervention (in the form of increased spending or reduced taxes) to stimulate the economy whenever it is operating below full capacity. Alternatively, when the economy is growing too fast, the government should increase taxes and/or decrease spending.
- **Supply-Side Economics** advocates minimum government intervention and the maintenance of low taxes and low government spending. It was the basis for many tax reductions initiated in the United States and other economies during the 1980s.
- **Rational Expectations Theory** suggests that government policy will have little effect on the economy since the economic agents will anticipate the future outcomes that will result from today's actions. For example, if the government cuts taxes today, agents will not spend the extra disposable income, but will save it since they

realize the government will have to raise taxes in the future to offset today's losses. Alternatively, if the government allows the money supply to increase in order to stimulate higher economic activity, workers will negotiate higher wage settlements and businesses will increase prices in order to offset the impact of inflation, thereby retarding growth.

FISCAL POLICY

- Fiscal policy is the use of government taxation, spending, and deficits to affect growth. One of the generally accepted duties is to "smooth out" the business cycle by spending more and taxing less when the economy is weak.
- The federal finance minister presents the federal government budget for the upcoming fiscal year (April 1–March 31) every year, usually in February. The budget includes projections for spending, revenue, deficits (or surpluses), and the level of debt for the upcoming year (and usually at least one additional year).

! Fiscal policy affects the economy in several ways:

1. Its **spending** and/or direct transfers to citizens.
2. **Taxes** of various types, including direct (income), sales, payroll, capital, and property taxes.
3. **Deficits**, which tend to stimulate the economy, while falling deficits (or surpluses) generally do the opposite.
4. **Automatic stabilizers**, which automatically move counter to the business cycle (e.g., **unemployment insurance** payments increase as unemployment rises, while **income taxes** rise as economic growth increases).

The existence of deficits on a continual basis has several consequences. It leads to increased borrowing needs, which in turn contribute to higher borrowing costs, which in turn raise costs and increase the chances of subsequent deficits—and the cycle continues. The Canadian government ran deficits from 1969 through to 1997, resulting in a continually increasing debt-to-GDP ratio that peaked at 68.4% in 1995–1996. The government had surpluses from 1997 to 2008, and the debt-to-GDP ratio declined considerably (to 32.8% in 2008–2009). As of the time of writing, we have been running deficits the last few years, as a result of the reduction of the GST and the financial crisis of 2008–2009.

MONETARY POLICY

! **Monetary policy** refers to the use of interest rates, the exchange rate, and the rate of money supply growth to influence demand and inflation. This function is performed in Canada by the **Bank of Canada**, which was founded in 1934.

- The Bank is governed by a board of directors that includes the governor, the senior deputy governor, and 12 directors (traditionally, there is at least one member from each province). The deputy minister of finance also sits on the board, but cannot vote.
- The responsibilities of the central bank include
    1. issuing the nation's currency;
    2. acting as banker to the central government; and
    3. operating monetary policy.
- Its general duties include
    1. regulating credit and currency;
    2. controlling and protecting the external value of the national monetary unit;
    3. mitigating, by its influence, fluctuations in the general level of production; and
    4. promoting the economic and financial welfare of Canada.

The major functions of the Bank are the following:

1. acting for the government in the issuance and removal of bank notes;
2. acting as the government's chief fiscal agent and financial advisor (As a fiscal agent, the Bank advises the government on financial matters; administers the deposit and fund accounts; manages international currency reserves and operates for the government in foreign exchange markets; acts as a depository for gold; and acts as the government's debt manager in issuing new debt securities and paying interest on them and retiring them.); and
3. conducting monetary policy, which is the Bank's most important function, and is discussed below.

- The Bank is responsible for maintaining stability in the general level of prices, employment, output and trade, and the external value of the Canadian dollar. In recent years, the Bank has focused on price stability, which it sees as the best way **monetary policy** can contribute to stability in employment, output, and the exchange rate. Currently the bank has a specific inflation target of 1%–3%.
- The Bank attempts to control inflation primarily through raising and lowering interest rates, although its open market transactions do affect money supply as well. The Bank recognizes that monetary conditions are the combined effect of interest rates and exchange rates.

Implementing Monetary Policy

- The Bank implements monetary policy by targeting interest rates in general. The mechanism it uses to do so is the **bank rate**. The bank rate is the rate at which the Bank of Canada is willing to lend short-term funds to the chartered banks and other members of the CPA, in its role as lender of last resort. Since 1996, the bank rate has been set equal to the *ceiling of its target range* for **overnight money rates**. Prior to that, it was set at 25 basis points (one-quarter of a percentage point) above the average yield on three-month treasury bills.

- The overnight money rate represents the rate at which money is lent overnight in the money market. Governments, financial institutions, and large corporations are the users and suppliers of overnight funds (due to excess or deficient cash balances). In 1994, the Bank established a 50-basis-point operating band (e.g., 3.0% to 3.5%) for overnight money rates. While the Bank targets the mid-point of this band, the upper limit is the bank rate.

! The Bank influences interest rates in a number of ways, the most important of which are described below:

1. **Cash Management**: This is the Bank's most important tool for influencing interest rates, and involves managing highly liquid reserves in the banking system through its "drawdown" and "redeposit" mechanism. All banks and other financial institutions that clear payments through the Canadian Payments Association (CPA) have accounts with the Bank.

   The CPA introduced the Large Value Transfer System (LVTS) in 1998 based on consultations with the Bank. This system permits participating institutions to track their LVTS receipts and payments electronically on an ongoing basis. Participants then achieve "zero-settlement" levels within the system through transfers to/from Government of Canada deposits at the Bank every day. At the end of the day, settlement of the positions is achieved through the overnight market (i.e., those who had deficit positions will borrow to achieve "zero," while those with surplus positions will lend).

   Generally, the Bank shifts federal funds between accounts at the Bank of Canada, and demand deposits at the clearing banks, in order to give institutions unexpected positive or negative settling balances. If the clearing banks find themselves with a positive balance, they will lend out the excess funds and buy securities, putting downward pressure on interest rates. The Bank achieves this using a "**redeposit**," which moves deposits from its own account to those of the clearing banks.

   The reverse happens if the clearing banks find themselves with a negative balance, which the Bank induces using a "**drawdown**" (which is the reverse of a redeposit). Financial institutions often use this information to make judgments regarding the Bank's short-term stance.

2. **Open Market Operations**: The Bank can also influence rates by trading money market securities in the open market. In recent years, the Bank has targeted the overnight borrowing (lending) rates. The Bank affects overnight rates by

   - offering to lend overnight money through a **special purchase and resale agreement** (**SPRA** or **repo**) at stated rates below existing market rates in order to **reduce rates**; and

- offering to borrow overnight from financial institutions through **sale and repurchase agreements (SRA)** (by selling securities to the chartered banks and agreeing to repurchase them the next day) at given rates that are higher than market rates (when it wants to **increase rates**).

In 1994, the Bank of Canada established a 50-basis-point **operating band** for overnight money by conducting repos (or specials) at the ceiling rate and SRAs 50 basis points below the ceiling. The target rate is the mid-point in this range. The Bank can also affect three-month treasury bill rates by buying and selling T-bills from its own inventory. When the Bank wants to **lower interest rates** through this mechanism, it **buys T-bills** by offering a price above the present market price, which lowers rates due to the inverse relationship between rates and prices. This action expands the Bank's balance sheet and effectively increases the money supply since the dealer it buys the T-bills from will likely lend out the funds it receives from the Bank. Since the Bank is targeting interest rates and not money supply, it will often "neutralize" the effect on money supply through "drawdowns." When the Bank **sells T-bills**, it exerts pressure designed to **increase interest rates**.

3. **Moral Suasion**: The Bank may simply ask financial institutions to tighten or loosen credit conditions in order to achieve its policy without action in the money market.

Two major challenges face the successful use of government policy to influence economic activity. First, the economy is often slow to react to interventions, which implies that even well-designed policies may be ineffective when needed the most. Second, many argue that the economy will achieve equilibrium on its own, without interference. If so, rather than assisting the economy, government intervention could in fact hinder, delay, or prevent this from occurring.

Chapter 5 Review Questions

1. _____________ is the term used when the Bank of Canada asks financial institutions to tighten or loosen credit in order to achieve its policy without action in the money market. ( )

   a) Moral suasion

   b) Indirect cash management

   c) Open market operations

   d) Moral persuasion

2. _____________ is an example of an automatic stabilizer. ( )

   a) The bank rate

   b) The use of open market operations

   c) Unemployment insurance

   d) A deficit

( ) 3. The Bank of Canada may use ____________ when it wants to increase interest rates.

a) redeposits
b) drawdowns
c) T-bill purchases
d) SPRAs

( ) 4. The Bank of Canada may use ____________ when it wants to decrease interest rates.

a) drawdowns
b) SRAs
c) neither (a) nor (b)
d) either (a) or (b)

( ) 5. Which of the following theories states that government intervention is critical to move the economy out of recession?

a) monetarist
b) Keynesian
c) supply-side
d) rational expectations

( ) 6. The collection of total government borrowing over time is referred to as:

a) budget surplus
b) budget deficit
c) national debt
d) balanced budget

Bonus Questions

( ) 7. Fiscal policy is:

a) an example of Monetarist theory
b) the use of government spending and taxation to pursue such economic goals as full employment and long-term economic growth
c) equal to government's revenues less its total spending
d) not accurately described by any of the above statements

( ) 8. The main source of federal government revenue in Canada is:

a) major transfers to persons
b) transfers to provincial governments

c) personal income tax
d) corporate income tax

9. If the bank rate is 6.50%, then: ( )
   a) the Bank of Canada target for the overnight rate is 6.25%
   b) the Bank of Canada will lend money to chartered banks at 6.50%
   c) the lower rate in the overnight operating band is 6.00%
   d) all of the above are true

10. Which of the following statements is true? ( )
    a) SPRAs are used to reinforce the lower limit of the operating band.
    b) SPRAs involve the government purchasing securities from a primary dealer and selling them back to the dealer the following day at a predetermined price.
    c) SPRAs involve the government lending money to chartered banks at rates outside of the operating band.
    d) None of the above are true.

11. Which of the following statements concerning drawdowns and redeposits is true? ( )
    a) A redeposit is the transfer of funds from the Bank of Canada to chartered banks.
    b) A drawdown is the transfer of funds from chartered banks to the Bank of Canada.
    c) A drawdown tends to put upward pressure on interest rates, while a redeposit tends to put downward pressure on interest rates.
    d) All of the above are true.

12. The debt-to-GDP ratio is: ( )
    a) viewed as a sound measure of Canada's overall ability to increase taxation of citizens
    b) viewed as a measure of a nation's debt relative to taxpayer's ability to repay it
    c) about 20% in Canada (as of 2009)
    d) decreasing in Canada over the past few years, which is a negative sign for the overall economy

chapter

6

FIXED-INCOME SECURITIES: FEATURES AND TYPES

CSC EXAM SUGGESTED GUIDELINES:

12 questions for Chapter 6

OVERVIEW AND TERMINOLOGY

A **fixed-income security** provides a known income stream to the holder and has a known maturity date. !

- A traditional fixed income security provides interim payments of interest or dividends. Examples include bonds, debentures, mortgages, swaps, and preferred shares. Discounted fixed-income securities are sold at a discount from their face value, with the face value being the amount that is repaid at maturity. The return is the increase in principal value, which is treated as income—not capital gains—for tax purposes. Examples include strip (or zero-coupon) bonds and most money market instruments (e.g., treasury bills, commercial paper, and bankers' acceptances).
- **Bonds** are debt instruments that are secured by real assets and are often called mortgage bonds. Details of the bond issue including payment, maturity, security, and bond covenants are included in a trust deed and written into the **bond trust indenture**, which represents a legal contract between the bondholders and the bond issuers. Interest payments are based on the coupon rate, which is stated on the face of the bond. This rate may be fixed or it may be floating, which means that it varies with changes in some underlying reference interest rate. Payments are usually made two times a year (i.e., every six months), with one of the payments made on the same day and month as the maturity date. **Debentures** are similar to bonds, but are generally unsecured, or else secured by a general floating charge over the company's unencumbered assets (i.e., those that have not been pledged as security for other debt obligations).
- Bond prices are quoted based on an index with a base value of 100. When bonds trade at 100, they are trading at par or face value. When they trade above this, they

are said to be trading at a **premium**, and when they trade below this they are trading at a **discount**.

- The face value or denomination (e.g., $1,000 or $10,000) represents the amount the issuer contracts to pay at maturity. The **term to maturity** is the remaining life of the bond. Canada Savings Bonds have minimum denominations of $100, while the minimum for most corporate bonds is $1,000.

! **Short-term bonds** have maturities of one to five years. **Medium-term bonds** have maturities ranging from 5–10 years, while **long-term bonds** have maturities beyond 10 years.

! **Liquid bonds** have significant trading volumes. **Negotiable bonds** are in deliverable form, and **marketable bonds** are those for which there is a ready market.

- Three main reasons for borrowing money are to match the term of assets with the term of liabilities, to benefit from the use of financial leverage, and to fund deficits.

- Secondary market trading of debt instruments in Canada is much larger than trading in equities, with 2007 figures of $7 trillion for debt and $1.7 trillion for equities.

BOND FEATURES

- Interest payments on bonds are based on the stated coupon rate and are generally paid semi-annually.

! **Floating-rate bonds** or debentures (floaters) have "adjustable" coupons that are typically tied to treasury bill rates or some other short-term interest rate. They are attractive for the protection offered in times of volatile interest rates and behave like money market securities in an investment portfolio.

! **Callable** (or **redeemable**) **bonds** give the issuer the option to "call" or repurchase outstanding bonds at predetermined **call prices** (generally at a premium over par) at specified times. This feature is detrimental to the bondholders who are willing to pay less for them (i.e., they demand a higher return) than for similar non-callable bonds. Generally, the issuer agrees to give 30 or more days' notice that the issue will be redeemed. **Call protection** refers to the period of time prior to the first call date during which callable bonds cannot be called. The **redemption price** is often based on a graduated scale, reflecting the fact that the hardship to the investor of having an issue called is reduced as the time to maturity declines. Provincial bonds are usually callable at face value plus accrued interest. Usually corporate issues have a mandatory call feature for sinking fund purposes. Most corporate bond issues have a **Canada yield call** feature attached to them. These permit the issuer to call the issue at the greater of par or a price based on the yield on a Government of Canada bond with the same maturity plus a yield spread (e.g., 0.45%).

Sinking fund provisions require the issuer to repurchase a certain amount of debt per year. **Sinking funds** represent the funds set aside by the company for this purpose. Sinking fund provisions benefit the issuer, because it helps them avoid having to come up with the entire face value of the issue at the maturity date. However, they are not always advantageous to debt holders, who may have their securities repurchased by the issuer, even if they had been planning on holding the security to maturity date. In addition, there is often no premium provided in the repurchase price. !

Purchase fund provisions are similar to sinking fund provisions; however, they require the repurchase of a certain amount of debt only if the debt can be repurchased at or below a given price. These provisions are generally advantageous to debt holders, since they provide some liquidity and downward price support for the market price of the debt instruments. !

Retractable bonds allow the bondholder to sell the bonds back to the issuer at predetermined prices at specified times. **Extendible bonds** allow the bondholder to extend the maturity date of the bond. Both of these bonds offer investors an additional privilege, which implies they will pay more for these bonds (i.e., accept a lower return). In other words, the market prices of retractables and extendibles are normally higher than those for similar bonds lacking these features. They both tend to trade similarly to short-term bonds during periods of rising interest rates, as it is likely that they will be redeemed (or not extended). Similarly, they tend to behave like long-term bonds during periods of decreasing interest rates. The holders generally must state their intentions to extend or redeem during the **election period**, which occurs 6–12 months prior to the extendible or retractable dates. !

Convertible bonds may be converted into common shares at predetermined conversion prices. This privilege is afforded to the investor in order to make the issue more saleable, and to reduce the interest rate that must be offered to purchasers. Most convertibles have "protection against dilution," which means that the conversion prices will be adjusted accordingly if the underlying shares undergo a stock split or stock dividend. Usually convertibles are issued with maturities of 5–10 years, although during periods of low interest rates, 10- to 20-year issues become more common. Most convertibles are callable and most also have a sinking fund. Most convertibles increase the conversion price through time to increase the chances of early conversion. Certain convertibles include a forced conversion clause, which forces conversion by affording the issuer the right to redeem the issue once the common share price goes above pre-specified levels. !

Convertibles typically trade similarly to straight debentures when the conversion price is well below the market price of the common shares. A **premium** appears as market price approaches conversion price, and it is said to "sell off the stock" once market price exceeds the conversion price. The payback period for a convertible measures how long it would take to recover its premium through the difference between its dividend yield versus the lower yield provided by the underlying stock (this will be discussed in depth in the next chapter). As a general rule of thumb, payback periods beyond two years are unattractive. !

Protective Provisions

! **Protective covenants** are clauses in the trust indenture that restrict actions of the issuer. Negative covenants prohibit certain actions (e.g., restrict dividend payments or prevent pledging of any assets to lenders). Positive covenants specify actions that the firm agrees to undertake (e.g., furnish quarterly financial statements or maintain certain working capital levels). Some common examples are described below.

! **Security**: Specify the details of the assets that support the debt.

! **Dividend Test**: Rules that restrict dividend payments.

! **Debt Test**: Limits the amount of additional debt that may be assumed by establishing maximum debt-to-asset ratios, etc.

! **Prohibition of a Prior Lien**: Prohibits the issue of securities that would rank senior to first mortgage bond payments. Debentures typically include **negative pledge provisions**, which preclude the issue of additional bonds that are secured by company properties unless the debentures receive similar collateral.

! Additional borrowing restrictions may be imposed through two mechanisms. The use of **closed-end mortgages** prevents the issue of additional bonds that would be backed by the same assets as the original bonds. An even stronger restriction is given if the mortgage includes an **after-acquired clause**, which implies that subsequent asset purchases would be covered by the original mortgage. It is customary to permit the assumption of **purchase money mortgages**, which are liens attached to new properties subsequently acquired that do not affect the original bondholders' security position. **Open-end mortgages** typically include general provisions limiting the issue of new bonds to provide a proper margin of safety.

- Covenants may also require that the issuer maintain certain working capital requirements and/or put restrictions on dividend payments. A **sinking fund clause** requires an issuer to set aside cash in a sinking fund for the purpose of repayment of future debt obligations.
- Covenants often prohibit companies from entering into sale and leaseback arrangements for certain assets, selling assets by sale or merger, disposing of shares of a subsidiary, issuing debt or shares by a subsidiary, disposing of debt or shares of a subsidiary, and merger of a subsidiary with an outside company.

GOVERNMENT SECURITIES

! **Marketable Bonds**: These have specified interest payments and maturity dates and are **transferable**. The Government of Canada is the single largest issuer, with $382 billion outstanding in July of 2010. Typically, they are non-callable (which will be discussed shortly). Government of Canada **Real Return Bonds (RRBs)** were introduced in 1991 to provide investors with a real yield that was initially set at 4.25%. This is achieved by pegging the face value to the CPI and having the coupon rate (e.g., 4.25%) apply to the inflation-adjusted face value.

Treasury Bills: These are short-term government obligations that are sold at a discount from face value. Traditionally, they were held by large investors, due to the large issue denominations. However, in recent years, the government has offered them in amounts as low as $1,000 to make them available to retail investors.

Canada Savings Bonds (CSBs): CSBs are offered for sale every year between October and April. Unlike other bonds, CSBs can be cashed out by the owner, at their full par value plus eligible accrued interest, at any bank in Canada at any time. They are **not transferable**, and their prices do not change over time. They are sold in **registered form** to provide protection against loss, theft, or destruction. In recent years, only individuals, estates of deceased persons, and trusts governed by certain types of deferred savings and income plans have been allowed to acquire CSBs.

- The rates of return on CSBs may be allowed to vary in order to avoid having holders "cash out" in times of rising interest rates. An effective program for selling CSBs is through the payroll savings plans of over 12,000 organizations, which reaches over 1 million employees. Since 1977 they have been available in two forms:
    1. regular interest, which pays annual interest to the holder; and
    2. compound interest, which reinvests the interest, so that interest is also earned on accumulated interest.
- One recent variation of CSBs are **Canada Premium Bonds (CPBs)**. These are similar to CSBs, but can only be redeemed once a year (on their anniversary date and for the 30 days following that). They usually provide a higher rate than CSBs when issued.

Provinces borrow to fund deficits and/or to provide funding for program spending. Similar to federal "bond" issues, these instruments are usually debentures in the true sense since they are not backed by specific assets. New issues of provincial direct and guaranteed bonds are usually sold at a negotiated price through a fiscal agent (using an underwriting syndicate). **Direct bonds** are issued directly by the government (e.g., Province of Quebec bonds), while **guaranteed bonds** are issued in the name of a Crown corporation, but are guaranteed by the provincial government (e.g., Ontario Electricity Financial Corporation).

Municipal governments usually issue **installment debentures** or **serial bonds** to raise money from the capital markets. These instruments have part of the issue maturing every year. As is the case with other types of governments, their credit rating is a function of their ability to pay (i.e., their tax base), as well as their level of indebtedness.

CORPORATE BONDS

Mortgage bonds are secured by real property such as land, buildings, or equipment. **First mortgage bonds** have first claim to such assets, and as such, they are referred to as "senior securities."

Collateral trust bonds are secured by a pledge of other financial assets such as common shares, bonds, or treasury bills.

! **Equipment trust certificates** are secured by equipment, such as the rolling stock of a railway. The assets pledged as security are owned by investors through a lease agreement with the railway until the loan has been retired. The certificates have serial numbers that dictate their maturity date, with a certain amount maturing every year.

! **Corporate debentures** are similar to bonds, but are generally unsecured, or else secured by a general floating charge over the company's unencumbered assets (i.e., those that have not been pledged as security for other debt obligations).

! **Subordinated debentures** are junior to some other security, in a manner that may be ascertained from the prospectus.

! **Floating-rate securities (or variable-rate securities)** have rates that automatically adjust to new rates. They have become more popular in recent years in response to volatile interest rates.

- **Corporate notes** are unsecured promises to pay interest and repay principal, and rank behind all other fixed obligations of the borrower. **Secured notes** or **collateral trust notes** are secured by notes pledging assets purchased with the loan proceeds, such as automobiles. Secured term notes are secured by a written promise to pay regular installments, and these notes trade in the money market.

! Bonds may be

1. **Domestic**: Issued in the currency and country of the issuer (e.g., a Canadian company that issues bonds in Canada in Canadian dollars).
2. **Foreign**: Issued in a country other than the issuer's, in the currency of the country in which it is issued (e.g., a Canadian company that issues bonds in the United States in U.S. dollars). **Foreign-pay bonds** are those whose payments are made in a foreign currency. Some offer the choice of payment in more than one currency, while others may provide interest payments in one currency and principal repayment in another.
3. **Eurobonds**: Issued in a country other than the issuer's, but not in the currency of that country (e.g., a Canadian company that issues bonds in Germany in U.S. or Canadian dollars). If the bonds are issued in Canadian dollars, they would be called EuroCanadian bonds; if issued in U.S. dollars, they would be called Eurodollar bonds.

- Warrants are sometimes attached to bonds or debentures (or preferred shares).

! **Strip (or zero-coupon) bonds** are formed when financial intermediaries "strip" coupons off bonds and sell the cash flows separately, creating zero-coupon bonds that pay no coupons, but repay maturity value at the maturity date.

- Subordinated debentures with very long maturities are sometimes referred to as **preferred debentures**. This reflects the fact that their characteristics fall somewhere between preferred shares and regular debentures. Their characteristics include
    - terms to maturity of 25–99 years;
    - a rank below all other debt, but a rank ahead of preferred shares;

- the option by management to delay interest payments for up to five years; and
- the ability to trade on exchanges in many instances.

Bankers' Acceptances (BAs) are commercial drafts that require borrowers to make a specified payment on a specified date. The payment is guaranteed by the borrower's bank, hence the name. They trade in the money market, and similarly to T-bills, they are sold at a discount from their face value, which is paid at maturity. They trade in multiples of $1,000 (minimum $25,000) with possible maturities of up to 365 days (30 or 60 days are the norm).

Commercial paper (CP) trades in the money market at a discount similar to T-bills or BAs (and trades in the same multiples, with the same minimum as BAs). Traditional CP is unsecured and can only be issued by top-grade credit quality corporations; however, in recent years they have been backed by asset-backed securities, which has not worked out too well, as trading in the non-bank asset-backed CP market in Canada ceased for over a year.

- Other fixed-income instruments are offered by intermediaries. Most of them focus on safety. Two of the most common instruments are term deposits and guaranteed investment certificates (GICs).

Term Deposits offer guaranteed rates for short-term deposits (usually up to one year), and usually levy penalties for early withdrawals.

Guaranteed Investment Certificates (GICs) offer fixed rates for specified periods of time, which may exceed one year. The interest and principal payments are both guaranteed. Non-redeemable GICs cannot be cashed prior to maturity except in the case of death or severe financial hardship. Redeemable GICs can be cashed before maturity, and typically provide lower returns than non-redeemable GICs.

- GICs are currently available with terms up to 10 years, with a variety of payment intervals (e.g., monthly, quarterly, etc.), and many provide compound interest. They may be used as collateral for loans, may be automatically renewed at maturity, and may be sold through an intermediary. Canada Deposit Insurance Corporation (CDIC) does not offer coverage for GICs with maturities beyond five years, and not all GICs are RRSP eligible.
- Some special features available with GICs include the following:
    1. **Escalating-Rate GICs**: The interest rates increase through time.
    2. **Laddered GICs**: The GIC is broken into equal terms to reduce interest rate risk (e.g., a three-year $6,000 GIC is divided into a one-year $2,000 GIC, a two-year $2,000 GIC, and a three-year $2,000 GIC).
    3. **Installment GICs**: The initial contribution is followed by regular periodic minimum deposits.
    4. **Index-Linked GICs**: The returns are linked to equity returns based on a particular domestic or global index.
    5. **Interest-Rate-Linked GICs**: The returns are linked to changes in other interest rates such as the prime rate or money market rates.

! The following depicts a typical bond quote for a regular bond:

Issue	Coupon	Maturity Date	Bid	Ask	Yield
XYZ Co.	3.0%	1 June/25	100.75	101.25	2.83%

The quote highlights the issuer (XYZ Co.), the associated coupon rate (3.0%), the date the bond matures (June 1, 2025), the highest bid price (100.75), the lowest ask price (101.25), and the associated yield to maturity of the bond (2.83%). The ask price represents the price the bond could be bought for, while the bid price is the price the bond could be sold for, based on $100 of face value. For example, if the face value of the bond was $10,000, you would have to pay $10,125 ($10,000 × 101.25) plus accrued interest (discussed later in this chapter) to purchase the bond.

! The quote for an extendible bond that is extendible at the holder's option would be similar to the one above except that the maturity date would be expressed differently. For example, if an extendible bond matured on June 1, 2020, but was extendible to June 1, 2025, the maturity date would be expressed as: 1 June 20/25.

! The quote for a retractable bond that allows the bond holder to sell the bonds back to the issuer prior to the stated maturity date would also have the maturity date expressed differently. For example, if a retractable bond matured on June 1, 2025, but could be redeemed by the holder on June 1, 2020, the maturity date would be expressed as: 1 June 25/20. *Notice the difference between extendibles and retractables: with retractables, the more distant maturity date is presented first, while for extendibles it is expressed last.*

! **Rating services** perform detailed analysis of bond issuers to determine their ability to maintain uninterrupted payments of interest and repayment of principal. Investment-grade bonds are those with bond ratings of BBB (Dominion Bond Rating Service [DBRS] and Standard & Poor's), or Baa (Moody's) or higher. Junk (or high-yield or low-grade) bonds have bond ratings below these. The following are the debt ratings categories for DBRS (which are virtually identical to those for Standard & Poor's).

DBRS:

- AAA: highest credit quality
- AA: superior quality
- A: good quality
- BBB: adequate quality
- BB: speculative, non-investment-grade quality
- B: highly speculative quality
- CCC/CC/C: very highly speculative quality
- D: default (a financial obligation was missed)

Ratings may also be modified by "high" or "low" to indicate the relative ranking within a category or the trend within the category.

Chapter 6 Review Questions

1. Which of the following statements regarding Canada Savings Bonds is true? ( )
   a) They are non-transferable.
   b) They are issued in bearer form.
   c) They may be issued only as compound interest bonds.
   d) None of the above are true.

2. A bond that is issued by a Japanese company in Canada that is denominated in U.S. dollars is an example of a: ( )
   a) domestic bond
   b) foreign bond
   c) Eurobond
   d) foreign-pay bond

3. ____________ are debt securities that are secured by financial assets. ( )
   a) Collateral trust bonds
   b) Equipment trust certificates
   c) Financial bonds
   d) Income bonds

4. Government of Canada Real Return Bonds provide holders with real returns by: ( )
   a) adjusting the notional value of the bond by inflation
   b) adjusting the coupon rate with inflation
   c) neither (a) nor (b)
   d) both (a) and (b)

5. ____________ bonds are those that are in deliverable form. ( )
   a) Marketable
   b) Negotiable
   c) Liquid
   d) Registered

6. A(n) ____________ prevents the issue of additional bonds against property that was pledged under a previous debt agreement. ( )
   a) open-end mortgage
   b) closed-end mortgage
   c) after-acquired clause
   d) both (b) and (c) are true

( ) 7. Sinking fund provisions:

a) are the same as purchase fund provisions
b) are generally advantageous to the bond holder
c) neither (a) nor (b) is true
d) both (a) and (b) are true

( ) 8. Financial leverage refers to:

a) the tax-deductibility of interest payments made by companies
b) the use of debt financing to magnify shareholder returns
c) the interest payment made regularly by bond issuers
d) the use of equity to finance growth

( ) 9. If a 15-year bond was issued 9 years ago, then today it is:

a) a medium-term bond with 15 years to maturity
b) a long-term bond with 15 years to maturity
c) a medium-term bond with 6 years to maturity
d) a long-term bond with 6 years to maturity

( ) 10. The redemption provision that allows the issuer to call a bond once the stock price associated with the particular debt issuance rises above a pre-specified level is referred to as:

a) a sinking fund
b) a convertible bond
c) a purchase fund
d) forced conversion

( ) 11. Safeguards in a bond contract designed to protect investors are referred to as:

a) covenants
b) protection against dilution
c) negotiable bonds
d) negative pledge

( ) 12. Which of the following statements about treasury bonds is FALSE?

a) Treasury bonds are zero-coupon bonds.
b) The interest earned on treasury bonds is taxed as a capital gain.
c) Treasury bonds come in denominations as small as $1,000.
d) Treasury bonds are sold every two weeks through the Bank of Canada.

Bonus Questions

13. Which of the following statements concerning fixed-income securities is FALSE? ( )

    a) BAs are discount securities that are guaranteed by the issuer's bank.
    b) Interest payments on preferred debentures can be deferred by management for up to five years.
    c) There is no secondary market for BAs or commercial paper in Canada.
    d) Commercial paper can be secured or unsecured.

14. Which of the following statements concerning GICs is true? ( )

    a) All GICs are RRSP eligible.
    b) CDIC covers GICs of less than five years.
    c) GICs are non-transferable.
    d) All of the above statements are true.

15. Which of the following statements concerning bonds and debentures is true? ( )

    a) Both bonds and debentures are secured by physical assets.
    b) Governments issue both bonds and debentures.
    c) Debentures are typically unsecured investments, with the exception of residual claims on assets.
    d) A firm can default on a bond, but not on a debenture.

16. If a bond that has a face value of $1,000 makes semi-annual interest payments, has a coupon rate of 6%, and a yield of 10%, then the bond will make interest payments of: ( )

    a) $30 twice a year
    b) $50 twice a year
    c) $60 twice a year
    d) $100 twice a year

17. Which of the following statements concerning callable bonds is true? ( )

    a) Corporate bonds, as well as all levels of government bonds, are typically callable.
    b) Call protection period refers to the period before the first possible call date.
    c) Issuers of callable bonds must repurchase a specific amount at set intervals.
    d) The call premium is typically set relative to the face value of the bond, and is fixed over the bond's life.

( ) 18. Which of the following statements concerning sinking funds and purchase funds is FALSE?

a) Purchase funds are set up to retire a specified amount of outstanding debt through purchase in the market.

b) Sinking funds and purchase funds are mutually exclusive.

c) Sinking funds are sums of money established from annual earnings to repay all or part of a debt issue by maturity.

d) Both the purchase fund and the sinking fund are used to reduce the amount of debt outstanding prior to maturity.

( ) 19. Which of the following statements concerning extendable and retractable bonds is true?

a) An extendable bond allows the investor to trade a shorter-term bond for a longer-term bond at the same or slightly higher interest rate.

b) Retractable bonds allow investors to return the bonds to the issuer in exchange for par value, prior to the original maturity date.

c) The decision to extend or retract an extendable or retractable bond must be made during the election period.

d) All of the above statements are true.

( ) 20. Which of the following statements concerning convertible bonds is true?

a) With the convertible bond, the holder has essentially locked in a known price at which they can buy common equity.

b) Issuers of convertible bonds typically have to pay a higher rate of interest than with otherwise similar bonds.

c) The conversion price generally declines over time, encouraging bond holders to delay conversion.

d) All of the above statements are true.

( ) 21. Which of the following statements concerning government securities is true?

a) Crown corporations issue debt that is backed by the Government of Canada.

b) The federal government is the largest issuer of marketable bonds in the Canadian bond market.

c) Bonds issued by the Government of Canada have the highest credit quality of all Canadian issuers.

d) All of the above statements are true.

22. Consider the following statements about Canada Savings Bonds. ( )

I. CSBs can only be cashed in by their holder in October and April of each year.

II. CSBs come in two forms: regular interest and zero-coupon bonds.

III. CSBs are registered bonds.

IV. CSBs can be cashed in by their owner at any bank in Canada at their prevailing market price.

a) None of the statements are true.

b) One of the statements is true.

c) Two of the statements are true.

d) All of the statements are true.

23. Which of the following statements concerning provincial bonds is FALSE? ( )

a) Provincial bonds are second in credit quality to only Government of Canada bonds.

b) Provincial bonds represent unsecured debt.

c) The amount and diversity of natural resources located in a province can influence the interest paid on provincial bonds.

d) Provinces borrow exclusively in the Canadian marketplace.

FIXED-INCOME SECURITIES: PRICING AND TRADING

chapter 7

CSC EXAM SUGGESTED GUIDELINES:

11 questions for Chapter 7

BOND PRICING PRINCIPLES

Regular coupon bonds pay regular interest payments or **coupons (C)** in semi-annual or annual installments, plus the **face** or **par value (P)** of the bonds, which is paid at the maturity date.[1] The amount of the coupons is determined when the bonds are originally issued and is calculated by multiplying the coupon rate by the face value.

!

The "fair price" of bonds is estimated by determining the **present value** of the cash stream provided by the bond (which consists of an ordinary annuity of interest payments and one lump sum repayment). To determine the fair bond price (PV) of a bond with an *n* period term to maturity, we determine the present value of all future cash flows when discounted by the appropriate discount rate [i.e., the market required rate of return, denoted as (r)] using the following equation:

!

$$PV = C \times \left[\frac{1 - \frac{1}{(1+r)^n}}{r} \right] + P\left[\frac{1}{(1+r)^n} \right]$$

Example 1:

!

(a) Determine the bond price of a $1,000 face value bond with four years to maturity that pays interest semi-annually at a coupon rate of 12%. Assume the appropriate discount rate is 10% (this will almost always be stated on an annual basis).

[1] For the actual CSC exam, unless you are told otherwise you should assume the coupons are paid **semi-annually**.

! **Solution:**

C = coupon rate/2 × face value = 12/2 × $1,000 = $60;

n = term to maturity = 4 years × 2 = 8 (*semi-annual periods*);

r = 0.10/2 = 0.05 (semi-annual rate)

$$PV = 60 \times \left[\frac{1 - \frac{1}{(1.05)^8}}{.05} \right] + P\left[\frac{1}{(1.05)^8} \right]$$

= 60(6.46321) + 1,000(0.6784) = $1,064.63

Using Financial Calculator:

PMT → 60; N → 8; FV → 1,000; I/Y → 5; compute PV → $1,064.63

Note: These bonds sell at a "premium" over par since market rates (10%) are less than the coupon rate (12%). If market rates were above the coupon rate of 12%, the bonds would sell at a discount.

This illustrates the basic "inverse" relationship between bond prices and interest rates:

As rates increase, bond prices decrease, and vice versa.

(b) Repeat (a) assuming six years to maturity, and nothing else changed. Everything else is the same as in (a) except that

n = 6 years × 2 =12

$$PV = 60 \times \left[\frac{1 - \frac{1}{(1.05)^{12}}}{.05} \right] + P\left[\frac{1}{(1.05)^{12}} \right]$$

= 60(8.86325) + 1,000(0.55684) = $1,088.64

Using Financial Calculator:

PMT → 60; N → 12; FV → 1,000; I/Y → 5; compute PV → $1,088.63 (difference due to rounding)

These bonds sell at a greater premium over par than the four-year bonds, which illustrates another important bond relationship: the prices of *longer-term bonds are more sensitive to interest rate changes* than shorter-term bonds (all else being equal).

! The **current yield** relates the cash flow of an investment to the price paid for the investment. It is computed using the following equation:

Current Yield = Annual Cash Flow/Amount Invested

Example 2:

Calculate the current yield for the bond in Example 1(a) assuming you can purchase the bond for the price determined in the solution to 1(a).

Solution:

Current yield = (\$60)(2)/\$1,064.63 = 120/1064.63 = 0.1127 = 11.27%

Notice that this differs from the yield to maturity (i.e., the discount rate) of 10%.

The discount rate (or required market rate of return) for bonds is determined by market activity and is generally referred to as the yield, effective yield, **Yield To Maturity (YTM)**, or the **average purchase/redemption yield**. The YTM is the discount rate that equates the present value of all future expected payments on the bond if held to maturity to its present market price. It can be found by solving the equation below for YTM, given the bond price, coupon rate, maturity value, and term to maturity:

$$PV = C \times \left[\frac{1 - \frac{1}{(1+YTM)^n}}{YTM} \right] + P\left[\frac{1}{(1+YTM)^n} \right]$$

It may be solved by a financial calculator, by using bond tables, or approximated using the following formula:

$$Approx.\ YTM = \left[\frac{Annual\ Coupons + \frac{P - PV}{n}}{(P + PV)/2} \right]$$

This is an approximation, based on the notion of dividing the average annual cash flows (as measured by the annual interest payments + average annual capital gain or loss) by the average investment in the bond.

Example 3:

Determine the yield to maturity for a six-year \$1,000 face value bond that pays semi-annual coupons at an annual coupon rate of 12%, if it is presently selling for \$980.

Solution:

By Financial Calculator:

PMT → 60; N → 12; FV → 1,000; PV → \$980; Compute I/Y = 6.242%

This is a semi-annual rate, so we multiply by two to get the annual YTM of 12.48% (6.24 × 2 = 12.48%).

! Using the approximation YTM formula, we get

$$\text{Approx. } YTM = \frac{120 + \frac{(1000-980)}{6}}{\frac{(1000+980)}{2}} = \frac{120+3.33}{990} = 12.45\%$$

(difference due to nature of approximation formula)

! The yield on treasury bills is determined in Canada using the following equation:

$$T\text{-}bill\ yield = \frac{Face - P}{P} \times \frac{365}{n} \times 100\%$$

where *Face* is the face value of the T-bill, *P* is its price, and *n* is the number of days to maturity.

! Example 4:

Determine the yield on 89-day Government of Canada treasury bills that are currently selling at a price (*P*) of 98 per 100 of face value:

Solution:

$$T\text{-}bill\ yield = \frac{100-98}{98} \times \frac{365}{89} \times 100\% = 8.37\%$$

! The YTM is calculated based on the assumption that all interest payments received are reinvested at the YTM. Of course, this will seldom be the case due to changing interest rates. **Reinvestment risk** refers to the risk associated with changing interest rates, which implies that the interest payments received from a bond could be reinvested at rates lower than the initial YTM. Hence, even if an investor holds the bond to maturity, their return could be less than the YTM. Of course, the opposite is also true—the investor could end up reinvesting at rates higher than the initial YTM and earn a rate higher than that YTM. It is also worth noting that this risk will be somewhat offset by the fact that when rates fall, the bond price itself will go up, which is of course a good thing for investors holding the bonds.

! The required market rate of return on bonds is determined by supply and demand. Fisher's Law suggests that nominal rates of return will change in accordance with changes in inflation rates, which implies that **nominal rates = real rates + expected inflation rates.** Real rates are determined by the forces of supply and demand for loanable funds. They tend to rise and fall during expansionary and recessionary phases of the business cycle.

THE TERM STRUCTURE OF INTEREST RATES

!

The term structure of interest rates or **yield curve** demonstrates the relationship between long- and short-term rates on similar debt instruments (e.g. Government of Canada bonds).

!

The three major explanations offered for the shapes of term structures include the following:

1. **Liquidity Preference Theory**: Suggests that investors prefer short-term bonds because they exhibit less interest rate risk; therefore, they must be provided with premiums to induce them to invest in longer-term bonds. As a result, yield curves will generally be upward sloping since long-term rates will be higher than short-term rates.
2. **Expectations Theory**: Argues that the yield curve reflects investor expectations about future interest rates. Therefore, an upward-sloping yield curve reflects expectations of interest rate increases in the future, and a downward-sloping curve reflects expectations of interest rate decreases in the future.
3. **Market Segmentations Theory**: Argues that there exist distinct markets (or segments) for interest rate securities of differing maturities, and rates are determined within these independent markets by the forces of supply and demand. When we aggregate these rates, we end up with a given term structure.

!

Some important properties of fixed-income securities are[2]

1. Prices are inversely related to interest rates.
2. Prices exhibit greater interest rate risk (sensitivity to changes in interest rates) the longer their term to maturity.
3. The smaller the coupon rate (all else remaining equal), the greater the interest rate risk.
4. Special features such as call provisions or convertible privileges lead to special pricing considerations (as previously discussed).
5. Prices are more volatile when interest rates are low, since the relative change of a 1% change in rates is more significant.
6. The current price is the net effect of all of these factors.

Duration is a calculation that equates coupon risk and term risk into a single measure of interest rate risk. It measures the responsiveness of bond prices to changes in interest rates over relatively small intervals of interest rate changes. The higher the duration, the more sensitive a bond will be to changes in interest rates. In particular, the price of a bond with a duration of five will fall approximately 5% if interest rates rise by 1% and will increase by approximately 5% if rates fall 1%. All else being equal, bonds with greater maturities and lower coupon rates will have higher durations than bonds with shorter maturities and/or higher coupon rates.

[2] Properties (1) and (2) were demonstrated in Example 1 and are the most important ones to remember, along with property (3).

Duration will always be *less* than the bond's term to maturity for coupon bonds. It will always *equal* the term to maturity for zero-coupon (strip) bonds.

- **Bond switches** occur when an investor sells one bond and replaces it with another. Potential benefits include
    1. an improvement in net yield (e.g., a high-tax investor may switch to bonds with lower coupons to reduce the interest income and increase the capital gains portion of income);
    2. term extension or reduction (e.g., a switch to longer-term bonds if the investor believes that rates will fall);
    3. improvement in credit (i.e., a flight to quality occurs, particularly during periods of higher market volatility);
    4. portfolio diversification benefits; and
    5. cash take-outs (i.e., if you are able to exchange bonds and pocket some cash in the process).
- Successful bond switching (i.e., achieving the desired results) requires success in forecasting the bond market, which is no easy task. One must be careful to take into account the following considerations:
    1. longer-term bonds with lower coupon rates are the most volatile, and
    2. transactions costs may be significant, particularly for less liquid issues.

DELIVERY, REGULATION, AND SETTLEMENT

Some typical settlement requirements for debt instruments

1. G of C treasury bills: Same day.
2. G of C bonds and guarantees with term <= 3 years (or to earliest call date if the transaction occurs at a premium): Second clearing day after transaction.
3. G of C bonds and guarantees with term > 3 years (or to earliest call date if the transaction occurs at a premium) and all provincial, municipal, corporate, and other bonds or debentures; stock; and other certificates of indebtedness (including mortgage-backed securities [MBS] except as described in point 4 below): Third clearing day after transaction.

Bond certificates may be in one of three forms:

1. **Bearer Bonds**: These are presumed to be owned by the party holding the bonds. Coupons are numbered and dated, and may be clipped and redeemed for cash.
2. **Registered Bonds**: The name of the owner is on the face of these bonds, and interest is paid to the registered owner by the issuer. This protects the holder in the event the bond is lost or stolen, because it is difficult for anyone else to redeem them.

3. **Bonds Registered in Book-Based Format**: An electronic record-keeping system, rather than physical certificates. Used with most bond issues around the globe today. In Canada, CDS Clearing and Depository Services Inc. provides these services.

- Today settlement for most bonds is handled by the Canadian Depository for Securities Limited (CDS) through a computerized settlement procedure called a book-based system. If a buyer wishes to receive a certificate, the settlement procedure is handled through a certificate-based system.
- Bond trading is regulated by IIROC in conjunction with the Toronto Bond Traders Association and Montreal Bond Traders Association. These associations are open to any member of IIROC, the bond departments of any chartered bank, and any other financial house whose application is acceptable to the board of governors. IIROC is the senior member and reserves the right of final decision. Trading and delivery regulations cover all major aspects of trading, including trading and delivery practices, and general regulations.

Accrued interest refers to the amount of interest earned, but not yet received, by the holder of a bond prior to selling it, and this amount must be paid by the buyer to the previous holder. This amount must be paid to the previous holders above the quoted bond price, the sum of which is referred to as the bond's cash price. Accrued interest is calculated using the following calculation:

Accrued Interest = Par Amount × Coupon Rate × (Time Period/365)

Example 5:

Determine the accrued interest on $250,000 face value as of June 12, 2013, if the bonds mature on August 31, 2028, and the coupon rate is 6%. Assume it is not a leap year.

Solution:

We assume these bonds pay semi-annual coupons, since it is not stated otherwise. Since they mature on August 31, coupons must be paid on August 31 and February 28 every non-leap year (February 29 in a leap year). This means the last coupon payment was made on February 28. Therefore, they have 104 days of accrued interest (31 days in March + 30 days in April + 31 days in May + 12 days in June)—in other words, it has been 104 days since the last interest payment. Thus,

Accrued Interest = $250,000 × .06 × (104/365) = $4,273.97

BOND INDEXES

Bond indexes have not been around as long as stock indexes (i.e., only since the 1970s). They serve similar functions as stock indexes:

1. to gauge performance of the bond market as a whole,
2. to assess the performance of bond portfolio managers, and
3. to construct bond index funds.

The major bond indexes in Canada are provided by PC Bond, a business unit of the TMX Group Inc., with the most widely used and recognized being the **DEX Universe Bond Index**, which includes a large cross-section of government and corporate bonds. The Universe Index is a market-cap weighted index that measures total returns based on realized and unrealized capital gains, and assuming interest payments are reinvested. RBC Dominion Securities, CIBC Wood Gundy, and Standard and Poor's also maintain Canadian bond indexes.

Merrill Lynch maintains a comprehensive set of bond indexes for the various segments of the U.S. bond market and also provide several international indexes. Morgan Stanley Capital International (MSCI) maintains several global bond indexes, in addition to their global equity indexes.

Chapter 7 Review Questions

( ) 1. The ____________ suggests that the yield curve represents the supply of and demand for bonds of various terms, which are primarily influenced by the bigger players in each sector.

a) Liquidity Preference Theory

b) Expectations Theory

c) Market Segmentation Theory

d) Term Extension Theory

( ) 2. What is the yield to maturity on a 10% bond that pays out coupons semi-annually and has 10 years to maturity if the bond is selling at $113.40?

a) 10.0%

b) 8.54%

c) 8.12%

d) none of the above

( ) 3. What is the yield on a 90-day T-bill purchased for $96,000 with a maturity value of $100,000?

a) 16.9%

b) 16.6%

c) 16.4%

d) 16.2%

( ) 4. What would be the market price of a 10% non-callable corporate bond with a face value of $1,000 and 14 years to maturity if it pays interest semi-annually and the required rate of return on similar bonds is presently 8.4%?

a) $1,130

b) $1,129

c) $1,000

d) $985

5. If the bond in Question 4 was a callable bond, we would expect it would sell for ____________ the price determined in Question 4. ( )

a) the same as

b) higher than

c) lower than

d) cannot say

6. How much accrued interest would have to be paid if you purchased 10% semi-annual pay bonds on February 8, 2013, if the bonds mature on June 30, 2027? ( )

a) $5.34

b) $10.41

c) $10.68

d) insufficient information

7. For risk-free securities, the nominal interest rate is the sum of: ( )

a) actual and expected inflation rates

b) expected inflation and expected return

c) the real rate of interest and expected inflation rate

d) the market rate of return and real rate of interest

8. A trade in a bond with two and a half years to maturity settles: ( )

a) the same day

b) the next business day

c) in two business days

d) in three business days

9. Duration will always be ____________ the bond's term to maturity for coupon bonds. ( )

a) more than

b) less than

c) equal to

d) unrelated to

Refer to the following bond quote to answer Questions 10 and 11:

XYZ Company	7.50%	1 June 25/20	102.10	103.50	8.21

10. Which of the following statements regarding this bond is FALSE? ( )

a) It is a retractable bond.

b) It is an extendible bond.

c) It has an associated coupon rate of 7.50%.

d) It pays coupons on June 1 and December 1 every year.

( ) 11. If you were to purchase this bond on the date this quote was available, and the date was January 1, how much would you have to pay the seller for the bond?

a) $1,021

b) $1,027.37

c) $1,035

d) $1,041.37

Bonus Questions

( ) 12. The quote of a bond that makes semi-annual coupon payments, has three years to maturity, a coupon rate of 8%, and a yield to maturity of 8% is:

a) 87.5

b) 92.5

c) 100

d) 105

( ) 13. The price of a 12 year, zero-coupon bond that has a face value of $100 and a yield of 6.5% is:

a) $41.33

b) $46.97

c) $49.63

d) $53.86

( ) 14. The yield on a 75-day T-bill with a current price of 96 is:

a) 4.17%

b) 6.87%

c) 18.45%

d) 20.28%

( ) 15. The yield to maturity on a bond refers to:

a) the number of years remaining in the life of the bond

b) the amount of income that you will receive each year

c) the average rate of return on the bond if purchased at the current price and held to maturity

d) the amount of interest income you will receive in relation to the price of the bond

16. Which of the following statements concerning real interest rates is FALSE? ( )
    a) Real rates are determined by the supply of funds and demand for loans.
    b) Real rates equal the nominal rate plus the inflation rate.
    c) When real rates are high, the supply of funds will also be high.
    d) Real rates tend to fall during recessions and rise during economic expansions.

17. Holding everything else equal, when interest rates fall: ( )
    a) the yield on a bond is unaffected
    b) the price of a bond rises
    c) the price of a bond falls
    d) none of the above are true

18. Holding everything else equal, which bond is LEAST sensitive to interest rate changes? ( )
    a) a bond paying an annual coupon with a coupon rate of 5%
    b) a zero-coupon bond
    c) a bond paying semi-annual coupons with a coupon rate of 7%
    d) we do not have enough information to answer the question

19. A 100-basis-point drop in yield: ( )
    a) will have a larger impact on bond prices when yields are high
    b) will have a larger impact on bond prices when yields are low
    c) will impact bond prices the same when yields are high as when they are low
    d) will in general cause bond prices to decrease

20. The measure of the sensitivity of a bond's price to changes in interest rates is referred to as: ( )
    a) yield curve
    b) duration
    c) convexity
    d) yield to maturity

21. If the duration of a bond is 6 and its price is 94, then for a 1% increase in interest rates the price of the bond will: ( )
    a) rise to 99.64
    b) fall to 88
    c) fall to 88.36
    d) be unchanged

( ) 22. If the duration of a bond is 6, then a 50-basis-point decrease in interest rates will cause the bond price to:

a) fall by approximately 6%
b) rise by approximately 6%
c) fall by approximately 3%
d) rise by approximately 3%

chapter 8

EQUITY SECURITIES: COMMON AND PREFERRED SHARES

CSC EXAM SUGGESTED GUIDELINES:
13 questions for Chapter 8

INTRODUCTION

- A **common share** provides proportionate ownership in the company's equity value, the value of which will change in response to changes in the value of the firm's equity and the number of shares outstanding. These shares will be attractive to investors looking to profit from the future accomplishments of the issuer.
- A **preferred share** provides the owner with a claim to a fixed amount of equity that is established when the share is first issued. These will be more attractive to investors who desire steady income and a more secure position than common shareholders hold with respect to claims on the assets and income of the company.

COMMON SHARES

- Common share capital is sometimes referred to as risk capital to reflect the possibility of total loss of investment if the issuer fails. Today, most share certificates are in "street form," which makes them easily transferable.

The following rights are associated with common share ownership:

!

1. **Potential for Capital Appreciation**: As earnings are reinvested in the firm, the asset base and common equity base grow.

   Stock splits have little effect on existing shareholders. For example, a two-for-one split doubles the number of shares authorized, issued, and outstanding, and will likely cause the market price to fall to half of the previous market price. They are typically used to obtain a price in a target range that will entice investors and prevent odd-lot problems that may be associated with

! high-priced shares. **Reverse splits** (or **consolidations**) occur when shares are trading at a value that may be unattractive to investors because it is too low.

2. **Right to Receive Common Dividends**: The firm's dividend policy is established by the board of directors, and dividend payout ratios vary across firms and industries. The board of directors decides whether to pay dividends, the amount of the dividend, and the payment date. Reductions or omissions occur sometimes and reflect the risks of common share investment. Sometimes these payments are restricted by provisions in outstanding bond and/or preferred share issues. **Regular dividends** are those that investors can reasonably expect will be maintained in the future. **Extra** (or **special**) **dividends** are those that may arise due to unusually favourable circumstances and cannot be assumed to persist into the future. Extra dividends should be included in the calculation of a firm's dividend yield only if there is strong evidence that they will be paid again.

   Payments are made to shareholders of record on the **dividend record date**. The **ex-dividend date** is set at the second business day before the record date, and shares trade without the right to the associated dividend on and after this date. This ensures that a purchaser of the share three days before the record date would settle by the record date (since common share trades settle on the third business day after a trade). Shares are said to trade **cum dividend** up to the ex-dividend date, and trade **ex dividend** thereafter. This will be reflected in the share price, which typically falls by an amount close to the dividend amount on the ex-dividend date.

- **Dividend Reinvestment Plans (DRIPs)** reinvest shareholders' dividends to purchase additional shares for them; although the shareholder is taxed as if they had received the actual cash dividends. In effect, these plans provide investors with an automatic savings plan that has the advantage of using dollar cost averaging. The shares are typically purchased through the open market by trustees, and the plan permits the purchase equivalent of fractional shares. Variations allow investors to contribute additional cash amounts to the plan and/or provide for the purchase of treasury shares at pre-specified discounts from the open market prices.
- **Stock dividends** may be offered when the firm wishes to preserve cash. They give the shareholder ownership of additional shares, which are taxed the same as cash dividends.

3. **Voting Privileges**: Shares may be normal voting, multiple voting, non-voting, subordinate voting, or restricted voting. Restricted voting shares are protected by certain rights and regulations designed to ensure their position is not abused. Since 2004, the TSX and the TSX Venture Exchange identify restricted stocks according to the type of voting structures: non-voting (NV); subordinate voting (SV); and restricted voting (RV).
4. **Tax Treatment**: Income from common shares is afforded favourable tax treatment through:
   - federal and provincial tax dividend credits, which reduce the effective tax rate on dividend income; (discussed in detail in Chapter 25);

- capital gains exemptions, which exempt 50% of capital gains from taxation; and
- stock savings plans, which entitle residents of several provinces to deduct up to specified annual amounts from (or obtain a tax credit for) the cost of certain stocks purchased in the respective provinces.

5. **Marketability**: Investors can buy or sell shares in the open market at any time. Occasionally, share trading may be suspended by securities commissions as a result of a material change in affairs. In addition, foreign ownership in certain companies (e.g., banks, trust, and insurance companies; broadcasting and communications companies) is restricted.

- Other rights and advantages include the right to elect directors, receive copies of annual and quarterly reports, examine certain company documents such as the bylaws, question management at shareholder meetings, and limited liability.

Stock quotations are provided in financial publications. They typically provide information regarding the following:

1. **High** or **low**: The highest (or lowest) trading price during the previous day (or week, or 52-week period).
2. **Close**: The last trading price of the day.
3. **Change**: The change from the previous day's closing price.
4. **Volume**: The number of shares changing hands during the day.
5. **Div.**: The total dividends per share paid over the past 52 weeks.

PREFERRED SHARE CHARACTERISTICS

- Preferred shares can be found on the right side of the balance sheet between debt and common equity. This reflects the fact that preferred shareholders rank behind creditors with respect to the right to income and/or assets but ahead of common shareholders. In addition, sometimes corporations will issue more than one class of preferred shares that may be ranked with respect to their position. If several preferred share issues all have equal rights, their ranking is described as **pari passu**.
- Most preferred shares have an associated "preference as to assets" clause and pay fixed dividend amounts (either as a fixed-dollar amount or as a stated percentage of par value). While payment of preferred dividends is not obligatory like interest payments, payments to common shareholders are prohibited until preferred shareholders have been paid in entirety. Failure to pay anticipated preferred dividends will weaken investor confidence in the issuer, and affect its general credit and borrowing power.
- Preferred dividends are paid from after-tax earnings, and unlike interest payments, they do not provide the issuer with a tax-deductible expense. Shareholders receive some relief in the form of a dividend tax credit, which implies they will pay lower taxes on a dollar of dividend income than on a dollar of interest income.

- Preferred shares are primarily fixed-income instruments that offer limited opportunity for capital gains in comparison to common shares. Interest rates have a larger impact on their value than do the earnings of the issuer, and their value tends to go up (or down) as interest rates decline (or increase).

! Companies issue preferred shares as a compromise between the demands created by debt and the dilution of equity caused by the issuance of additional common shares, or when market conditions are unfavourable for new common share issues.

! Investors may be attracted to preferred shares when they desire dividend income, which offers tax advantages over interest income. In addition, sometimes there are special features that make preferred shares attractive to investors (which are discussed below).

Types of Preferred Shares

! **Fixed-Rate** (or **Straight**) **Preferreds**: May have some or all of the features discussed in the section below entitled "Preferred Features." Generally, they have a stated par value and pay a fixed dividend rate.

! Advantages and disadvantages of straight preferreds include

1. tax advantage of dividends;
2. less safety than debt, but greater safety than common shares;
3. "fixed" income;
4. no voting privileges;
5. no maturity date;
6. less marketable than common shares; and
7. less appreciation potential than common shares.

Note to students: The material on the following page (up to Convertible Preferreds) is no longer "directly" in Chapter 8, but it used to be tested frequently so I have left it in (just in case).

! Similar to bonds, straight preferred shares can be valued according to the present value of their future dividends. Since the dividends are for a fixed amount and there is no maturity date, the future dividends represent a perpetual annuity (or perpetuity). Denoting P_{ps} as the market price, D_p as the dividend amount, and k_p as the market required rate of return on the preferred shares, they can be valued according to the following equation:

$$P_{ps} = D_p/k_p$$

This equation can be rearranged to determine the required rate of return on the preferred shares as

$$k_p = D_p/P_{ps}$$

Example 1:

(a) Determine the market price of a preferred share that pays an annual dividend of $2, when market rates are 10%.

Solution:

P_{ps} = $2/.10 = $20

(b) Repeat (a) assuming market rates are 12%.

Solution:

P_{ps} = $2/.12 = $16.67 (notice that the price falls as rates rise just like with bonds)

(c) Repeat (a) assuming market rates are 8%.

Solution:

P_{ps} = $2/.08 = $25 (notice that the price rises as rates fall just like with bonds)

Example 2:

Determine the market yield on preferred shares that provide a $5 annual dividend and are presently selling for $60.

Solution:

k_p = $5/$60 = 0.0833 or 8.33%

Convertible Preferreds: Are convertible into common shares at a conversion price that is generally set at a modest premium (10% to 15%) above its converted value to discourage early conversion.

The **conversion "premium"** may be calculated as the cost of purchasing the required amount of convertible preferreds that could be converted into common shares, over and above the cost of purchasing the common shares directly in the market.

Example 3:

Determine the premium of a convertible preferred share that is presently selling for $50 and is convertible into two shares of common shares that are presently selling for $23.

Solution:

It would cost $50 to buy two common shares using the convertible versus $46 (2 × $23) to purchase them directly. Therefore

Dollar premium = $50 − $46 = $4 Percentage premium = premium/cost of purchasing common = 4/46 = 8.70%

The **payback** is the number of years it takes the buyer to pay back the premium from the convertible's higher dividend stream. In other words

Payback = (%premium) ÷ (convertible yield ÷ common yield)

Example 4:

Determine the payback for the preferred share in Example 3 if the annual dividends are $2.00 for the preferred shares, and $0.80 for the common shares.

Solution:

The dividend yield for the preferred shares = 2/50 = 4.0%

The dividend yield for the common shares = 0.80/23 = 3.48%

Therefore, payback = (8.70%)/(4.0% – 3.48%) = 16.73 years

Generally investors prefer convertibles with *lower premiums* and *shorter paybacks*; however, this will be dependent on the circumstances (which should be investigated).

- No commission is charged on conversion, and a capital gain or loss is not recorded until the common shares are actually sold.
- Investors must consider
  1. the outlook for the common stock;
  2. the life of the conversion privilege;
  3. the reasonableness of the premium; and
  4. the selling price in relation to the call price.
- Advantages and disadvantages of convertible preferreds include the following:
  1. They are two-way securities.
  2. They generally provide higher yields than the underlying common shares.
  3. They provide the right to obtain common shares without paying commission.
  4. They provide lower yields than straight preferreds.
  5. They may provide for less than "board lots" of common shares, which makes them harder to séll.
  6. They revert to straight preferreds after conversion period if not converted.

Retractable Preferreds: Can be tendered by the holder to the issuer for redemption at one or more retraction dates. Investors must consider

1. the life of the retraction privilege; and
2. the relationship of the market price to the retraction price.

- Advantages and disadvantages of retractable preferreds include the following:
    1. They are less vulnerable to interest rate changes (short maturity potential).
    2. There exists the potential for capital gains if bought at a discount from retraction price.
    3. They sell above retraction price and at least as high as call price when rates drop.
    4. They do not retract automatically.
    5. They become straight preferreds if not retracted.

- The yield on a retractable may be calculated as follows:
    1. when selling above retraction price:

       Yield = annual dividend/market price
    2. when selling below retraction price:

       Yield = (annual dividend + annualized capital gain) ÷ ([market price + retraction price]/2)

Example 5:

!

(a) Calculate the yield for a 7% $100 par value preferred share that is retractable at $100 in 6 years and 6 months' time when it sells for $103.

Solution:

Yield = $7/$103 = 6.79%

(b) Repeat (a) when the preferred share is selling for $97.

Solution:

Yield = ($7 + [100 – 97]/6.5) ÷ ([97 + 100]/2) = 7.462/98.5 = 0.07576 or 7.58%

!

Variable or **Floating-Rate Preferreds**: Dividend payments vary with interest rates over certain time periods.

Companies issue variable-rate preferreds for several reasons, including the following:

1. Straight preferreds are not selling well and the issuer does not want to issue convertible or retractable preferreds.
2. The issuer believes rates will not increase (and may decrease).
3. The issuer is trying to match the nature of their assets.

Sometimes firms issue **delayed floaters**, **fixed-reset**, or **fixed floaters**, which provide fixed dividends for a certain period of time, after which they become variable.

- Advantages and disadvantages of variable or floating-rate preferreds include
  1. higher income if rates rise;
  2. variable income amounts that may be difficult to predict; and
  3. prices will be relatively unresponsive to changes in rates.

! **Preferreds with Warrants**: Often warrants are sold along with preferreds in a unit, to provide a *sweetener* for investors.

Other Preferreds

! **Participating Preferreds**: Have certain pre-specified rights to share in company earnings over and above their specified rate.

- **Foreign-Pay Preferreds**: Pay dividends in foreign currencies. Benefits or costs depend on the resulting exchange rates, and beliefs regarding future exchange rates factor greatly in assessing the desirability of holding such instruments. One advantage of these is that while payment is received in a foreign currency, the dividend is still eligible for the dividend tax credit. They may be attractive to sophisticated investors who wish to diversify the currencies in their portfolio and/or to Canadian investors who require foreign currency for some other reason (e.g., extensive travel abroad).
- **Auction Preferreds**: Their dividend rate is determined by an auction between the holder and the issuer, and they usually offer minimum and maximum reset dividend rates.
- **Deferred Preferreds**: Do not pay dividends until some specified future maturity date, at which time the accrued dividends are treated as interest income. If they are sold prior to the maturity date, the income is treated as a capital gain (or loss). These provide investors with an opportunity to defer taxes paid on income earned until a later date.
- **Split Shares**: Also known as **structured preferreds** or **equity dividend shares**. These represent common shares that have been split into two different shares: the *equity dividend share* that receives the dividends, and the *capital share* that receives the greatest potential for capital gains. Most of these are redeemable; however, if redeemed prior to maturity, the investor foregoes dividend income.

Preferred Features

! Preferred shares usually have a **cumulative** feature associated with their dividends. This requires the firm to pay all preferred dividends (current and arrears) before paying any dividends to common shareholders, which makes the preferred less risky than common shares from the investor's point of view.

- **Callable** (or **redeemable**) **preferred shares** are generally callable at a premium over par value, similar to callable debt, which benefits the issuer.

! Generally, preferred shares are **non-voting**. However, if a pre-specified number of dividend payments are not made, they may receive voting privileges.

- Some preferreds have **purchase funds** that require the company to purchase a specified amount of preferreds in the open market, if they are available at or below the stipulated price. This provides built-in market support for these shares.
- Sinking fund provisions are less common for preferred share issues. They have the potential disadvantage to investors that the required purchases may be called in by lot at the sinking fund price plus accrued and unpaid dividends, if the fund's open market operations are unsuccessful.
- Generally, both purchase and sinking funds improve the position of remaining preferred shareholders, by reducing the number of shares outstanding.
- **Protective provisions** generally include
  1. restriction of common dividends unless working capital and/or purchase or sinking fund requirements are met;
  2. the right to vote is provided in event of arrears beyond a stipulated amount; and
  3. restrictions on further preferred issues, sale of assets, or changes in the terms of the original issue.

STOCK INDICES AND AVERAGES

An **index** is a number that measures a number of stock prices so that a percentage change in this index may be calculated over time. They are used for performance comparisons and to gauge overall movements in the stock market. They are also important for creating index mutual funds and serve as the underlying assets for options, futures, and exchange-traded funds. An **average** is used for the same purposes as an index, but it is unlike an index because it is determined by summing a number of prices and dividing this sum by the number of items composing the average; therefore it is composed of equally weighted items. !

The TSE 300 Composite Index System was introduced in 1977. The value of the **S&P/TSX Composite Index** is determined by the total market capitalization (the number of common shares outstanding times the market price per share) of a portfolio of the largest and most actively traded Canadian stocks. In other words, it is *a market- or value-weighted index.* Thus, a stock's weight changes in response to changes in share price and/or the number of shares outstanding. The stocks that are included in the index are reviewed every quarter, and new stocks are added to replace those that no longer satisfy the criteria for inclusion. !

- The stocks included in the S&P/TSX Index are classified by industry to form 10 sector indices, based on the Global Industry Classification Standard (GICS), which was developed by S&P and MSCI. There are also three Canadian-specific subsector indices (Diversified Mining, Real Estate, and Gold). The base value of 1,000 was set for all indices for the base year of 1975.
- Total Return indices were introduced in 1980 and measure the return on the indices if all dividends had been reinvested. As such, they measure the actual total

returns that would have been achieved by holding those stocks on a continuous basis. Their base value is set at 1,000 as of December 31, 1976.

The **S&P/TSX 60**, which is also a market-weighted index, was introduced on December 31, 1998. It is managed by S&P and the index base value was set equal to 100 as of January 29, 1982. This base period was chosen due to concerns regarding data reliability prior to this date. This is the index upon which the value of i60 units is based. It is also the basis for equity index option and futures products that trade on the ME.

The **S&P/TSX Venture Composite Index** is a market-cap weighted index measuring the performance of the TSX Venture Index. It has been in existence since December 2001. It is revised quarterly and does not contain a specified number of companies. It includes companies that are incorporated in Canada and represent at least 0.05% of the total market capitalization of the index.

The **Dow Jones Industrial Average (DJIA)** is the most widely quoted measure of NYSE stock performance, despite the fact that it includes only 30 of over 2,300 stocks that trade on the NYSE. It is a *price-weighted average* and is therefore affected more by changes in higher priced stocks. It is calculated by adding the prices of the 30 stocks together and dividing by a divisor, which has been revised downward through the years to reflect the impact of stock splits. The DJIA is composed of the highest quality blue chip stocks that trade in the United States. These stocks have relatively low risk and have tended to underperform broader based indices such as the S&P 500 Index (discussed below) in the long-term as a result. Other Dow Jones indices include the Transportation average (20 companies), a Utility average (15 companies), and a Composite average (65 companies), which are all price-weighted.

The **S&P 500 Index** is a broader based market-weighted index that measures U.S. stock performance. It is widely used to measure the investment performance of institutional investments.

- The NYSE maintains market-valued indices which include all listed equities for a given group: composite; industrials; transportation; finance and real estate; and utilities. The AMEX index is a market value-weighted index, based on the market capitalization of all 800 or so stocks that trade on the American Stock Exchange. The NASDAQ Composite Index includes over 4,000 OTC stocks (market cap around 13% of NYSE stocks) and is market-valued. The Value Line Composite Index measures the average percentage change in about 1,700 stocks that are mainly second tier issues. It is maintained by Wilshire Associates and represents one of the broadest measures of U.S. stock market activity.
- Important international indices include
    1. the Nikkei Stock Average (225) in Japan, which is price-weighted and has been available since 1950;
    2. the FTSE 100 Index in the United Kingdom, which is market-weighted;
    3. the DAX in Germany, which consists of 30 blue chip stocks and is value-weighted (assuming reinvested equity income);
    4. the CAC 40 Share Price Index in France; and
    5. the Swiss Market Index in Switzerland.

Chapter 8 Review Questions

1. The settlement date for convertible preferred shares is the ____________ the transaction. ( )
   a) second clearing day after
   b) third clearing day after
   c) same day as
   d) next clearing day after

Refer to the following information to answer Questions 2 to 4:

A convertible preferred share is presently selling for $35 and is convertible into three shares of common shares which are presently selling for $11. The annual dividends are $2.00 for the preferred shares and $0.22 for the common shares.

2. What is the conversion premium percentage? ( )
   a) 5.7%
   b) 6.1%
   c) 6.3%
   d) there is insufficient information

3. What is the dividend yield on the common shares? ( )
   a) 0.7%
   b) 1.0%
   c) 2.0%
   d) 5.0%

4. What is the payback for these convertibles? ( )
   a) 0.6 years
   b) 1.1 years
   c) 2.3 years
   d) none of the above

5. The cumulative feature, associated with some preferred shares, requires the company to do which of the following? ( )
   a) pay all current dividends on preferred shares prior to paying dividends to common shareholders
   b) pay all dividends, both current and arrears, on preferred shares prior to paying dividends to common shareholders
   c) accumulate and set aside funds in order to pay preferred share dividends
   d) none of the above

( ) 6. Which of the following are examples of protective provisions associated with preferred shares?

I. the right to vote if a specified number of dividends are omitted

II. restrictions placed on the sale of assets

III. the callable feature

IV. the issue of Class A shares

a) I and II

b) I and III

c) II and III

d) II and IV

( ) 7. A company has one million shares outstanding before it undergoes a one-for-four consolidation. After the consolidation, the number of shares outstanding will be:

a) unchanged

b) 0.25 million

c) 2 million

d) 4 million

( ) 8. A company declares a dividend that is payable on January 25 to holders of record on December 8. In order to be entitled to receive this dividend, you must buy the shares prior to:

a) January 25

b) December 7

c) December 6

d) December 5

( ) 9. Which of the following statements about the DJIA and the S&P/TSX Composite Index is true?

a) The DJIA is more greatly affected by stocks with a higher market cap than is the S&P/TSX Index.

b) S&P/TSX is more greatly affected by stocks with a higher market cap than is the DJIA.

c) Both are equally affected by stocks with a higher market cap.

d) None of the above are true.

( ) 10. The ____________ is the most widely used benchmark by investment professionals in the United States.

a) DJIA

b) S&P 500

c) Value Line Composite Index

d) NASDAQ Composite Index

11. A potential disadvantage of common shares is: ( )
    a) dividends are payable at the discretion of management
    b) they rank behind many other stakeholders in receiving payment in the event of default
    c) they suffer from limited liability
    d) statements (a) and (b) are true, but (c) is false

12. The most predominate measure of the Japanese stock market is: ( )
    a) the CAC 40 Share Price Index
    b) the German DAX Index
    c) the Nikkei Stock Average (225) Price Index
    d) the FTSE 100 Index

13. Which of the following is NOT a subsector index in the Canadian market? ( )
    a) Diversified minerals
    b) Financials
    c) Gold
    d) Real Estate

Bonus Questions

14. If an index starts with a value of 500 and increases in value to 550, then ____________ is the percentage change and ____________ is the point change. ( )
    a) 50; 10
    b) 5; 25
    c) 10; 50
    d) 110; 550

15. Under the current Canadian tax system, capital gains are: ( )
    a) fully tax deductable
    b) taxed at a rate equal to 50% of regular income
    c) taxed as regular income
    d) included in the dividend tax credit offered to shareholders of taxable Canadian companies

16. Pari passu refers to: ( )
    a) the ranking of preferred shares relative to common shares
    b) the ranking of preferred shares relative to debt holders
    c) when different classes of preferred shares have different rank in relation to asset and dividend entitlement
    d) when different classes of preferred shares have the same rank in relation to asset and dividend entitlement

( ) 17. ABC Inc., a Canadian firm, has outstanding preferred shares that pay a fixed annual dividend of US$1.525 per share. This is an example of:

a) a fixed floater
b) a foreign-pay preferred
c) a COPrS
d) a soft retractable preferred

( ) 18. Which of the following is NOT a benefit to owning common shares?

a) limited liability
b) potential for capital gains and dividend income
c) marketability
d) the right to fire managers

( ) 19. Which of the following statements about regular and extra dividends is true?

a) Companies increase a regular dividend in a given year by instituting an extra dividend, the combined value of which is the regular dividend in the following year.
b) The company can, at its discretion, decrease or eliminate an extra dividend, but not a regular dividend.
c) Regular dividends are expected to be maintained by the company, while the extra dividend is likely to be reduced in future years.
d) Regular and extra dividends are synonyms for cash dividends.

( ) 20. If the dividend record date on a share is March 23 (a Friday), then the ex-dividend date is:

a) March 21
b) March 22
c) March 23
d) March 24

( ) 21. Subordinate voting restricted shares:

a) have no voting rights
b) have the right to vote, but on a lower per share basis than other types of shares outstanding
c) have the right to vote, but are limited in the number or percentage of shares that may be voted by a person, company, or group
d) have voting rights similar to common shares, but rank behind common shares in settlement given liquidation

( ) 22. The dividend tax credit:

a) is designed to avoid the double taxation of dividends
b) provides debt holders with a tax incentive, as interest payments made by corporations are tax deductible

c) is now obsolete, as the tax treatment of interest and dividend payments is now equivalent in Canada

d) none of the above statements are true

23. Which of the following statements concerning stock splits and consolidations is FALSE? ( )

a) Splits and consolidations are used to keep stock prices within a price range deemed optimal by management.

b) A shareholder who owns 500 shares valued at $30 will own 1,500 shares valued at $10 each after a three-for-one split.

c) A shareholder who owns 500 shares valued at $10 will own 1,250 shares valued at $4 each after a two-for-five consolidation.

d) Stock consolidations are used, among other reasons, to avoid delisting of a stock from an exchange.

24. Preferred shares with a cumulative dividend feature require: ( )

a) the company to pay any preferred dividends in arrears before they pay any common dividends

b) the company to pay the fixed preferred dividend in every year, regardless of its financial position

c) the company to declare a dividend before it is paid in a given year

d) the company to pay preferred dividends equal in value to the amount of common dividends

25. Which of the following statements concerning floating rate preferreds is FALSE? ( )

a) They rank behind other types of debt but ahead of common shares in the event of default.

b) They trade on listed stock exchanges.

c) Their price is very sensitive to interest rate changes.

d) Their quarterly distributions are treated as dividend income for income tax purposes.

26. Which of the following statements concerning the DJIA is FALSE? ( )

a) It is the most widely used stock market average in the United States.

b) It is composed of the shares of 30 industrial companies.

c) Its value is calculated by summing the prices of the stocks in the average and dividing by the number of companies in the average.

d) Changes in the price of shares which have a higher price have more impact on the DJIA than price changes of low priced shares, regardless of their relative market value.

EQUITY SECURITIES: EQUITY TRADING

chapter 9

CSC EXAM SUGGESTED GUIDELINES:
10 questions for Chapter 9

CASH AND MARGIN ACCOUNTS

!

Clients who open **cash accounts** are not granted credit by the securities firm and are expected to make a full payment for purchases by the settlement date. The **settlement date** is

1. the same day as the trade for government T-bills;
2. two business days after the trade for other Government of Canada direct and guaranteed bonds/securities up to three years; and
3. three business days after the trade for all other securities (including preferred and common shares).

A **long position** is when an investor owns the underlying security, whereas a **short position** is created when an investor sells securities they do not own.

Margin accounts are established for clients to enable them to buy (or short sell) securities by initially contributing only part of the full price of the transaction, with the remainder being borrowed from the member (with interest being charged on the borrowed amount).

- Investment firms are allowed the use of customers' free credit balances, but must give them written notice to this effect.
- The term "margin" refers to the amount of funds the investor must contribute to the margin account.

Maximum loan values by exchange and IDA members for securities other than bonds and debentures, expressed as maximum percentages of market value, are[1]

- 70% for securities eligible for reduced margin;
- 50% for prices of $2 and over that are not eligible for reduced margin;

[1] Member firms may establish more stringent margin criteria if they so choose.

!
- 40% for prices of $1.75–$1.99;
- 20% for prices of $1.50–$1.74; and
- no loan value for prices under $1.50.

- When the margin falls below the specified level (due to a decline in market value of the underlying security), the client receives a "**margin call**" from the member firm requiring the client to deposit additional funds (or securities) to the account, or else shares will be sold to bring the account within margin. If the security rises in value, the account may have excess margin in the account, which may be utilized by the client.

!
Example 1:

(a) Determine your margin requirement if you purchase 1,000 common shares of company A on margin when it is trading at $2.00 and is not eligible for special margin.

Solution:

Total cost A = $2 × 1,000	= $2,000
Less: ID max. loan (@50%)	= $1,000
Equals: Margin requirement	= $1,000

(b) If the price of A immediately decreases to $1.50, how much (if any) will you be required to deposit into your margin account?

Solution:

Notice that the new percentage limit on the maximum loan is now 20%.

Original cost A	= $2,000
Less: Revised ID max. loan A (@20%)	
= 0.20 × $1.50 × 1,000	= $300
Gross Margin Requirement	= $1,700
Margin deficit (surplus)	= deficit $700
(since there was only $1,000 in the account)	

Therefore, the required deposit is $700, which will increase the margin contribution to $1,700 and reduce the loan amount to $300 (the allowable amount).

(c) What if, instead of falling, the price had risen to $3? In other words, repeat (b) assuming the new price was $3.

Solution:

Original cost A	= $2,000
Less: Revised ID max. loan A (@50%)	
= 0.50 × $3.00 × 1,000	= $1,500
Gross Margin Requirement	= $500
Margin deficit (surplus)	=surplus $500
(since there was already $1,000 in the account)	

Therefore, you may withdraw $500, which will reduce the margin contribution to $500 and increase the loan amount to $1,500 (the allowable amount).

SHORT SALES

!

Short sales occur when an investor sells securities they do not own. The investor is said to be in a "short" position since he or she must repay them in the future (hopefully they can be repurchased after prices have fallen). The investor must leave the proceeds of the short sale with the dealer (who then has free use of these funds), and deposit a certain portion of the market value in addition to the proceeds. It is, in essence, the reverse of buying a stock on margin.

Required account balances, expressed as percentages of market value, are

- 130% for securities eligible for reduced margin;
- 150% for prices of $2 and over that are not eligible for reduced margin;
- $3.00 per share for prices of $1.50–$1.99;
- 200% of market value for prices of $0.25–$1.49; and
- 100% of market plus $0.25 per share for prices under $0.25.

Example 2:

!

(a) Determine the amount that an investor must deposit in their account if they short sell 1,000 shares of a stock that is eligible for reduced margin and is trading for $10.

Solution:

Minimum account balance (@130%)	= 1.30 × $10 × 1,000	= $13,000
Less: Proceeds from short sale	= $10 × 1,000	= $10,000
Equals: Minimum margin requirement		= $3,000

(b) What will happen if the price of the shares which were sold short immediately increases to $12?

Solution:

Minimum account balance (@130%)	= 1.30 × $12 × 1,000	= $15,600
Less: Proceeds from short sale	= $10 × 1,000	= $10,000
Equals: Minimum margin requirement		= $5,600
Required deposit = margin deficit = 5,600 – 3,000		= $2,600

(c) Instead of (b), what would happen if the price of the shares had immediately decreased to $8?

Solution:

Minimum account balance (@130%)	= 1.30 × $8 × 1,000	= $10,400
Less: Proceeds from short sale	= $10 × 1,000	= $10,000
Equals: Minimum margin requirement		= $400
Required deposit (surplus) = margin surplus = 400 – 3,000		= ($2,600)

The $2,600 represents surplus funds, which may be withdrawn.

! Profits and losses are calculated based on the difference between the initial selling price and the subsequent purchase price. For example, if you short sold 100 shares for a price of $5 per share and repurchased the shares when the price was $4 per share, you would gain $1 per share, for a total of $100.

- There is **no time limit** on the maintenance of a short position; however, the client must buy the necessary shares to cover the position if the broker is unable to borrow sufficient shares to do so. Because of this potential problem, many experienced traders confine short sales activities to stocks that are actively traded. Members are required to disclose which trades are short sales, and the TSX compiles and publicly reports total short positions twice a month.

! Difficulties and hazards of short selling include

  - difficulties in borrowing a sufficient number of shares;
  - responsibility of maintaining an adequate margin;
  - liability for any dividends paid;
  - threat of buy-in requirements if margin is not maintained and/or if originally borrowed stock is called by its owners and cannot be replaced;
  - difficulty in obtaining up-to-date information on total short sales;
  - possibility of volatile prices should a "rush" to cover occur; and
  - the unlimited potential loss.

EQUITY TRANSACTIONS

- Traditional equity transactions involve a buyer, who is represented by an investment advisor (IA) as their agent, and a seller, who is also represented by an IA as their agent. The respective IAs report the current bid and ask prices to their clients. Assuming that the bid price is $20, and the ask price is $21, the buyer knows he can purchase at least one board lot (100 shares) if he is willing to pay the current ask price of $21 per share. Similarly, the seller can sell at least one board lot if she is willing to accept the current bid price of $20 per share. The clients may then decide to inform their IA to obtain the best possible price for the stock, which is referred to as a market order (discussed in the next section). A transaction occurs if the buyer is willing to accept a seller's price, or vice versa.
- After a transaction has occurred, both the buyer and the seller must receive a confirmation of the transaction, which describes the transaction details, as well as the amount of commissions due and payable. The parties involved are then required to "settle" the transaction (within three business days if it is an equity trade).
- An alternative transaction format that is very common is to have one IA act as an agent for both the buyer and seller.

- IAs can also act as principals in an equity transaction when they fill a customer's order from their own inventory in a security. In this situation, the trade is executed at the market price as determined by the exchange, which is based on detailed procedures designed to protect the investor.

Buy and Sell Orders: !

1. **Market orders** are executed at the best available price.
2. **Limit orders** are executed only if a specific price or better can be obtained.
3. **Day orders** are limit orders that are valid only for the day.
4. **Open** or **Good Till Cancelled (GTC) orders** are limit orders that remain open until executed or until the date specified in the order. Usually they are held open for 30, 60, or 90 days.
5. **All Or None (AON) orders** are executed only if the total number of shares specified in the order can be obtained or sold. Alternatively, the investor may specify a minimum number of shares that is acceptable.
6. **Any part orders** are the opposite of AON orders. They will accept any amount of shares, whether in round or odd lots, up to the total amount of the order.
7. **Good through orders** remain valid orders for a specified period of time, after which they are automatically cancelled if not yet filled.
8. **Stop-loss orders** are orders that generate *market orders* to sell if the price drops below a certain level. They are used to limit losses on long positions.
9. **Stop buy orders** are the opposite of stop-loss orders. A *market buy order* is generated if the price rises above a certain level to limit losses on short positions.
10. **Professional (Pro) orders** are transactions involving partners, directors, officers, shareholders, IAs, or specified employees. These orders must be appropriately labelled as **Pro** or **N-C** (non-client) or **Emp** (employee).

- The **preferential trading rule** requires IAs to give priority to client orders over those of non-clients, which may include professional orders from partners, directors, officers, shareholders, IAs, and in some cases, specified employees.

Chapter 9 Review Questions

1. The minimum required margin deposit as a percentage of the market value of securities that are purchased of shares with a market price of $1.91 per share is: ( )

   a) 30%

   b) 40%

   c) 50%

   d) 60%

( ) 2. You purchase five board lots of the common shares of company A on margin. The share is presently trading for $1.50. How much cash must you deposit with your broker?

a) $375

b) $450

c) $600

d) $750

( ) 3. Refer to the information given in Question 2. If the price of A dropped immediately to $1.40, how much will you be required to deposit into your margin account?

a) $10

b) $50

c) $100

d) $150

( ) 4. A friend of yours decides to short sell 1,000 shares of security B that is eligible for reduced margin and is trading at $8. What amount must she deposit into a margin account?

a) $2,400

b) $4,000

c) $4,800

d) $6,400

( ) 5. Refer to the information given in Question 4. If the price of B dropped immediately to $7, how much would your friend be required to deposit into her account?

a) $1,500

b) she can withdraw $1,500

c) $1,300

d) she can withdraw $1,300

( ) 6. Refer to the information given in Question 4. What profit (loss) does your friend realize if she closes her short position when the price of the underlying share is $5?

a) profit of $3,000

b) loss of $3,000

c) profit of $5,000

d) loss of $5,000

7. Which of the following statements regarding stop-loss orders and stop buy orders are true? ( )

   I. A stop-loss order is used to reduce losses on a short sale, while a stop buy order is used to limit losses on long positions.

   II. A stop-loss order is used to limit losses on long positions, while a stop buy is used to reduce losses on a short sale.

   III. Both involve margin deposits.

   IV. Both generate market orders.

   a) I and II

   b) I and III

   c) II and III

   d) II and IV

8. If you call up your broker and tell her to sell 100 shares at the best available price, she will execute a: ( )

   a) good through order

   b) market sell order

   c) limit sell order

   d) GTC order

9. What is the difference between a market order and a day order? ( )

   a) Market orders are executed at the best immediately available price, while day orders are executed at the best price available during the entire day.

   b) Market orders are those that occur when the client sets a specific price at which the transaction can be executed, while day orders have certain restrictions placed upon them before they can be executed.

   c) Market orders are executed at the best available price, while day orders are executed only if a specific price or better can be obtained.

   d) Market orders are those that occur when the client sets a specific price at which the transaction can be executed, while day orders are executed only if a specific price or better can be obtained.

10. What difficulties and hazards are associated with short selling a stock? ( )

   I. There can be difficulties borrowing the required quantity of the security sold short to cover the short sale.

   II. The short seller is not liable for any dividends paid during the period the account is short.

   III. There are difficulties in obtaining up-to-date information on total short sales on a security.

   IV. The short seller is responsible for maintaining adequate margin in the short account.

a) I, II, III, IV
b) I, II, IV
c) II, III
d) I, III, IV

Bonus Questions

( ) 11. A ____________ position refers to the ownership of a security, whereas a ____________ position refers to the sale of a security that an investor does not own.

a) long; short
b) cash; margin
c) short; long
d) margin; cash

( ) 12. A bond with more than three years to maturity settles ____________, whereas a Government of Canada treasury bill settles ____________.

a) two business days after the trade; the next business day
b) three business days after the trade; the next business day
c) two business days after the trade; the same day as the trade
d) three business days after the trade; the same day as the trade

( ) 13. If an investor wishes to short sell 100 shares of a security currently trading at $1.50 a share, then the minimum account balance is:

a) $150
b) $225
c) $300
d) $450

( ) 14. An investor short sells 500 shares of a security, currently valued at $2.50 a share, but which are eligible for reduced margin. If the share price increases by $1.00, then the investor:

a) is able to remove $650 from the margin account
b) will receive a margin call for $650
c) will receive a margin call for $500
d) is able to remove $500 from the margin account

( ) 15. An investor short sells 1,000 shares of a security that is not eligible for reduced margin, currently valued at $2.75 a share. If the share price falls to $1.75 a share, then the investor is able to withdraw:

a) $125 from the margin account
b) $250 from the margin account
c) $1,125 from the margin account
d) $2,750 from the margin account

16. Which of the following is NOT a danger of short selling? ( )

a) The short seller may have to increase their margin.

b) The losses from short selling are potentially limitless.

c) The short seller may have to replace the asset even if they desire to maintain the short position.

d) The stock price may be above the original short sale price on the maturity date of the short sale certificate.

17. Which of the following statements concerning investment dealers acting as principals is true? ( )

a) The investment dealer matches a buyer (seller) with a seller (buyer) at another firm.

b) The investment dealer matches a buyer (seller) with a seller (buyer) within their own firm.

c) The investment dealer buys or sells securities from their own inventory.

d) Investment dealers are prohibited from acting as principals in trades as a result of potential conflicts of interest.

18. ______________ refers to a trade order to buy or sell at the current price. ( )

a) Market order

b) Limit order

c) Day order

d) Good through order

19. If an investment order does not specify the time in which the investment advisor has to fill the order, then: ( )

a) the order remains open until filled

b) if the order cannot be filled immediately, it is cancelled

c) the order remains open until the close of the business day, or until filled, whichever is sooner

d) the order cannot be accepted, as investment advisors cannot accept orders that do not have a specified expiry date

20. The maximum that an investor can borrow to purchase a security currently priced at $1.55 is: ( )

a) zero

b) 20% of the market value of the transaction

c) 40% of the market value of the transaction

d) 50% of the market value of the transaction

DERIVATIVES

chapter

10

CSC EXAM SUGGESTED GUIDELINES:

10 questions for Chapter 10

INTRODUCTION

- Derivatives are so called because they derive their value from the price of another underlying asset, such as a stock, stock or bond index, commodity price, etc. They are suitable for hedging or speculative purposes by more sophisticated investors and are used extensively by institutional investors. Investment advisors dealing in derivatives require additional research, specialized knowledge, and particular skills, and are required to take special courses to deal in some of these products. Conversion, retraction, or extendible features that are attached to debt and preferred equity securities are securities that include embedded options, and are also derivative securities.

While derivatives can take on many complex forms, most fall into one of two categories:

1. **Options**: Contracts that provide the buyer the right, but not the obligation, to buy or sell a certain quantity of some underlying asset at a predetermined price for a predetermined period of time. The seller of the contract is obligated to buy or sell if called upon to do so.
2. **Forwards**: Contracts that obligate both parties to exchange a certain quantity of an underlying asset at a specified future point in time at a predetermined price.

! Derivatives trade on exchanges and in the over-the-counter (OTC) market. The key differences between these derivatives are listed below:

Exchange-traded	OTC
standardized contracts	customized contracts
public (transparent)	private
ease of early termination	early termination more difficult
clearinghouse provides third-party guarantee	default risk—no third-party guarantee
gains/losses "marked-to-market" daily	gains/losses settled at end of day
heavy regulation	much less regulation
delivery rarely occurs	delivery or cash settlement often
visible trading costs (i.e., commission)	trading costs less visible (dealer spread)
used by retail, institutional, corporations	used by corporations and financial institutions

There are two main categories of underlying assets: **commodities** (e.g., wheat, corn, soybeans, canola, livestock, forest products, food products, precious and industrial metals, and energy products), and **financials** (e.g., equities, interest rate products, and currencies).

Derivatives are used by **individual investors**, **institutional investors**, **corporations and businesses**, and **derivative dealers**. The main reasons they use them are for speculative or hedging purposes, which will be discussed in greater detail later in the chapter. They are also used for yield enhancement, market entry and exit, and for arbitrage purposes.

OPTIONS

! **Options** are contracts between a buyer and a seller, based on an underlying security. Unlike rights and warrants, they are not issued by a company as a form of capital. The **buyer** pays a "**premium**" or fee and *receives the right, but not the obligation,* to exercise certain rights provided in the contract. Each equity option contract is for *100 underlying shares,* therefore if the quoted price is $2, the cost of purchasing the option contract would be $2 × 100 = $200. The **seller** or "**writer**" of the option contract is "*obligated*" to undertake certain actions specified in the contract, when notified to do so by the buyer (or the clearing corporation).

! The **expiration** (or **expiry**) **date** is the date at which the option contract expires. Options expire on the *third Friday* of the stated expiration month.

! The "**exercise**" or "**strike**" **price** refers to the price specified in the contract at which the underlying security may be *bought* (in the case of a "**call**" option) or *sold* (in the case of a "**put**" option).

European-style options can be exercised *only* at the expiry date, while **American**-style options can be exercised *any time up to and including the expiry date.* Most exchange-listed equity options are American style, while index options and OTC options are typically European.

Options can be bought or sold through an exchange facility or privately arranged (OTC options).

- Exchange-traded options alleviate some problems that plague the OTC options markets by
    1. standardizing option contracts; and
    2. introducing a clearing corporation that guarantees the performance of the seller of an options contract (i.e., effectively it becomes the buyer and seller for each option contract).

The **Canadian Derivatives Clearing Corporation (CDCC)** is the sole clearing corporation in Canada, and issues and guarantees all equity, bond, and stock index option positions. In the United States all listed options are cleared through the Options Clearing Corporation (OCC).

When an investor initially buys or sells option contracts, it is referred to as an opening transaction. When they buy the option(s), they establish a "long" position, and when they sell them, they establish a "short" position.

Investors close their positions on or before the expiration date in one of three ways:

1. They can enter into an "offsetting" transaction, which involves selling identical options if they were originally a buyer, or buying identical options if they were originally sellers. This is easy to do for exchange-traded options since all transactions go through the clearinghouse. It is more difficult for OTC options, since it requires direct negotiation between the buyer and seller.
2. The buyer can exercise the option (described below).
3. The buyer can let the option expire.

Exercise is accomplished by submitting an exercise notice to the clearing corporation, which "assigns" the exercise notice to a member firm, which then assigns it to one of its accounts.

The following depicts a typical equity option quotation as it would appear in the media:

ABC Co.	$20.50				450	5500
		Bid	**Ask**	**Last**	**Opt Vol**	**Op Int**
May	$20.00	1.00	1.20	1.15	200	3500
	$20.00P	0.75	0.90	0.80	100	1000
July	$22.50	0.60	0.75	0.65	50	600
	$20.00	1.50	1.75	1.70	60	400
	$20.00P	1.40	1.70	1.50	40	500

The quotes above can be interpreted as follows:

- ABC Co. represents the name of the underlying equity.
- \$20.50 is the closing market price for the security (i.e., ABC Co.).
- Opt Vol is the day's trading volume in each option series (450 is the total for all five series).
- Op Int represents the total number of contracts outstanding for each series (with 5500 being the total outstanding for all five series).
- May and July are the expiration months.
- \$20.00 is the exercise price for the May call.
- \$20.00P is the exercise price for the May put (as indicated by the P).
- 1.00 is the closing bid price for the May 20.00 call series; 1.20 is its closing ask price; and 1.15 is the last sale price for that option series.

Investors buy calls to speculate on price increases (and take advantage of the leverage provided by options, which is demonstrated in the example below).

! Example 1:

Investor A buys one share for \$20, while investor B buys one option to buy one share at a cost of \$4. Find the percentage return on each of their investments: (a) if the share price goes to \$24 and the option price goes to \$8.50; and (b) if the share price goes to \$16 and the call price goes to \$0.60. Ignore transaction costs.

Solution:

(a) A's return = (24 – 20)/20 = 0.20 = 20%; B's return = (8.50 – 4)/4 = 1.125 = 112.5%

(b) A's return = (16 – 20)/20 = –0.20 = –20%; B's return = (0.60 – 4)/4 = –0.85 = –85%

Notice how the returns are magnified (or leveraged) in either direction by using options.

- Investors may also buy calls to hedge risk by establishing a maximum purchase price for the underlying stock, or to limit potential losses on short positions. For example, consider a fund manager who wants to buy 1,000 shares of a stock that is presently trading for \$20 a share, but will not have the funds to do so for a month. She could lock in a purchase price today by purchasing 10 call option contracts (for 100 shares each) with an exercise price of \$20 at a cost of \$1.20 per option. If the share price rose to \$25 during the month, she would exercise the options and buy the shares for \$20 through the contracts rather than paying \$25 per share in the market. Her net cost would be \$21.20 per share (i.e., \$20 plus \$1.20 per option). Notice that if the price fell to \$15, she would let the contract expire, and buy the shares for $15 per share in the market, for a net cost of $16.20 (i.e., $15 plus $1.20 per option).

Call writing may be done

1. to generate additional income;
2. to close out a position (i.e., for a call that was previously purchased); and
3. as protection against a price decline in the underlying security.

!

- **Naked (uncovered) call writers** do not own the underlying security and are subject to a great deal of risk since they are obligated to buy the underlying security for delivery at market prices, which can increase substantially. As such, they are required to maintain margin accounts. **Covered call writers** already own the stock, and thus are not required to maintain margins since they merely have to deliver their own shares if required.

Example 2:

Determine the payoff (profit) to an investor who writes a "naked" call with an exercise price of $20 under the following scenarios: (a) the share price is $25 at expiration date and the option is exercised; and (b) the share price is $15 at expiration date and the option expires worthless.

Solution:

(a) Profit = 4 (premium received) – (20 – 25) (loss on option) = –$1

(b) Profit = 4 – 0 = $4

- Consider an investor who owns a share they bought for $20 who subsequently writes a "covered" call and receives a $4 premium. If the share price rises to $25 at expiration date and the option is exercised, they are effectively selling the stock for $24 (i.e., the $20 sale price through the option contract plus the $4 premium they received). While this is below the $25 market price, the investor "locked in" this selling price when they wrote the option. On the other hand, if the share price declined to $15 by the expiration date, the option would expire worthless, and the investor would keep the $4 premium, thus effectively lowering their purchase price to $16 (i.e., the $20 price originally paid – the $4 premium).

Buying a put may be done

1. to speculate on price decreases;
2. to create leverage;
3. as insurance against a drop in the underlying security's price (i.e., to manage risk); and
4. to close out a "short" put position.

! **Example 3:**

Determine the payoff to the buyer of a put with a $20 exercise price at a cost of $2 who does not own the underlying stock under the following scenarios: (a) the stock price falls to $16 at expiration date and the put is exercised; (b) the stock price increases to $24 at the expiration date and the option expires worthless.

Solution:

(a) Payoff (profit) = (20 – 16) (payoff from the put) – 2 (cost of the put) = $2

(b) Payoff (profit) = 0 – 2 = –$2

- Alternatively, an investor may purchase a $20 put for $2 on a share that they already own—this strategy is referred to as a **married put** or a **put hedge**. This strategy allows the investor to manage risk by locking in a minimum future selling price. They are protected from price declines because if the price drops below $20 (say to $16), they sell the share for $20 through the put contract—this is better than selling it for $16, but notice that they receive a net of only $18 per share (i.e., $20 – the $2 option price). On the other hand, if the share price rose (say to $24), they would let the put expire and sell in the market for $24 (netting $22 per share). The $2 is the cost of insurance.

! Writing a put may be done

1. to earn additional income;
2. to close out a "long" put position; and
3. to acquire the underlying security (at desired prices).

- Similar to call option writers, put writers can be either naked or covered; however, "covered" puts involve having a "short" position in the underlying stock, and hence are not that common. It is more common to enter into "cash-secured" put writing, which involves investing cash in a low-risk, highly liquid investment such as T-bills so that the money will be available to buy the shares through the put contract if it is exercised. Notice that the cost to the put writer in either situation is that they will have to buy shares at the exercise price (say $20) that is higher than what they are worth in the open market (say $16). However, if the stock price is above the exercise price at the expiration date, the writer gets to keep the premium they received, with no offsetting expense.

Corporations do not usually (nor should they) speculate with options, but rather use them for hedging purposes. For example, a company may agree to purchase goods from a European supplier for delivery in two months' time, with a two-million euro payment due on delivery. In order to eliminate the risk that the euro will appreciate against the Canadian dollar, the firm could purchase a two-month call option arrangement in the OTC market to buy euros at a predetermined price. If the euro is above the price (exchange rate) on that date, they would exercise the option, and if it is below the exercise price, they would buy euros in the open market and let the call option expire.

Another company, say a gold producer, could purchase a put option, giving them the right to sell their gold at a predetermined price. This provides them protection against a decline in the price of gold, but of course will not be exercised if the price of gold increases.

- New option contracts are created in the primary market. The contracts must be issued under the option prospectus, which is a short-form prospectus that is a generic publication from the clearing corporation outlining the risks of options trading. There is no fixed number of options outstanding and they do not have certificates.

Option sales settle the next business day. Exercise of options settle in three days. !

An existing option holder (or writer) enters into a **closing transaction** by selling (or buying) an identical option, thereby closing their previous open position in the option. It is one of the functions of the clearing corporation to match all buy and sell orders. !

Call options are said to be **"in-the-money"** when the price of the underlying security (P_0) is greater than the strike price (S) (puts – when $P_0 < S$). !

Call options are said to be **"out-of-the-money"** when $P_0 < S$ (puts – when $P_0 > S$).

Call options are said to be **"at-the-money"** when $P_0 = S$ (puts – when $P_0 = S$).

The **intrinsic value (IV)** of an option is the amount it is in-the-money, or zero if it is at-the-money or out-of-the money (since exercise is optional, the IV can never be negative). It is obviously determined by the relationship between share price and exercise price. !

For calls: $IV = Max(P_0 - S, 0)$

For puts: $IV = Max(S - P_0, 0)$

- The **time value** of an option is the difference between the option premium and the intrinsic value. It is affected by time to maturity, dividends, interest rates, and volatility of the underlying security. For puts and calls, we can say

Time value = Option price – IV

Example 4: !

An investor obtains the following market prices for a call and put option on a common share that is presently trading at $7.00 per share:

call option: exercise price is $8 and the call premium is $1.00

put option: exercise price is $9 and the put premium is $2.50

(a) Determine the intrinsic values and time value premiums for each option, and state whether they are in-, at-, or out-of-the-money.

Solution:

Call: IV = Max (7 – 8, 0) = 0; Time value = 1 – 0 = $1.00; out-of-the-money

Put: IV = Max (9 – 7, 0) = $2.00; Time value = 2.50 – 2.00 = $0.50; in-the-money

! (b) Determine the net profit (ignoring transactions costs) for an investor who purchases one contract of each of these options if they hold the options to expiration date, at which time the share price is $9.00.

Solution:

Call: Cost = 100 × $1.00 = $100; Profit = ([$9 – $8] × 100) – $100 = $0

Put: Cost = 100 × $2.50 = $250; Profit = 0 – 250 = –$250 loss

Net profit = $0 – $250 = –$250 (loss)

- Exceptions to these short-term maturities are **Long-Term Equity AnticiPation Securities (LEAPS)**, which are **long-term options** that can be exercised any time up to the expiry date. Technically, equity options expire on the Saturday following the third Friday of the month, and clients must make their exercise decisions on the Friday.
- Available option products include the following:
    1. **Equity Options**: These are traded on the Bourse de Montreal (Bourse), along with index and exchange-traded fund (ETF) options and futures, bond options and futures, and financial futures. Options on agricultural futures trade on the IntercontinentalExchange (ICE).
    2. **Currency Options**: These trade on the Philadelphia Stock Exchange.
    3. **Bond Options**: These trade on the Bourse on Government of Canada bonds.
    4. **Stock Index Options**: Index options trade on the Bourse on the S&P/TSX 60 Index. In the United States, index options exist on Standard & Poor's 500 Index, plus many other indices. Index options are "cash-settled," based on a multiple (often 100) of the value of the index.
    5. **OTC Options**: These can be tailor-made and are used a great deal by larger institutional investors (note that default risk is more of a concern for these options since there is no clearing corporation to guarantee performance).

FUTURES AND FORWARDS

Futures and **forwards** are used to reduce risk or for speculation purposes. Futures contracts are legal contracts to deliver or take delivery of a specified quantity and quality of a specified asset at a specified future time period at a predetermined price. Unlike options, both sides of the contract must satisfy their side of the contract (i.e., there is no option to be exercised).

Futures are standardized with respect to the amount and quality of the underlying asset, expiration dates, and delivery locations. A long position in a futures contract is an obligation to buy the underlying asset in the future at the contract price, while a short position represents an obligation to sell the underlying asset. If a futures contract is not offset and is held to the expiration date, the short party must deliver the underlying asset to the long party according to the terms of the contract. Financial futures are often "cash-settled," rather than delivering the actual asset, which is often complicated (e.g., stock index futures).

- Both buyers and sellers of futures must deposit and maintain margins in their futures accounts. The margin accounts essentially represent good-faith deposits or performance bonds to ensure the parties fulfill their part of the contract. The **initial margin** is the amount that must be deposited initially, while the **maintenance margin** represents a level below which the margin cannot fall. If it does, they must deposit additional cash or securities, referred to as the addition margin. The accounts are "marked-to-market" daily, with the "losing" party making payments and the winning party receiving them.
- **Swaps** are OTC contracts that are used extensively by large corporations and financial institutions, primarily to manage currency and interest rate risk. Swaps are essentially forward contracts that involve an agreement to exchange a "series" of future cash flows (rather than just one future cash flow).
- Futures are traded in the trading pit of a commodity or futures exchange by means of public outcry. Delivery time periods can range from one day for an index contract to a window of four or five weeks for some commodity futures contracts.
- A futures contract is set at today's prices, but is for delivery at some future point in time. Most contracts are closed out in the market ahead of time, so that physical deliveries are rare (roughly 2% of all contracts).
- Futures trade on agricultural products; commodities including some metals, lumber and plywood, and heating oil; and financial instruments such as interest rate products and stock indices.[1] Options on futures contracts have also become popular because they entail more limited risk than the underlying futures contract (where exercise is NOT optional).
- In Canada, the only commodity exchange is the **IntercontinentalExchange (ICE)**, where canola futures are by far the most active commodity future traded.
- The Bourse trades financial futures contracts, most of which call for cash delivery. The underlying assets for the financial futures that presently trade on the Bourse include single stocks, indices, 10-year Government of Canada bonds, three-month bankers' acceptances, and the overnight repo rate.

Hedgers are generally participants who deal in the underlying commodity or financial asset and wish to manage their risk by

1. selling futures contracts to effectively pre-sell inventories at current market prices; or
2. buying futures to lock in a future purchase price for the underlying asset.

[1] In 2000, the Bourse began offering futures contracts on the stock price of Nortel Networks. This endeavour met with limited success and no other such futures contracts have been issued since.

- The hedging effect can be achieved without delivery taking place, as illustrated in the following example. Suppose a farmer grows canola and wishes to pre-sell his expected harvest at current prices. This can be achieved by selling a futures contract promising November delivery of 10,000 tonnes at $365 per 100 tonnes. In November, if the price of canola is $365 per 100 tonnes, the futures contract will be worth nothing and the farmer will sell the harvest in the open market. If the price has fallen to $335 (which is the risk that was being hedged), he can close out his futures position at a profit of $30 per 100 tonnes, which will offset the lower price he obtains for selling the canola in the market. If the price has risen to $385, the farmer loses $20 per 100 tonnes on the futures contract. This offsets the higher selling price for the canola; however, this is the cost of obtaining "insurance."

Speculators invest through futures to exploit the leverage and flexibility afforded by these contracts. In the example above, the farmer may have sold the futures contracts to a speculator who was speculating that the price of canola would increase. Therefore, we observe that the futures market can serve as a mechanism for transferring risk from those wanting to avoid it to those willing to accept it.

- Financial futures contracts permit investors to hedge their equity or debt instruments relatively inexpensively, since only a margin deposit is required. In addition, they are ideal for speculation due to the leverage they provide.

Mutual fund companies and portfolio managers use derivatives for the following reasons:

1. **Hedging**: Managers use many of the techniques discussed previously for this purpose.
2. **Market Entry and Exit**: Derivatives provide managers with a cost-effective method of effectively entering or exiting markets on a temporary basis. Trying to do so by purchasing or selling the underlying securities would be more costly due to the transaction costs involved, especially when the dollar amounts are substantial.
3. **Yield Enhancement**: Managers may sell covered call options to enhance their yield on a long position in an underlying asset they own.

Futures markets use a **clearing corporation** to reduce default risk and to arrange deliveries as required. They also ensure that futures traders maintain adequate margin deposits.

Forwards are the *OTC equivalent of futures*. Unlike futures, the contracts are not standardized and may be tailor-made. There is no clearing corporation, so default risk is a concern to the parties involved, and forwards can also suffer from illiquidity.

- The largest users of forwards are banks, who issue these contracts to hedgers such as pension funds, manufacturers, and corporations. The banks trade foreign exchange and interest rate products, often in the form of swaps.

RIGHTS AND WARRANTS

Rights and **warrants** are similar to call options (discussed later in this chapter) because they both *give the holder the right to purchase shares at specified prices until the expiration date.* Unlike options, they are *issued by the corporation itself,* and result in dilution of the common equity capital base.

Rights are generally *short-term* in nature, while warrants tend to be issued with *three to five years to maturity.*

A right provides a shareholder the opportunity to acquire additional shares at a predetermined (subscription) price which is generally *lower* than the current market price. This creates value for the shareholder and induces them to exercise this option.

Rights are usually transferable, and certificates are mailed to shareholders on the **record date**. Shares trade **ex rights** *two business days prior to a record date,* and the stock is said to be **cum rights** before the ex-rights date. Typically the share price will drop by the theoretical intrinsic value of the right on the ex-rights date.

Rights may be offered because

1. Current market conditions are not conducive to traditional common share issues.
2. Management wants to give existing shareholders the opportunity to acquire shares, possibly at a discount to present market price.
3. It enables new funds to be raised while providing existing shareholders the right to maintain their proportionate ownership of the company (which is known as the **pre-emptive right** associated with common share ownership).

- No commission is levied on the exercise of rights, and a ready secondary market can develop, which provides holders who do not wish to exercise their rights the option to sell their rights. If the shares trade on an exchange, the rights are listed on the exchange automatically and trading takes place until they expire.

Regular delivery requires settlement within *three business days* on the TSX and the TSX Venture Exchange *up to three days* before the expiry date. On the TSX, they settle in *two days* for trades *three days prior to expiry,* the *next day* for trades *one and two days prior* to the expiry date, and must be settled in *cash* on the expiry date. For the TSX Venture Exchange, rights are settled on a cash basis from three days prior to, and including, the expiry date. Because of their short lifetime, they are often bought and sold on a "when issued" basis, which implies that sellers agree to deliver the rights when they are received.

A rights holder may take four courses of action:

1. Exercise some or all of the rights.
2. Sell some or all of the rights.
3. Buy additional rights for trading or exercise purposes.
4. Do nothing and let the rights expire: This would represent suboptimal behaviour since the investor would gain no benefit through this action and would lose the value of the rights they were provided with.

Usually *each shareholder receives one right* and a certain *number of rights* (*N*) *is required to purchase one share* (purchase of fractional shares may or may not be permitted, depending on the details of the issue).

The theoretical **Intrinsic Value (IV)** of a right is calculated using two methods:

1. During the cum rights period:

   IV = (market price of the stock – subscription price) – (N+1)

   The addition of 1 to N reflects the fact that the market price of the share includes the value of one right during this period.
2. During the ex-rights period:

   IV = (market price of stock – subscription price) – (N)

Example 5:

(a) Determine the intrinsic value of a right for a share that is trading for $40 cum rights. Four rights are required to purchase a share at the subscription price of $35.

Solution:

IV = (40 – 35)/(4 + 1) = $1.00

(b) Determine the intrinsic value of the right in part (a) two days after the ex-rights date if the share price above has fallen to $39.20.

Solution:

IV = (39.20 – 35)/4 = $1.05

The term *warrants* may have two meanings, which are described below. The first definition is by far the most common, and it is the one that the remaining discussion is based upon.

1. Warrants are certificates that contain an option to buy shares from the issuer at a given price for a predetermined period of time. Companies often attach warrants to debt or preferred share issues as *sweeteners* (i.e., to make the issue more attractive to investors). Most are *detachable* either immediately or after a certain holding period, after which time they may be traded separately from the original security to which they were attached.

2. Warrants may also be referred to as certificates that provide ownership of rights, although this is much less common.

Investors may be attracted to warrants because they provide **"leverage,"** which is attractive to speculators. In other words, the market price of a warrant is generally much lower than the price of the underlying security, yet its price moves together with the underlying asset price. The result is greater swings in prices for warrants than for the underlying asset, which magnifies gains (or losses) in percentage terms.

A ratio that may be used to measure this leverage potential is

leverage potential = (market price of the underlying) ÷ (market price of the warrant)

In general, larger ratios imply a greater leverage effect; however, other factors such as the amount of over-valuation must also be considered.

Example 6:

Determine the leverage potential of the following warrants:

(a) share price is $50, warrant price is $8, and exercise price of warrants is $52

(b) share price is $40, warrant price is $15, and exercise price of warrants is $30

Solution:

(a) leverage potential = 50/8 = 6.25

(b) leverage potential = 40/15 = 2.67

- Some other factors that investors should consider before purchasing warrants include *marketability* and *protection against stock splits and/or stock dividends* (which are usually covered).

Similar to rights, the intrinsic value (IV) of a warrant is the amount by which the market price of the underlying asset (P_0) exceeds the exercise or subscription price (S) of the warrant. It may never go below zero since exercise is at the option of the warrant holder. It is also typical to estimate the **time value** of a warrant, which refers to the amount by which the price of the warrant exceeds its intrinsic value. We can express these relationships using the following equations:

$IV = Max (P_0 - S, 0)$

Time Value = Price of warrant – IV

Example 7:

Determine the intrinsic value and time value for the warrants in Example 2.

Solution:

(a) IV = Max (50 – 52, 0) = 0; Time Value = 8 – 0 = $8

(b) IV = Max (40 – 30, 0) = 10; Time Value = 15 – 10 = $5

Warrants and options are similar in the following ways:

1. They are both leveraged equity investments.
2. Owners of either type of security do not receive dividends or voting rights.
3. Their prices are determined by similar factors, and option pricing models are often applied to warrants.

Warrants and options differ from one another in the following ways:

1. Options are issued by individuals, not the underlying corporations.
2. New shares are created when a warrant is exercised, which is not true for options.
3. The number of option contracts that may be outstanding is not limited.
4. Option exercise prices never change, while some warrants may provide for changing exercise prices.

Chapter 10 Review Questions

( ) 1. Rights trade ex rights ____________ business days prior to a record date.

a) two
b) three
c) four
d) five

( ) 2. Most OTC options are ____________ style.

a) European
b) American
c) Canadian
d) British

Refer to the following information to answer Questions 3 and 4:

An investor obtains the following market prices for a call and put option on a common share that is presently trading at $12.00 per share: (i) call option—exercise price is $15.00 and the call premium is $3.00; and (ii) put option—exercise price is $16.00 and the put premium is $4.50.

( ) 3. What is the intrinsic value of each option?

a) call: $3; put: 0
b) call: $3; put: $4
c) call: 0; put: $4
d) call: 0; put: 0

4. What is the total profit for an investor who purchases one contract of each of these options if they hold them to expiration date, at which time the share price is $16.00? ( )

a) loss of $650

b) gain of $100

c) gain of $650

d) loss of $100

Use the following information to answer Questions 5 and 6:

A company has issued warrants that are presently outstanding. One warrant is required to purchase one common share. The common share price is presently $10, the warrant price is $3, and the exercise price of the warrant is $12.

5. The intrinsic value of one warrant is: ( )

a) $0

b) $2

c) $5

d) none of the above

6. The time value of one warrant is: ( )

a) $0

b) $2

c) $3

d) none of the above

7. Which of the following statements are true? ( )

I. Futures markets use a clearing corporation to reduce default risk and to arrange deliveries as required.

II. Forward contracts are not standardized and may be tailor-made.

III. Forward markets use a clearing corporation similar to the future markets.

IV. Futures markets suffer from illiquidity.

a) I, II, III

b) I, III, IV

c) I, II

d) I, II, III, IV

Refer to the following information to answer Questions 8 and 9:

Suppose ABC Company issued rights with a subscription price of $35 with an ex-rights date of June 6 where four rights are required to purchase one common share and:

(a) June 5: share price is $40; (b) June 6: share price is $38; and (c) June 10: share price is $21.00.

( ) 8. What is the intrinsic value of the rights on June 5?

a) $1.25
b) $2.50
c) $5.00
d) none of the above

( ) 9. What is the intrinsic value of the rights on June 6?

a) $3.00
b) $1.50
c) $0.75
d) $0.60

( ) 10. Which of the following are reasons that portfolio managers use derivatives?

I. hedging
II. market entry and exit
III. yield enhancement
IV. price adjustment

a) I, II, III
b) I, III, IV
c) II, III IV
d) I, II, III, IV

Bonus Questions

( ) 11. Which of the following statements concerning options is FALSE?

a) Options give the holder the right to buy or sell the underlying asset at a pre-specified price.
b) The seller of the option has the right, but not the obligation, to fulfill the option contract.
c) Options have an expiry date.
d) Options derive their value mainly from the price of an underlying asset.

( ) 12. Which of the following is NOT a commonly used financial derivative?

a) bond derivatives
b) equity derivatives
c) currency derivatives
d) interest rate derivatives

13. An option's strike price is the: ( )
    a) price that the option sells for in the marketplace
    b) agreed upon future price of the underlying asset as written in the option contract
    c) fee that buyers must pay to sellers to obtain the right to buy or sell the underlying asset
    d) commission paid to the derivative dealer involved in the option trade

14. Which of the following statements concerning North American exchange-traded stock options is FALSE? ( )
    a) They have a trading unit of 100.
    b) If the premium is $3.50, each option will cost the buyer $350.
    c) The writer of the option is typically the exchange on which the underlying stock trades.
    d) They can trade as either market or limit orders.

15. ____________ can only be exercised on the expiration date, whereas ____________ can be exercised on any date prior to, and including, the expiration date. ( )
    a) Forward contracts; futures contracts
    b) Warrant contracts; right contracts
    c) American-style options; European-style options
    d) European-style options; American-style options

16. Which of the following is NOT a reasonable action to take for in-the-money options? ( )
    a) Exercise the option.
    b) Sell the option.
    c) Let the option expire.
    d) All of the above are reasonable actions to take.

17. A(n) ____________ option is in-the-money when the price of the underlying asset is below the strike price. ( )
    a) put
    b) call
    c) LEAPS
    d) assigned

18. A put option with an exercise price of $10 is currently priced at $5. If the time value of the option is $3, what is the price of the underlying asset? ( )
    a) $5
    b) $8

c) $10
d) $12

( ) 19. Marking to market of futures contracts refers to the:
a) daily settlement of gains and losses between those long and those short futures contracts
b) requirement for investors to deposit additional margin in their margin account
c) minimum account balance that must be maintained while the contract is open
d) calculation of the settlement value of the futures contract upon expiration

( ) 20. The exercise price of a right is:
a) typically above the current market price of the underlying stock
b) referred to as the subscription price
c) set so that the rights have zero intrinsic value when issued
d) all of the above statements are true

FINANCING AND LISTING SECURITIES

chapter 11

CSC EXAM SUGGESTED GUIDELINES:

7 questions for Chapter 11

BASIC FORMS OF BUSINESS ORGANIZATION

1. Proprietorship

!

- Proprietor is owner and operator of a business.
- It is NOT recognized as a separate legal entity.
- Income is taxed as personal income.
- Owner/operator has complete control and claim to profits.
- Owner faces **unlimited liability**, which means that he/she is personally liable for all debts, losses, and obligations arising from business activity.
- This form of business faces capital generation restrictions.

2. Partnership

!

- It is very similar to proprietorship, except that two or more owners are involved.
- There must be at least one general partner who is involved in the day-to-day operations of the business, and who is personally liable for all business debts and obligations.
- Partners in **general partnerships** face unlimited liability and usually joint and several liability (this means that all partners are "jointly" liable for all obligations, but also that each general partner is severally liable for all obligations on his or her own).

! • **Limited partnerships** must include at least one general partner who faces unlimited liability and is involved in running the business. Limited partners cannot be involved in the daily business activity, and liability is limited to the partner's investment.

3. Corporation

- This is the "dominant" form measured by dollar volumes of sales.
- Corporations are recognized as **separate legal entities**.
- The business structure allows for **separation of ownership from management**.
- Corporate tax rates are applicable.
- Corporations have an **unlimited life**.
- Owners (shareholders) face **limited liability** and can personally sue the corporation.
- Shareholders can easily **transfer ownership** by selling their shares.
- The characteristics above suggest that corporations have greater **access to capital** than other forms of business organizations.

Advantages of incorporation include

1. recognition of a corporation as a separate legal entity that can sue and be sued;
2. limited liability of shareholders;
3. continuity of existence;
4. ease of ownership transfer;
5. professional management;
6. possible tax benefits;
7. a general enhanced capability of accessing capital; and
8. growth potential, due to the ability to obtain large amounts of capital.

Disadvantages of incorporation include

1. a loss of flexibility;
2. the possibility of double taxation (of corporate profits and dividend income to shareholders);
3. additional administrative costs; and
4. complications involving withdrawal of capital.

THE INCORPORATION PROCESS

The incorporation process begins when one or more persons file documents with the appropriate federal or provincial department. The corporation comes into existence when it is issued a **charter** by the government. Charters may be issued as

1. letters patent;
2. memorandums of association; or
3. articles of incorporation.

The charter includes the corporate name, the date of incorporation, maximum authorized capital, and other pertinent data. The name of a corporation must identify the business as a corporation through the use of the words limited, corporation, or incorporated (or abbreviations).

- The decision to incorporate federally or provincially will depend primarily on where the business activities will take place. A provincially incorporated corporation may need further licensing or registration to carry on business in other provinces. A federally incorporated corporation is subject to general provincial laws, provided they do not deprive it of the rights associated with being federally incorporated.

Private corporations restrict the right of shareholders to transfer shares, limit the number of shareholders to fewer than 50, and prohibit inviting members of the public to subscribe for their securities. **Public corporations** face no such restrictions. While the *Canada Business Corporations Act* (CBCA) and many provincial acts no longer distinguish between the two, some securities regulations provide exemptions for private corporations (i.e., those whose shares do not trade on a stock exchange or over-the-counter).

- A corporation is regulated by
    1. the government act under which it was incorporated;
    2. its own charter; and
    3. its by-laws.

- By-laws are passed by directors and approved by shareholders. They deal with items such as determining the specifics of shareholders' and directors' meetings; qualification, election, and removal of directors; appointment, duties, and remuneration of officers; declaration and payment of dividends; date of fiscal year-end; and signing authority for documents.

Shareholder Rights

- Significant events such as the acquisition or liquidation of businesses, or those requiring amendments to the corporate charter require shareholder approval. Usually each common share entitles the holder to one vote, which implies any parties owning more than 50% of outstanding shares could elect every board director. However, sometimes different classes of shares may vote separately for a certain number of directors, while other shares have no voting privileges, and others may have multiple voting rights.
- All shareholders have the right to attend shareholders' meetings and must receive related materials such as proxies and audited financial statements. Some of the important matters dealt with at such meetings include the election of directors, the appointment of independent auditors, and the presentation and discussion of the company's financial statements and auditor's report for the previous year.

! A **proxy** represents a power of attorney that allows another party to vote on behalf of the shareholder. It is compulsory for management to solicit proxies by sending a proxy form and information circular to shareholders along with notification of the shareholder meeting. If management obtains a sufficient number of proxies it can control the board of directors. "**Proxy fights**" occur when challengers attempt to solicit proxies before a meeting. These are rare, but can lead to the removal of management if the challengers obtain sufficient support.

! During a period of restructuring due to financial difficulties, a corporation may establish a **voting trust**. This involves having shareholders deposit their shares with a trustee to transfer voting control to a few individuals under the terms of a voting trust agreement. These are generally in effect for a limited period of time, or until given objectives have been accomplished.

Corporation Structure

- Usually, corporations are required to have a minimum number of outside directors that are not officers of the corporation or related companies. Directors are required to attend periodic meetings, where they are normally responsible for
  - appointing and supervising officers;
  - appointing signing authorities for banking;
  - authorizing important contracts;
  - approving budgets, financing, and expansion plans; and
  - the declaration of dividends.
- Many corporate statutes require that directors *exercise care, diligence, and skill that a reasonably prudent person would exercise* in comparable circumstances. They may be liable under securities statutes for misrepresentations contained in prospectuses and other statutory filings, as well as for violations of insider trading provisions.
- The board elects a chairman, who may also be a senior officer of the company. In addition to presiding over board meetings, the chairman is influential regarding

the management policies followed by the corporation. Typically, either the chairman or the president will be the chief executive officer.

- The president is appointed by, and responsible to, the board of directors and may serve as chairman if necessary.
- An executive vice-president is often the next in line below the president and may sometimes be the chief operating officer. In addition, companies generally have a number of vice-presidents in charge of specific functional areas such as marketing, production, or finance.

The maximum number of common (or preferred) shares that the corporation may issue under the terms of its charter is referred to as the number of **authorized shares**. Changes in this amount require revisions to the charter. **Issued shares** refer to the number of shares issued by the corporation, while **outstanding shares** are those that are held by investors. If no shares are redeemed and the company does not repurchase any shares, the number of issued shares will equal the number of outstanding shares. !

Par value shares have a stated face value that may be misleading, since it has no relationship to either market value or entitlement to some amount of corporate assets. Under the current federal act, shares must be without par value. !

- Mortgage bonds are secured by real property, while debentures are not.

GOVERNMENT AND CORPORATE FINANCING

- Governments need financing for many reasons, such as
  1. to finance deficits;
  2. to finance infrastructure projects (e.g., roads and bridges); and
  3. to fund services (e.g., schools and hospitals).
- Most investment firms have separate government finance departments to act as intermediaries and advisors to the government regarding the issue of new securities. The investment advisor tries to reach a deal that is acceptable to the government issuer and prospective investors. The issue must be structured to accommodate the investors' interest of trying to ensure an adequate return and acceptable level of risk, as well as the issuers' interest in trying to obtain the cheapest source of financing.
- The investment dealer advises the government regarding several matters, including
  - the size of the issue, the interest rate offered, and the currency in which the issue is to be denominated;
  - the timing of the issue;
  - whether it should be a foreign or domestic issue;

- what possible impact the issue may have on the market; and
- whether it should be a new maturity issue, or if a previous issue should be re-opened.

- The premarketing phase involves soliciting informal advice from market participants and potential investors regarding how the market would react to a particular issue. It occurs before all of the final details of the issue are specified.

! The auction or **competitive tender system** is used for most issues by the federal government. **Government securities** (or **primary**) **distributors** that are eligible to tender include Schedule I and II banks (which may only tender for trading accounts and client orders and not for head office accounts such as pension funds); investment dealers; and active foreign dealers. **Competitive bids** may consist of up to seven bids in multiples of $1,000 (minimum $100,000 per individual bid) that are submitted (usually electronically) by 12:30 p.m. on the date of the auction. The bid must state the yield to maturity to three decimal places. Bidding limits of 40% of the total are imposed on dealers. Primary distributors may also submit one non-competitive tender, in multiples of $1,000, with a minimum bid of $1,000, and a $3-million limit on non-competitive bids per customer. These bids are executed at the average price of the accepted competitive bids.

! Generally the coupon rate is set to *within 25 basis points of the average yield* of the accepted competitive tenders, producing an average issue price at (or slightly below) par. When existing issues are being supplemented by additional offerings, bonds are sold at the price equivalents of the bid yields, plus accrued interest if applicable.

The following example illustrates how the bidding process works.

! Example 1:

The following are the "top four" competitive bids, which are listed in order of the yield bid for a $1 billion auction of government bonds:

Number	Bid Yield (%)	Amount
(1)	4.701	$600 million
(2)	4.704	$200 million
(3)	4.707	$200 million
(4)	4.708	$300 million

There was also $70 million in non-competitive bids submitted.

The bonds would be allocated as follows:

Bidder 1 would receive $600 million at the 4.701% yield, bidder 2 would receive $200 million at the 4.704% yield, and bidder 3 would receive only $130 million at the 4.707% yield, with the other $70 million being allocated to non-competitive bidders at the average yield of 4.704%.

- The Bank of Canada may bid to meet its own requirements. It also stands ready to absorb the entire tender if required, which implies the Bank could theoretically set the yield at each tender. Around 2:00 p.m. on the day of the auction, the Bank releases all pertinent information about the tender so that bidders can determine their net position. The dealers who purchase the bonds receive no commissions, and there are no selling price restrictions for the successful bidders.
- Thirty-year bonds are auctioned semi-annually while 2-, 5-, and 10-year government bonds are offered separately by quarterly auctions in denominations of $1,000, $5,000, $100,000, and $1 million. Treasury bills are offered every other Tuesday by the Bank through a competitive tender in maturities of 91, 182, and 364 days, and in denominations of $1,000, $5,000, $100,000, and $1 million.
- Canada Savings Bonds are sold every year, beginning in October, through investment dealers, banks, trusts, and on a commission basis. There is no set limit on the size of the issue; however, investors are restricted in the number they can purchase. Since these instruments are medium-term maturity but are cashable at any time, the rates are generally set in accordance with prevailing short-term rates.

New issues of provincial direct and guaranteed bonds are usually sold at a negotiated price through a fiscal agent (underwriting syndicate). !

Direct bonds are issued directly by the government (e.g., Province of Ontario bonds), while **guaranteed bonds** are issued in the name of a Crown corporation but are guaranteed by the provincial government (e.g., Hydro-Québec). Similar to corporate issues, there may be an exempt list (which is discussed later in this chapter). !

- Municipal bond and debenture issues are generally purchased by institutional portfolio managers and pension funds.

Corporations need new financing for many reasons, including !

1. to increase working capital,
2. to fund bank loans,
3. to purchase fixed assets, and
4. to expand production.

Financing may also be required to purchase other companies or for restructuring purposes. !

- A competitive tender is an auction by a number of dealers to buy an issuer's new securities. **Negotiated offerings** are more commonly used for corporate issues. They involve negotiations between the investment dealer (ID) and the issuing company regarding the type of security, price, interest or dividend rate, special features, and protective provisions.

THE FINANCING PROCEDURE

- Before entering into a formal arrangement to market a corporation's securities, an investment dealer will undertake a thorough investigation of the corporation, including: an extensive industry analysis; an analysis of the corporation's position within that industry; and an analysis of the financial record and financial structure of the corporation.

! The dealer advises the issuer regarding the amount, timing, pricing, and attributes of the issue. The dealer also advises the clients regarding the method of distribution (discussed below) and how the issue is to be marketed. Close relationships often develop, and sometimes a dealer or broker may become the **broker of record**, which provides them with the right of first refusal on new financing.

- A **private placement** is an arrangement with private investors (usually institutional investors) and does not require a full prospectus, only a specific contract (**offering memorandum**). Under these conditions, the dealer usually acts as an agent for the issuer. These will be marketed to exempt institutions in Canada and/or the United States.

! **Public offerings** are regulated by the *Canada Business Corporations Act* (CBCA) and provincial securities regulations. They require that prospectuses be prepared that include "*full, true and plain disclosure of all material facts relating to the securities offered.*" A material fact is one that significantly affects, or has the potential to have a significant impact on, the securities' market price.

! Public issues can be classified as one of the following:

1. **Initial Public Offerings (IPOs):** These occur when a growing firm or Crown corporation decides to "go public."
2. **Secondary Issues:** These are follow-up issues or redistribution of previously issued stock (typically large blocks that have been held by institutional investors).

- The dealer will consider the corporation's existing financing structure, the stability of earnings, and prospects for the future, as well as current market conditions, before recommending an appropriate financing alternative, as well as appropriate protective provisions (for debt and preferred shares) and voting restrictions (for common shares).

! Some of the advantages of debt financing include the following:

1. Interest payments are tax deductible for corporations.
2. Debt is not a permanent commitment.
3. It does not dilute equity ownership.
4. Some or all of the issuing discount may be tax deductible.
5. It is generally the lowest cost financing alternative for a company.

! Some of the advantages of equity financing include the following:

1. There is no obligation to pay any portion of earnings as dividends.
2. Repayment of capital is not required.

3. Assets are not encumbered nor are management's actions restricted. !
4. It provides a greater cushion against insolvency and can improve the company's credit rating.

Prospectuses are lengthy legal documents that contain relevant financial statements, proposed use of funds from the issue, future growth plans, and the relevant information regarding the share issue. Normally, before a final prospectus may be issued, it is necessary to prepare and distribute copies of a **preliminary prospectus**, or **red herring**, to the securities commission and prospective investors. This contains most of the information to be included in the final prospectus (except the price) to the dealers and public, and sometimes the auditor's report. A statement, in red, must be displayed on the front page to the effect that it is not final and is subject to completion or an amendment before shares can be issued. The dealer may also prepare a **green-sheet**, which is an information circular, for in-house use only. It highlights the most important features of the issue and can be used by the sales department to solicit interest in the new issue. !

- During the 90-day **waiting period** (between the issuance of red herrings and the receipt of final prospectuses), dealers are prohibited from entering into purchase and sale agreements; however, they can solicit expressions of interest. Meanwhile, the dealer typically proceeds along other lines, attempting to formalize the details of items such as the Trust Deed or Indenture (for debt issues); the underwriting or agency agreement between issuer and distributor; the Banking Group Agreement; the Selling Group Agreement; and final price to the public and to the dealer.
- Once completed, the prospectus is filed with the relevant securities commissions, and approval generally takes three weeks. If the issuers agree to any proposed changes, the issue is said to be "blue skyed" and may then be distributed to the public. It must be accompanied by the consent of all experts whose opinions are referred to in the prospectus. The prospectus is required to be mailed or delivered to all purchasers of the securities, no later than midnight on the second business day after the trade.

The **Short-Form Prospectus Distribution (SFPD) System** (formerly the Prompt Offering Qualification [POP] System) allows senior reporting issuers, who have made public distributions and who are subject to continuous disclosure requirements, to issue short-form prospectuses. The rationale is that there is already a great deal of information available on the company that would normally be included in a prospectus. These short-form prospectuses save issuers a great deal of time and money and generally focus on details of the securities being issued such as price, distribution spread, use of proceeds, and security attributes.

Issuers under the SFPD System !

1. file electronically using SEDAR;
2. are reporting issuers in at least one Canadian jurisdiction;
3. are "up to date" in their filings;
4. have filed or will file an Annual Information Form (AIF) with the appropriate administrator;

! 5. are not issuers whose operations have ceased or whose principal asset is cash (i.e., capital pool companies); and
6. have equity shares listed and trading on an exchange (e.g., TSX, TSX Venture Exchange, or CNSX).

! Short-form prospectuses are commonly used for "**bought deals**," and have contributed to the growth of these arrangements, which are a popular form of underwriting in Canada. The issuer sells the entire issue to one investment dealer or to a group that attempts to resell it and accepts all of the price risk. Generally, the dealer has premarketed the issue to a few large institutional investors. Issuers are usually large, well-known firms that qualify for the use of SFPD; therefore, bought deals are generally executed very swiftly.

- The first step in the **underwriting process** has the issuing company selling the securities to the **Financing Group** (also known as managing underwriters or syndicate managers), which consists of one or two firms. The Financing Group accepts the liability of the issue on behalf of the **Banking Group** members, which includes themselves as well as other dealers who have agreed to participate, based on certain terms.
- Second, the Financing Group sells the securities to the **Banking Group** at a "draw down" price that is slightly above the price paid by the Financing Group in order to provide that group with a differential. They also obtain an "**override**," which is an additional payment for their advisory and lead services. At this point "tombstone advertisements" may begin in newspapers that indicate all members of the Banking Group selling the issue.
- Third, the securities are distributed for sale to the public, with a certain proportion being allocated to
    1. the **Banking Group** (the largest proportion);
    2. the **exempt list**, which usually includes only large professional buyers, mostly financial institutions, who are exempt from prospectus requirements;
    3. the **Selling Group**, which consists of other dealers who are not part of the Banking Group;
    4. **casual dealers**, who are not members of the Banking or Selling Groups, and may be brokers, broker dealers, foreign dealers, banks, etc.; and
    5. **special groups**, which may include the issuer's banker or dealer, etc.
- Lead underwriters generally provide **after-market stabilization** of the issuer's market price. If they intend to do so, it must be disclosed on the first page of the prospectus, with additional details provided within the prospectus. Three possible types of stabilization activities are the following:
    1. Initially sell more than the original amount of securities offered by the issuer, then buy shares back if the price drops below a certain value. If the price does not fall below this value, the firm can cover its short position by exercising an **over-allotment** (or **green shoe**) option. This option allows the dealer to obtain additional securities from the issuer.

2. Penalize members of the Selling Group by reducing the proportion of shares they are allocated in future offerings, if their customers sell their shares in weak issues in the period immediately following the issue.
3. Establishing a "stabilizing bid" to purchase shares at a price less than or equal to the offer price if the issue is not complete. This is the least common type of support.

Junior company distributions occur when listed junior companies (usually junior mining and oil companies) raise new capital by issuing treasury shares to the public, which requires them to find an underwriter.

- Listed companies can issue securities to the public using a prospectus, or through the exchange itself by filing an exchange offering prospectus or a statement of material facts. This form of distribution is unique to Canada, and is used primarily by junior mining and oil companies. These treasury share underwritings are usually priced below the prevailing market price (but discounts are restricted to be less than 10%–25% depending on the market price). They must also be used to raise minimum amounts of new capital (from $100,000 to $350,000). Often these shares are required to be held "in escrow" (by a trustee) until certain provisions have been met. **Escrowed shares** typically maintain associated voting and dividend privileges; however, they are not transferable during the period of escrow.
- The **Capital Pool Company (CPC)** program offers businesses an opportunity to raise early-stage financing. It permits an IPO and TSX Venture Exchange listing for a newly formed company that has no current business, operations, or assets, other than cash. The funds raised by these IPOs can be used to identify and acquire businesses that would qualify for a regular Tier 1 or Tier 2 exchange listing. The directors and officers of the CPC must contribute a significant amount (e.g., $100,000) in seed capital; the issuer must raise between $200,000 and $1.9 million in the IPO; and the offering price must be between $0.15 and $0.30. The total amount of capital raised from director and officer contributions plus the IPO cannot exceed $700,000. The shares may have their trading suspended or be delisted from the exchange, if the CPC does not identify businesses that can be acquired with the funds through a Qualifying Transaction (QT).

Companies that fall below TSX Venture Exchange listing requirements trade on the newly created NEX board, which provides a trading forum for (i) companies that no longer meet TSX Venture Exchange Tier Maintenance Requirements (known as Inactive Issuers); (ii) CPCs that did not complete a QT as required by the exchange; and (iii) TSX issuers that no longer satisfy listing requirements.

THE LISTING PROCESS

New share issues are usually traded OTC initially and are considered for listing on an exchange only after proof of satisfactory distribution becomes available. Often, the !

underwriting agreement requires the underwriters to provide some market support for the new security issue for a specified time period.

Advantages of listing include

1. prestige and goodwill;
2. established value in mergers and acquisitions;
3. excellent market visibility;
4. more available information;
5. facilitation of valuation for tax purposes; and
6. increased marketability and attention of investors.

Disadvantages of listing include

1. additional controls on management;
2. additional costs to the company;
3. market indifference (i.e., if trading volumes turn out to be very low);
4. additional disclosures required; and
5. the need to keep market participants informed.

- Companies wishing to become listed must apply to the appropriate exchange. The application requires disclosure of detailed company information including

1. the company's charter and any current prospectus;
2. the financial statements for the past three to five years;
3. a written opinion from the company's legal counsel, verifying the organizational matters as presented;
4. sample share certificates; and
5. annual reports.

- Once the application has been approved, the company enters into a formal **listing agreement**. The agreement specifies regulations and reporting requirements that the company must follow to maintain its listing. Some of these requirements include

1. the submission of annual and interim financial statements and other corporate reports;
2. prompt notification to the exchange(s) about dividends and other distributions;
3. the company's proposed stock options for employees only, underwritings, and sale or issue of treasury shares; and
4. notification of proposed material changes in the business or affairs of a listed non-exempt company.

- Exchanges have the power to suspend the trading or listing privileges of an individual security temporarily or permanently.

Temporary withdrawals of privileges include

1. **delayed opening** (which may arise if there exists a large number of buy and/or sell orders);

2. **halt in trading** (to allow significant news to be reported, such as merger activity); and
3. **suspension of trading**, which may occur for more than one session until an identified problem is rectified by the company to the exchange's satisfaction (if the company fails to meet requirements for continued trading or does not comply with listing requirements).

A listed security can be cancelled or delisted for a variety of reasons such as the following:

1. It no longer exists (e.g., a preferred share issue that has been redeemed).
2. The company has no assets or is bankrupt.
3. Public distribution of the security is no longer sufficient.
4. The company no longer complies with the terms of its listing agreement.

Chapter 11 Review Questions

1. Bought deals are typically offered in conjunction with companies that: ( )
   a) trade in the OTC market
   b) wish to issue new securities through a private placement
   c) issue full prospectuses
   d) issue short form prospectuses

2. The second step in the underwriting process involves: ( )
   a) the issuing of securities to the Financing Group
   b) the selling of securities to the Banking Group
   c) the selling of securities to the general public
   d) the waiting period

3. The following are all advantages to issuing debt EXCEPT for: ( )
   a) It is generally the lowest cost financing alternative.
   b) It provides greater financing flexibility.
   c) Some or all of the issuing discount may be tax deductible.
   d) All of the above are advantages to issuing debt.

4. The following are all disadvantages of listing shares for trading on a public exchange EXCEPT for: ( )
   a) additional costs
   b) additional controls
   c) established collateral value
   d) market indifference

( ) 5. Competitive bids for government bond issues must be in multiples of:
a) $5,000 subject to a maximum bid of $500,000
b) $5,000 subject to a minimum bid of $25,000
c) $1,000 subject to a maximum bid of $500,000
d) $1,000 subject to a minimum bid of $100,000

( ) 6. Three features of corporations that allow them greater access to capital are:
a) limited liability, limited life, and ease of transfer of ownership
b) limited liability, unlimited life, and ease of transfer of ownership
c) unlimited life, separation of ownership from management, and voting privileges for shareholders
d) unlimited liability, separation of ownership from management, and voting privileges for shareholders

( ) 7. A corporation's ____________ is responsible for declaring dividends.
a) chief executive officer
b) chief operating officer
c) president
d) board of directors

Bonus Questions

( ) 8. Which of the following statements concerning sole proprietorship is FALSE?
a) The business is protected by limited liability.
b) The structure involves one person owning the business.
c) The income earned from the business is taxed as personal income.
d) The resources of the business tend to be limited.

( ) 9. Which of the following is NOT a potential advantage of incorporation?
a) Limited liability of shareholders.
b) Ease with which funds can be withdrawn from the firm.
c) Ease with which ownership of the firm can be transferred to another individual.
d) Ease with which new capital can be raised.

( ) 10. All corporations whose shares trade on an exchange or OTC are:
a) private corporations
b) partnerships

c) public corporations

d) sole proprietorships

11. Which of the following may NOT be an advantage of debt issuance versus equity issuance? ( )

a) after-tax cost

b) ownership dilution

c) credit rating improvement

d) magnification of rate of return earned by shareholders

12. A red herring prospectus refers to: ( )

a) the final prospectus

b) the preliminary prospectus

c) the in-house information circular prepared by dealers

d) none of the above

13. The ability of the underwriter to buy additional shares from the issuer at the offer price, in excess of the original number of shares offered, is referred to as: ( )

a) escrowed shares

b) override

c) a green shoe option

d) share flipping

14. A separate board of the TSX Venture Exchange, on which companies that have fallen below the Venture Exchange's listing standards can trade, is the: ( )

a) CPC

b) Grey market

c) NEX

d) MEX

CORPORATIONS AND THEIR FINANCIAL STATEMENTS

chapter 12

CSC EXAM SUGGESTED GUIDELINES:
8 questions for Chapter 12

UNDERSTANDING FINANCIAL STATEMENTS

Financial statements demonstrate what a firm owns and what it owes, as well as how profitable it has been in the past. A firm's past performance is important to potential investors since it may provide insight into the company's future prospects, which are difficult to predict accurately.

The reader may refer to the "sample" financial statements provided in Chapter 14 for illustration purposes.

STATEMENT OF FINANCIAL POSITION

- The **Statement of Financial Position** (formerly the **Balance Sheet**) is divided into two sections:
  1. **assets**, which shows what the firm owns and is owed; and
  2. **liabilities**, which shows what the firm owes, and **shareholders' equity** or net worth, which represents the shareholders' interest in the company.

Shareholders' equity is often referred to as the "book value" of the company, which in general does not correspond to its market value.

Assets

- Assets are generally presented in order of increasing liquidity, with the most liquid assets appearing at the top of the balance sheet, and the least liquid assets appearing at the bottom.
- **Current assets** include cash, marketable securities, accounts or notes receivable (net of an allowance for doubtful accounts), inventories, and prepaid expenses (which represent payments made by the company for services to be received in the near future).

! **Inventories** are generally in the form of raw materials, work-in-process, or finished goods. They are valued at the lower of original cost or current market value. Two common methods for valuing inventory are

1. **average cost** of all items in inventory; and
2. **First-In-First-Out (FIFO)**, which is the most commonly used method in Canada.

! During periods of increasing prices, FIFO will produce higher inventory values and higher profits than the average cost method. This is illustrated in the example below.

! Example 1:

A firm currently has three inventory items on hand, which were purchased in the following order for the following prices: $10, $15, and $20. If the firm sells one item today for $30, determine the ending inventory value and profit using each of the two inventory valuation approaches discussed above.

	Inventory Value	Profit
FIFO:	15 + 20 = $35	30 – 10 = $20
Average Cost:	[(10 + 15 + 20)/3]× 2 = $30	30 – 15 = $15

- **Prepaid expenses** account for payments made in advance for goods or services to be received in the future.
- **Miscellaneous items** are neither current nor fixed and commonly include the cash surrender value of life insurance policies; amounts due from company employees, officers, or directors; investments of a long-term nature; and investments and advances to subsidiary and affiliated companies.
- **Property, plant, and equipment** (or **capital assets**) consist of land, buildings, machinery, and equipment that are long-term in nature. Their value lies in their contribution to producing goods and services, rather than their resale value. The proportion of capital to total assets varies widely across companies.

! **Amortization** (or **depreciation**) is a *non-cash expense* charged against capital assets to reflect their decline in value through time. Amortization allocates the net cost of assets through time to provide better "matching" of the revenues they generate with the initial cost of said assets. It is generally charged using

1. the "**straight-line method**," which charges an equal amount each period based on the initial cost of the asset and its estimated useful life; or
2. the "**declining balance method**," which applies a fixed percentage (usually double the straight-line rate) to the outstanding undepreciated balance.

As a result, the timing of the amortization charged differs from each of these methods, as illustrated in the example below.

Example 2:

A company purchased a $100,000 piece of equipment that has an estimated useful life of 10 years. Determine the amortization charge and book value for this asset for the first three years using (a) the straight-line method; and (b) the declining balance method.

Straight Line Declining Balance (@20%)

Year-end	Amortization	Book Value	Amortization	Book Value
1	10,000	90,000	20,000	80,000
2	10,000	80,000	16,000	64,000
3	10,000	70,000	12,800	51,200

Depletion is similar to amortization and is used by mining, oil, natural resource, and timber companies to reflect the fact that as these assets are developed and sold, the company loses part of its assets with each sale. An allowance for depletion recognizes the fact that companies must recover their initial costs of acquiring these assets in addition to extraction costs.

Amortization is the term used when applied against deferred charges and intangible assets, which are described below.

- When a company records an expenditure as an asset, rather than expensing it on the income statement, it is referred to as "**capitalizing**" the expenditure. This procedure spreads the associated expense claim over more than one period.
- Capitalized leases are those that are viewed as another means of financing the acquisition of an asset. Consequently, these leases are recorded as if the company had assumed ownership of the asset (which is recorded like any other fixed asset) and assumed a liability, which is recorded at the present value of future lease payments.
- Capitalizing interest occurs when interest costs are capitalized and added to the cost of the asset, rather than expensed. This process is sometimes used by oil and gas companies that are active in exploration, or by utilities companies during periods of construction. This policy should not be changed once adopted, since it effectively increases current income and asset value and lowers future income amounts.
- **Deferred charges** are similar to prepaid expenses, except that the benefits will extend over a period of years. The cost of such items is spread out over several years by gradually writing off the asset (i.e., amortization).

- **Intangible assets** include goodwill, patents, copyrights, franchises, and trademarks. While they are not tangible in the typical sense, they have the potential to create value by enhancing earnings capability. Creditors often assume these assets will be worth nothing if a company is liquidated. While it is common to think of goodwill as the probability of obtaining repeat customers, from an accounting perspective, it arises when a purchaser pays a price for a company above the value of the company's assets (i.e., is willing to pay for its "good name").

Liabilities and Shareholders' Equity

- **Current liabilities** typically include bank advances (short-term loans from financial institutions); accounts payable; dividends payable; income taxes payable; long-term debt obligations that are due within one year; and many other items such as wages payable, legal fees, pension payments, etc.

!

- **Future income taxes** (or **deferred tax**) occur when the tax figure on a company's income statement differs from tax reported in its tax return. These instances usually result from "**timing**" **differences** due to the use of different procedures for Canadian Institute of Chartered Accountants (CICA) reporting purposes, versus those used for income tax purposes. The major source of these timing differences is the use of straight-line amortization for accounting purposes, and declining balance amortization, which is used for income tax purposes (capital cost allowances or CCA). The net effect is that assets are "written off" or expensed faster for tax purposes, which causes the taxes payable figure on tax returns to be lower than the tax expense figure in the financial statements. This gives rise to a deferred tax credit (liability) on the balance sheet.
- Some analysts treat deferred tax as a liability, since it represents taxes that must be repaid in the future. Others view it as equity, because the company is unlikely to have to repay such taxes as long as they are continually purchasing assets for given CCA asset classes. Others disregard this account, treating it as neither debt nor equity in determining net worth or debt ratios.
- **Permanent differences** also exist between income statement and tax return reporting such as the following:
    1. Dividend income received by a Canadian corporation from another Canadian corporation is not taxable for filing purposes; however, it is considered income for accounting purposes.
    2. Interest and penalties on taxes are not deductible for tax purposes; however, they are considered accounting expenses.

These differences do not show up in the deferred tax account.

Non-controlling (or **minority**) **interest in subsidiary companies** is reported on consolidated balance sheets only. It is calculated as the interest that "outsiders" have in the subsidiary firm, which is viewed as a "quasi-liability," which must be deducted in arriving at the consolidated shareholders' equity position of the parent company.

- **Other liabilities** typically include provisions for estimated losses (e.g., from a lawsuit). Contingencies based solely on conservative thinking, and not to a specific loss, are more properly reported as a note to the financial statements.
- **Deferred Revenue** is the opposite of a deferred charge and arises when a company has received payment for goods or services that it has not yet provided (e.g., prepaid magazine subscriptions).
- **Long-Term Debt** typically consists of long-term bank loans, mortgage bonds, and/or debentures. These items are usually described in detail in a note, including a description of repayment, maturity, and sinking fund provisions.

Shareholders' equity consists of

1. preferred share capital;
2. common share capital (issued and outstanding);
3. retained earnings, which belong to shareholders and represent reinvested profits;
4. contributed surplus (sometimes), which also belongs to shareholders, but originates from a source other than earnings. Any excess received for shares that are issued above par or stated price is shown in contributed surplus; and
5. foreign currency translation adjustments, which may appear on consolidated statements of companies that have foreign subsidiaries and reflects a significant change in the value of the subsidiary due to a favourable (or unfavourable) change in the exchange rate.

!

Total common equity is made up of items (2) through (5).

STATEMENT OF COMPREHENSIVE INCOME

- The major component of the Statement of Comprehensive Income is the traditional **Earnings Statement** (or **Income Statement**, or **Profit and Loss Statement**, or **Statement of Revenue and Expense**), which reveals
  1. where company income comes from and how it is spent; and
  2. the adequacy of earnings to assure continued successful operation and income generation for its security holders.

In short, it is a "*flow*" statement that provides evidence regarding the company's earning power, which is of primary interest to investors.

- It is generally broken down into four broad categories, including
  1. the operating section;
  2. the non-operating section;
  3. the creditors' section; and
  4. the owners' section.

The first two sections show the origin of income, while the other two show its distribution. It is important to distinguish between operating and non-operating sources of income to get a true reflection of the firm's true earning power.

- The operating section shows the source of income and associated expenses, as well as the resulting net operating profit or loss, and includes
  1. **net sales** (gross sales less excise taxes, returns and allowances, and discounts);
  2. **cost of goods sold** (labour, raw materials, and other associated costs);
  3. **gross operating profit** ([1]–[2]);
  4. **operating expenses** (selling, general and administrative expenses, depreciation, and other expenses such as pension fund contributions, directors' fees, legal fees, and management compensation); and
  5. the **net operating profit or loss**, which results after deducting the expenses in (4).
- The non-operating section contains income from sources including interest and dividend payments received, rents from no-longer-required properties, royalties on patent fees, finance charges earned, etc.
- **Earnings Before Interest and Taxes (EBIT)** equals the sum of operating profit and non-operating income and is a widely used profitability measure in ratios and other company analysis.
- The creditors' section shows distribution of income to creditors in the form of interest or lease payments, which is important since they represent a fixed legal obligation.
- The owners' section shows taxes (both current and deferred) and minority interest amounts.

! Non-controlling (or minority) interest arises from the **consolidation method of accounting**, which is required whenever the parent *owns more than 50%* of the voting shares of a subsidiary. When the parent owns *less than 20%* of the subsidiary, the **cost method** of accounting is utilized, while when the parent owns *between 20% and 50%*, it will use the **equity method**. The equity method may lead to the reporting of *equity income* (or losses) by the parent company even though no cash was received (or distributed). On the other hand, the parent may receive dividends from the subsidiary, which represents cash received, but is not treated as income. As a result, cash earnings calculations should subtract equity income and include dividends received from the subsidiary (however, this is not always done in practice).

Additional items on the income statement include

1. "**unusual items**" that are typical for the normal business activity of the firm, but were caused by unusual circumstances (e.g., unusual bad debt or inventory losses); and
2. "**extraordinary items**" that are not likely to reoccur such as a loss due to disposal of an operating division.

After making all of the adjustments above, and adjusting for **income tax expense**, we are left with the **net income** (or **net profit**).

When net income is adjusted for other items such actuarial gains and losses on defined benefit plans, and gains and losses on foreign currency translations, then we end up with **comprehensive income**. Comprehensive income is then transferred to the Statement of Financial Position through the **Statement of Changes in Equity** (discussed below).

OTHER COMPONENTS

- The **Statement of Changes in Equity** (or **Retained Earnings Statement**) is the link between the earnings statement and balance sheet. It provides a record of the profits kept in the company year after year and accounts for dividends paid every year. It also accounts for adjustments to retained earnings that may occur from time to time as retained earnings are appropriated as reserve against possible events (e.g., such as a decline in the value of raw materials purchased at a time of high commodity prices). The term *reserve* must be used for federally incorporated companies under such circumstances; however, it does not mean that a cash fund has been set aside for this provision. Rather, it means that a portion of retained earnings has been earmarked as unavailable for distribution to shareholders.
- The **Statement of Changes in Financial Position** (or **Cash Flow Statement**) provides financial statement users with important information regarding the liquidity and solvency of a company by showing the sources and uses of funds over a certain period. It is broken down into the following three areas:
  1. **operating activities**, which shows cash flows from profits and temporary accounts such as receivables and payables;
  2. **financing activities**, which shows cash flows from debt and equity issues or retirements; and
  3. **investing activities**, which shows cash flows from net investment in fixed assets and/or investment assets.

The concluding section of the cash flow statement reconciles the total change in cash with the beginning cash balance and the end-of-period cash balance.

When the indirect method is used to construct the cash flow statement, the firm must disclose information regarding cash interest and income taxes paid, since this method does not identify these items directly.

- The **Notes to Financial Statements** provide users with important information regarding items such as accounting policies; description of fixed assets, share capital, and long-term debt; and commitments and contingencies. They should also disclose information regarding significant segments of the company's operations by industry and geographical location (including earnings statements and capital expenditures).

- The **Auditor's Report**, which is required by Canadian corporate law, typically has four sections. The first describes the statements examined. The second provides a description of the individual responsibilities of management and the auditors. The third describes how the audit was conducted and the scope of the examination, and usually indicates that the examination was made in accordance with generally accepted accounting principles (GAAP). The fourth gives the auditor's opinion on whether the statements fairly present the firm's financial position. If the auditor finds discrepancies from GAAP, they may be unable to give an opinion or may offer a "qualified" opinion that refers to any dubious points. A qualified report can be viewed as a signal that the statements may not fairly represent the company's financial condition and are not allowed in some provinces.

Auditors are appointed at the annual meeting by a shareholders' resolution. In Canada, qualified auditors are members of the Institute of Chartered Accountants in the appropriate province. Certified General Accountants (CGAs) and Certified Management Accountants (CMAs) may also serve as auditors in some provinces. In the United States, the auditor must be a Certified Public Accountant (CPA).

The **Canadian Public Accountability Board (CPAB)** was set up in 2003 to increase public confidence "in the integrity of financial reporting" and "[promote] high-quality, independent auditing." This board was established around the time the United States created their own board, which emanated from the *Sarbanes-Oxley* (*SOX*) *Act* of 2002. Among the new SEC requirements is that CEOs and CFOs must personally attest to the accuracy of public corporations' financial statements.

Chapter 12 Review Questions

( ) 1. During periods of falling prices, FIFO will produce ____________ inventory values and ____________ profits than the average cost method.

a) higher; lower

b) higher; higher

c) lower; lower

d) lower; higher

( ) 2. Non-controlling interest in subsidiaries arises due to the use of the ____________ method of accounting.

a) consolidated

b) equity

c) cost

d) GAAP

3. A fixed asset is purchased for $50,000. The amortization expense in year two, if it is amortized on a declining balance method at a rate of 10%, will be: ( )

a) $4,500
b) $5,000
c) $6,000
d) $10,000

4. The equity method of accounting is used whenever firms acquire: ( )

a) the common shares of another corporation
b) more than 10% of the voting shares of another corporation
c) more than 50% of the voting shares of another corporation
d) between 20% and 50% of the voting shares of another corporation

5. Deferred charges and prepaid expenses are similar to one another in that they are both charges that represent payments made by a company for which the benefit will last into the future. The main difference between the two is that: ( )

a) a deferred charge is recorded as an asset on the balance sheet, while a prepaid expense is recorded under the liability heading
b) deferred charges are included as current assets, while prepaid expenses are included as long-term assets
c) the benefit of deferred charges will be received in the near future, while the benefit of prepaid expenses will extend over a period of years
d) the benefit of prepaid expenses will be received in the near future, while the benefit of deferred charges will extend over a period of years

6. What is the difference between "extraordinary items" and "unusual items" on the earnings statement? ( )

a) Unusual items are typical for the normal business activity of the firm, but were caused by unusual circumstances, while extraordinary items are not likely to reoccur, such as a loss due to disposal of an operating division.
b) Extraordinary items are typical for the normal business activity of the firm, but were caused by unusual circumstances, while unusual items are not likely to reoccur, such as a loss due to disposal of an operating division.
c) Extraordinary items are always reported "above" unusual items.
d) There is no difference; they refer to the same thing.

7. If a company has liabilities of $5 million and assets of $7 million, then its shareholders' equity is: ( )

a) $1 million
b) $2 million

c) $12 million

d) $35 million

( ) 8. Which of the following statements concerning current assets is true?

a) Current assets are typically listed in order of liquidity, with the least liquid assets listed first.

b) The only acceptable method for determining the cost of inventory under GAAP is FIFO.

c) Accounts receivable is an example of a current asset.

d) All of the above statements are true.

Bonus Questions

( ) 9. ____________ refers to the recording of an expenditure as an asset rather than an expense.

a) Amortization

b) Capitalizing

c) Deferred charge

d) NIBT

( ) 10. Current liabilities are debts incurred by the company that are due within the next:

a) three months

b) six months

c) nine months

d) year

( ) 11. The income tax equivalent of amortization is referred to as:

a) CICA

b) CRA

c) CCA

d) GAAP

( ) 12. The purpose of amortization is to:

a) reduce the level of income tax payable by a firm in a given year

b) encourage firms to purchase assets that have a longer useful life

c) allocate the cost of an asset over its useful life

d) solidify the cash positions of Canadian firms relative to their international counterparts

13. A company purchased 200 units of inventory two years ago for $300 and last year purchased 500 units for $500. Under the average cost method, if the company sells 150 units today, the unit cost of the goods will be: ( )

a) $300

b) $443

c) $500

d) $1,550

14. Suppose that a company purchases an asset for $250,000. The asset has a useful life of 10 years, after which time it has a salvage value of $50,000. If the company uses straight-line depreciation, then the amount of amortization in the first year will be ____________ whereas if the company uses declining balance depreciation, with a depreciation rate of 10%, the amount of amortization in the first year will be____________. ( )

a) $25,000; $25,000

b) $20,000; $20,000

c) $20,000; $25,000

d) $30,000; $20,000

15. Which of the following statements about cash flow and the cash flow statement is FALSE? ( )

a) The cash flow statement provides information concerning how the company generated and used cash through the fiscal period.

b) Under GAAP, firms have flexibility in their financial reporting, and this flexibility allows firms to change their earnings without actually changing their cash flow.

c) The cash flow statement consists of three sections: operating activities, financing activities, and investing activities.

d) An example of an investing activity on the cash flow statement would be the repayment of outstanding debt.

16. ____________ should be regarded as a signal that the financial statements of a firm may not present fairly its financial position or results. ( )

a) An unaudited report

b) A CPAB report

c) A qualified report

d) An unqualified report

FUNDAMENTAL AND TECHNICAL ANALYSIS

chapter 13

CSC EXAM SUGGESTED GUIDELINES:

12 questions for Chapter 13

OVERVIEW

- This chapter deals with the factors that affect equity and bond markets, including the economy and the business cycle, industry cycles, interest rates, and government policies. The objective is to determine the risks and rewards associated with investing in these securities.

Expected profitability and **interest rates** are the two most important factors affecting the value of a security. However, they are affected by the other factors identified above. !

Fundamental analysis looks at the economy, the industry, and the company. The most important factor affecting security prices is considered to be the expected future profitability of the issuer. **Technical analysis** looks at stock trading prices, trading volumes, and other market data, in the hopes of identifying recurring patterns. Both methods may use **quantitative analysis** to identify historical patterns of interest rates, economic variables, and industry or stock valuations to measure the factors influencing investment decisions. !

- Investors are assumed to be rational, profit-seeking individuals who react quickly to, and try to anticipate, new information.

The **Efficient Markets Hypothesis** (**EMH**) states that asset prices fully reflect available information. !

The Random Walk Theory suggests that in efficient markets, prices will follow a "random walk" where prices change randomly (in response to new information, which by nature is unpredictable). In other words, there should be no persisting patterns in asset returns. !

! **The Rational Expectations Hypothesis** assumes that people are rational and make intelligent economic decisions that are consistent with the evaluation of all available information. It assumes everyone has access to the same information and uses it wisely to best serve their own interest.

- Many studies have been conducted that suggest markets are in general efficient, despite the existence of temporary or small inefficiencies or anomalies. However, it seems unlikely that new information is available to all investors at the same time, that they will react immediately to all information in the same way, and that everyone has the ability to make accurate forecasts and correct decisions. Therefore, it is reasonable to assume that there may exist "opportunities" to earn abnormal returns, and intelligent investors will be ready to exploit them as they arise. With this in mind, a better understanding of how macroeconomic, industry, and company factors influence asset valuation should lead to better investment results.

FUNDAMENTAL MACROECONOMIC ANALYSIS

- Some of the macroeconomic factors that affect investor expectations and thus security prices include the following:
  1. **External Effects**: Include international events such as wars and election results, as well changes in the forces of demand and supply, which affect commodity prices and currency markets.
  2. **Fiscal Policies**: Taxes, government spending, and accumulated government deficits affect securities prices through their impact on investment and corporate profitability.
  3. **Monetary Policy**: Changes in monetary policy affect interest rates and corporate profitability in several ways. U.S. monetary policy decisions made by the U.S. Federal Reserve Board are a crucial factor affecting Canadian securities prices. This is partially attributable to our reliance on foreign funding to finance our large accumulated debt. The large amount of outstanding government debt has led to substantial growth in bond markets. In addition, monetary policy has a large impact on inflation, which in turn affects the level of T-bill and bond yields. When inflation concerns mount, the Federal Reserve Board must do something to calm bond market uncertainty (i.e., by raising short-term rates to combat inflationary pressures), which can lead to more moderate economic growth or even a growth recession. Since equity markets compete directly with bond markets, this affects the value of all securities.

     A "**tilting of the yield curve**" refers to a situation where short-term rates rise while long-term rates fall. This tends to be good news for equity markets, since the short-term rate increase relieves inflationary pressures, while the decline in long-term rates enhances the attractiveness of equities relative to bonds, whose yields are falling. Strong evidence suggests that U.S. and Canadian equity markets rally when the yield curve tilts, and the gains increase as the degree of tilt increases. These tilts have occurred more frequently since the 1980s.

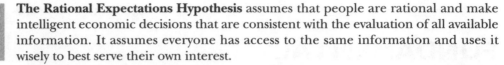

4. **Flow of Funds**: Large capital flows from one asset class to another are determined by shifts in Canadian retail and institutional investors' demand for stocks and bonds, and by changes in the demands by foreign investors. Net Canadian equity mutual fund purchases are often cited as an important factor influencing the S&P/TSX Index. Since falling interest rates lead to increased stock prices, we would expect equity fund purchases to rise as interest rates fall, which is generally the case.
5. **Inflation**: Inflationary pressures cause uncertainty regarding the future, which often leads to higher interest rates, lower profitability, and lower price-earnings (P/E) multiples. Inflation causes higher inventory and labour costs to manufacturers, who may not be able to pass on the total increase in these costs. The growth in the level of the return on equity (ROE) for the S&P/TSX Index (which serves as a proxy for the general level of corporate profits) is highly correlated with changes in GDP and changes in inflation.

INDUSTRY ANALYSIS

- Industry and company profitability may be as much a function of industry structure as it is of the product which the industry sells. This structure, in turn, reflects the strategies pursued by companies within the industry.
- The S&P/TSX Composite Index is classified into 10 major sector groups. It is important for investors to try to assess the prospects for growth and degree of risk associated with different industries. Three basic questions to examine are the comparison of industry growth in sales with that of nominal GDP; the comparison of volume sales with real GDP; and how an industry price index compares with the overall inflation rate.

In order to sustain a competitive advantage that will enable them to survive in both the short and long run, companies generally strive to become either

- a low-cost producer, or
- a producer of a "differentiated" product, which has perceived distinct advantages or features from potential competing products.

Generally all industries exhibit a **life cycle**, which includes the following stages:

1. **Emerging** or **Initial Growth**: These industries are generally in the process of introducing new goods or services and may be experiencing negative cash flows and profitability. As a result, these industries may exhibit low or meaningless P/E ratios, provide low dividend yields, and are very risky in nature.
2. **Rapid Growth**: During this stage, sales and earnings are growing more rapidly than most other industries, and profit margins and cash flows may increase. Typically, growth will be financed to the extent possible from reinvested earnings, and these industries will exhibit low dividend yields. They may exhibit high P/E ratios to reflect the growth opportunities available; however, they may also exhibit above-average risk.

! 3. **Mature Industries**: These are characterized by a dramatic slowing of growth and a "squeeze" on profit margins as competition escalates. These industries are characterized by slower, more stable growth rates in sales and earnings, and firms usually have greater financial resources available to them. As a result, dividend yields tend to be higher.
4. **Declining Industries**: Growth rates may begin to decline, and profit margins may fall.

! **Five competitive forces** determine the attractiveness of an industry, and its prospects for future growth:

1. ease of entry or exit,
2. degree of competition,
3. availability of substitutes,
4. ability to exert pressure over selling price of products, and
5. ability to exert pressure over the purchase price of inputs.

! The **Return On Equity** (**ROE**) is a financial ratio of particular importance to shareholders of a company because it measures the profitability of the business, relative to the equity investment in that business. It is calculated as

Return on Total Equity = (net earnings before extraordinary items) ÷ (total equity)

! This ratio shows how well the capital contributed by equity holders has been used to generate profits.

! Industries are often classified as **cyclical**, **defensive**, or **speculative**. Cyclical industries are those whose earnings are affected to a larger-than-average amount by downturns in the business cycle. As a rule, the ROE of cyclical industries would vary by at least 100% over a complete business cycle, versus one-third for defensive industries, and about 55% for the S&P/TSX Index.

- Most S&P/TSX Index cyclical companies are large international exporters of commodities such as lumber, nickel, copper, and oil. **Commodity-based cyclicals** include industries such as forestry products, mining, and chemicals. **Industry cyclicals** include transportation, capital goods, and basic industries (steel, building materials), while **consumer cyclicals** include merchandising companies and automobiles.
- Defensive stocks are those whose sales and earnings are less affected by swings in the business cycle, resulting in more stable values of ROE. **Blue chip stocks** are those that can be considered of superior investment quality, and their earnings are more stable during periods of growth or recession. Usually they have a solid record characterized by a dominant market position, strong internal financing, and effective management. While Canadian banks fit the profile of blue chip stocks in many regards, their earnings fluctuate a great deal in response to changes in interest rates. This is true because they are forced to offer higher savings rates when interest rates rise, but they are locked in to fixed rates for mortgage income,

which results in a squeeze on profits. Also, as with utility companies, they pay out relatively high dividend amounts, and their prices will decline as a result of increasing interest rates.

- Speculative industries are usually so called because there is a great deal of risk and uncertainty associated with them due to the absence of definitive information. Penny stocks and/or high-technology stocks may fit this profile.

FUNDAMENTAL VALUATION MODELS

The Dividend Discount Model (DDM) assumes that we value common shares according to the present value of expected future cash flows associated with the security. If we assume dividends are the relevant cash flows, we can express the relationship as

$$P_0 = \frac{Div_1}{(1+r)^1} + \frac{Div_2}{(1+r)^2} + \frac{Div_3}{(1+r)^3} + \ldots + \frac{Div_t}{(1+r)^t} \ldots,$$

where P_0 is the intrinsic value of share price today, Div_1 is the expected dividend at the end of year one, and the required rate of return by the common shareholders (r) is the appropriate market-determined risk-adjusted discount rate. If we make the assumption that dividends will grow at a constant rate (g) indefinitely, the equation above reduces to the following equation, which is often referred to as the constant-growth version of the DDM or Gordon's Dividend Growth Model:

$$P_0 = \frac{Div_1}{r - g}$$

Notice that the discount rate depends largely on the general level of interest rates.

Example 1:

Determine the share price of a stock that is expected to pay an annual year-end dividend of $1.00, which is expected to grow indefinitely at an annual rate of 5% per year, if the required return on these shares is 15%.

Solution:

$$P_0 = \frac{Div_1}{r - g} = \frac{\$1.00}{.15 - .05} = \$10.00$$

- The DDM has a great deal of intuitive appeal, because it links equity prices to three important "fundamentals": corporate profitability (through their link with dividends); the general level of interest rates; and risk (the latter two through their impact on the discount rate).

! In particular, all else being equal, the model predicts that the intrinsic value of common shares will **increase** as a result of

1. increases in expected dividends as measured by Div_1, which are closely related to profitability;
2. increases in the growth rate (g) of these dividends; and
3. decreases in the appropriate discount rate (r), which will be an increasing function of the general level of interest rates, as well as the riskiness of the underlying security.

! The constant-growth version of the DDM can be rearranged in the following manner, using the present market price in place of intrinsic value, to obtain an estimate of the return required by investors on a particular share:

$$r = \frac{Div_1}{P_0} + g$$

! Example 2:

Determine the required rate of return on a stock that is expected to pay an annual year-end dividend of $2.00, which is expected to grow indefinitely at an annual rate of 4% per year, if the shares are trading at $20.

Solution:

$$r = \frac{2.00}{20} + .04 = .140 \text{ or } 14\%$$

! An expression for the P/E ratio can be derived from the DDM, by determining the payout ratio (b) associated with a given dividend. In other words, if we define EPS_1 as the expected earnings per share during year one, we can express the DDM as

$$P_0 = \frac{EPS_1 \leftrightarrow b}{r - g}$$

Dividing both sides of this by EPS_1, we get

$$P/E = \frac{b}{r-g}$$

This equation implies, all else being equal, that P/E ratios will increase

1. as a firm increases its payout ratio;
2. as the discount rate falls—which could be caused by falling inflation (which will cause the general level of interest rates to decline), and/or a decline in the riskiness of expected cash flows; and
3. as the growth rate in dividends (or earnings) increases.

- Generally, existing shareholders like to see high P/E ratios as they indicate good growth prospects and/or lower riskiness associated with the firm's cash flows. It is important to remember the phrase "other things being equal" because usually other things are not equal and the preceding relationships do not hold by themselves. It is quite obvious, upon reflection, that if a firm could increase its estimated P/E ratio, and therefore its market price, by simply raising its payout ratio, it would be very tempted to do so. However, such an action would in all likelihood reduce future growth prospects, lowering *g*, and thereby defeating the increase in the payout. Similarly, trying to increase *g* by taking on particularly risky investment projects would cause investors to demand a higher required rate of return, thereby raising *r*. Again, this would work to offset the positive effects of the increase in *g*. Variables 2 and 3 are typically the most important factors in the preceding determination of the P/E ratio because a small change in either can have a large effect on its value.

Example 3:

Determine an appropriate P/E ratio for a stock, if the company maintains a payout ratio of 53.5% under the following conditions:

(a) r = 15%, and g = 7%

(b) r = 16%, and g = 7%

(c) r = 15%, and g = 8%

Solution:

(a) $$P/E = \frac{0.535}{0.15-.07} = 6.69$$

(b) $$P/E = \frac{0.535}{0.16-.07} = 5.94$$

(c) $$P/E = \frac{0.535}{0.15-.08} = 7.64$$

- Often people say that a share represents a "buy" opportunity due to a low P/E ratio. The implication is that the share is undervalued relative to its earnings. However, market efficiency implies that this need not be (and in fact should not be) the case, as each security should be priced to reflect all relevant information about the firm.

! • Empirical evidence suggests that P/E levels in general (as measured by broad market indexes such as the S&P/TSX Index and the S&P 500 Index) are inversely related to inflation. In other words, when inflation increases, P/E ratios tend to decrease on average. This is consistent with what one would expect by looking at the formula above for determining P/E ratios, since the discount rate (*r*) (which is in the denominator) increases with increases in interest rates, and increases in inflation rates cause interest rates to increase.

- P/E ratios can be very volatile because earnings can vary significantly and sometimes be negative, especially for highly cyclical or economically sensitive companies. The P/E ratios are uninformative in such situations.

TECHNICAL ANALYSIS

! Technical analysis is based on three main assumptions:

1. All market actions are automatically accounted for in price activity; therefore, fundamental analysis is a fruitless exercise.
2. Prices move in a series of trends and patterns that tend to persist through time.
3. The past repeats itself in the future.

- Some commonly used tools in technical analysis are discussed below. They include the following:

  1. chart analysis,
  2. quantitative analysis,
  3. sentiment indicators, and
  4. cycle analysis.

! 1. **Chart Analysis**: This technique uses graphs to examine where security prices have been in order to determine in which direction they may be heading. These charts are used to try to identify support and resistance levels, as well as to identify normal trading patterns. **Resistance levels** are price levels that stock prices have difficulty exceeding, because investors begin to sell the underlying securities as the prices approach these values (i.e., supply increases and demand falls at these points). **Support levels** are price levels that stock prices have difficulty falling below because investors begin to buy the underlying securities as the prices approach these values (i.e., demand increases and supply falls at these points). Some of the commonly used tools and patterns are described below.

   - The most commonly used graph is a **bar chart**. Bar charts plot the range of prices over a particular interval, such as a day or a week. They also usually include trading volume at the bottom of the chart.

- **Reversal patterns** are those that often precede a substantial price swing. For example, a **Head-and-Shoulders Bottom** formation refers to a stock price pattern that depicts an accumulation range. Once the price breaks out of this accumulation range, by breaking through the "neckline" from below, it begins a *bull* surge (i.e., prices are expected to increase). The **Head-and-Shoulders Top** formation implies the opposite. Once the price breaks through the neckline from above, prices are expected to decline significantly.
- **Continuation patterns** represent "sideways" patterns that are thought to represent pauses in a prevailing price trend. They are often referred to as "consolidations," with the triangle pattern representing one of the most important patterns.

2. **Quantitative Analysis**: This approach focuses on identifying trends or providing early signals that a given trend is losing momentum. There are two general categories:
   - **Moving Averages (MAs)**: These are calculated by adding the closing prices for a stock (or index) over a given period of time (usually 40 weeks or 200 days to attempt to align with the market primary trend). If the overall trend has been down, the MA line will be above the current individual prices, and if the price "breaks through" the moving average line from below, it generates a "buy" signal. If the overall trend has been up, the MA line will be below the current individual prices, and if the price "breaks through" the moving average line from above, it generates a "sell" signal.
   - **Oscillators**: Oscillator indicators generally fluctuate in values between 0 and 100, or from 21 to 11. They may be used to provide
     - a signal of when a market is "overbought" or "oversold," which would be indicated when the values are near the extreme values;
     - a warning regarding a weakening trend, which may occur when the oscillator diverges from the underlying price; or
     - important trading signals when the oscillator crosses the zero line.
   - One of the most important oscillators is the **Moving Average Convergence-Divergence (MACD)** indicator. It finds the difference between two moving averages (such as the 20-day MA and the 30-day MA) and generates a smoothing line based on the difference.
3. **Sentiment Indicators**: These indicators focus on measuring investor expectations. **Contrarians** invest based on the premise that the majority of market beliefs will be wrong, on average. Therefore, they take the opposite position from prevailing confidence indicators. For example, if a survey indicated that 90% of market participants were bearish (i.e., believed markets would decline in the near future), a contrarian would buy on such information, based on the belief the market is currently "oversold."
4. **Cycle Analysis**: This approach focuses on identifying the overall direction of market movements. They tend to focus on four different cycle lengths:
   - long-term (greater than two years),
   - seasonal (one year),

- primary/intermediate (9–26 weeks), and
- trading (four weeks).

One of the most popular theories is the **Elliot Wave Theory**. This theory suggests that the market moves in a series of large waves and cycles, which are superimposed by smaller waves, and so on. In particular, it suggests that the market moves up in a series of five waves and down in a series of three waves, all of which have smaller waves superimposed upon them.

- **Equity Market Analysis** may use some of the following indicators of the soundness of equity markets in general, which are discussed below:
  1. volume changes
  2. breadth of market
     - advance-decline line and
     - new highs and new lows.
  3. sentiment

1. **Volume Changes**: When volume is increasing during a bull (bear) market, it indicates a lot of buying (selling) pressure, which confirms support for the trend. If volumes are lower, the trend is not well-supported and may begin to reverse.
2. **Breadth of Market**: Measures the number of different issues being traded, an increase in which suggests *bullish* conditions. There are two important breadth measures:
   - **The Advance-Decline Line**: The cumulative advance-decline line adds the difference between advances and declines every day to its starting value, an increase in which suggests *bullish* conditions.
   - **New Highs and New Lows**: When new highs are increasing (and new lows are decreasing), it is a *bullish* signal, while the opposite provides a *bearish* signal.
3. **Sentiment**: As discussed above.

- Many of the demand and supply factors that technical analysts monitor change in response to fundamental factors that affect earnings. Therefore, technical analysis is related to fundamental analysis in some sense, and it may help in timing purchases or sales, since it may indicate turning points. Its main disadvantage is the subjectivity involved in interpreting the charts and signals.

Chapter 13 Review Questions

( ) 1. All of the following would likely exert a positive influence on the general level of stock prices EXCEPT for:

a) A minority government is replaced by a majority government.

b) Short-term interest rates rise, while long-term interest rates fall.

c) Unemployment approaches the full-employment unemployment rate.

d) The government announces a significant cut in corporate tax rates.

2. The rationale for the use of technical analysis is *inconsistent* with: ( )

a) the Random Walk Theory

b) the Efficient Markets Hypothesis

c) neither (a) nor (b)

d) both (a) and (b)

3. Technical analysis involves looking at: ( )

a) stock trading prices, trading volumes, and other market data

b) P/E ratios and dividend yields

c) the economy, the industry, and the company

d) none of the above

4. What is the intrinsic value of a common share that has an expected payout ratio of 37.5% and has expected earnings per share of $4.00, if earnings and dividends are both expected to grow indefinitely at an annual rate of 5% per year, and the required return on the shares is 11%? ( )

a) $25.00

b) $30.00

c) $66.67

d) there is insufficient information

5. What is the implied P/E ratio for a stock that has an expected EPS of $5.00 and an expected year-end dividend of $2.00, if the appropriate discount rate is 12%, and the expected annual growth rate in dividends is 4%? ( )

a) 3.0 times

b) 5.0 times

c) 10.0 times

d) 25.0 times

6. Which of the following *increases* the attractiveness of an industry, with regard to the prospects for enhanced profitability of the companies within the industry? ( )

a) Entry into the industry entails limited technological requirements.

b) There are many competitors.

c) There are very few complementary products available.

d) There are very few substitute products available.

( ) 7. Rising inflation causes P/E ratios to ____________ due to the upward pressure it exerts on ____________.

a) increase; interest rates
b) decrease; interest rates
c) increase; corporate profits
d) decrease; corporate profits

( ) 8. Which of the following situations represents a *bearish* signal?

a) an increase in the advance-decline line
b) new lows are decreasing
c) head-and-shoulders bottom formation
d) none of the above

( ) 9. An investor whose primary investing objective is income would be most interested in common shares of a company in an industry in the ____________ life cycle stage.

a) emerging
b) initial growth
c) rapid growth
d) mature

( ) 10. What is the implied rate of return on common shares that are trading at $50 if they are expected to pay a year-end dividend of $4.00 that is expected to increase at an annual rate of 4% per year?

a) 8%
b) 12%
c) 14%
d) none of the above

( ) 11. The basic factor affecting shifts in demand for stocks and bonds by institutional investors is:

a) the level of interest rates
b) net purchases by nonresidents
c) the level of P/E ratios
d) external effects

( ) 12. "Tilting of the yield curve" is a common phrase that refers to:

a) substituting long-term bonds for short-term bonds in a portfolio
b) substituting short-term bonds for long-term bonds in a portfolio
c) short-term rates rising while long-term rates fall
d) long-term rates rising while short-term rates fall

Bonus Questions

13. The two most important tools of fiscal policy are: ( )
    a) short-term interest rates and money supply
    b) money supply and levels of government spending
    c) levels of government spending and taxation
    d) taxation and short-term interest rates

14. A drop in short-term interest rates would: ( )
    a) slow economic growth
    b) reduce inflationary pressure
    c) attract capital from foreign investors
    d) none of the above

15. Emerging growth, rapid growth, maturity, and decline are stages of what cycle? ( )
    a) life cycle
    b) industrial cycle
    c) business cycle
    d) none of the above

16. Which of the following is a consequence of inflation? ( )
    a) widespread uncertainty and lack of confidence in the future
    b) lower corporate profits
    c) higher interest rates
    d) all of the above

17. Inflation results in: ( )
    a) lower P/E multiples
    b) lower consumer good prices
    c) lower production costs
    d) none of the above

18. Which of the following is NOT typically a characteristic of a blue chip company? ( )
    a) top investment quality
    b) strong internal financing
    c) exceptional growth in sales and earnings
    d) none of the above

( ) 19. Why might a firm have a high P/E ratio?

a) It is in a growth industry.
b) It is in a speculative industry.
c) Investor confidence is high.
d) All of the above.

( ) 20. If true, the Random Walk Theory could be considered particularly damaging to which group?

a) fundamental analysts
b) quantitative analysts
c) industry analysts
d) technical analysts

( ) 21. Which of the following is NOT an implication of the efficient market hypothesis?

a) The market reacts quickly to new information.
b) Transaction costs are minimized.
c) A stock's price fully reflects all available information.
d) The stock price is the best estimate of the stock's true value.

( ) 22. Which of the following analyses is NOT used by technical analysts?

a) chart analysis
b) cycle analysis
c) macroeconomic analysis
d) analysis of sentiment indicators

( ) 23. A resistance level is when:

a) supply exceeds demand and the price begins to rise
b) supply exceeds demand and the price begins to fall
c) demand exceeds supply and the price begins to rise
d) demand exceeds supply and the price begins to fall

( ) 24. Which indicator is generally used to confirm other indicators, rather than on its own?

a) sentiment
b) volume
c) price
d) oscillator

COMPANY ANALYSIS

chapter 14

CSC EXAM SUGGESTED GUIDELINES:
11 questions for Chapter 14

FUNDAMENTAL COMPANY ANALYSIS

- Fundamental company analysis involves quantitative analysis, which focuses on financial statement and market data; and qualitative analysis, which assesses less tangible factors such as the quality of management and firm reputation. The objective is to gain insight into the factors that affect company profitability. A good starting point is an examination of the company's financial statements.
- **Statement of Comprehensive Income Analysis** examines trends, and reasons for trends, in variables such as
  - sales;
  - operating costs and profitability;
  - key financial ratios relating to profitability such as the pre-tax profit margin, net profit margin, ROE, cash flow measures, and earnings per share (EPS); and
  - the company's dividend record.
- **Statement of Financial Position** (or **Balance Sheet**) **Analysis** provides a picture of the company's overall financial position and examines
  - the effect of leverage on earnings;
  - the company's capital structure, which provides a picture of the company's overall financial soundness; and
  - what types of securities have been or might be issued.

Qualitative analysis of management effectiveness and other company intangibles can often be one of the most critical parts of fundamental analysis.

- Investors will also be concerned with the degree of liquidity associated with corporate securities.
- Timing of share transactions may be a crucial factor in successful investments. Changing market sentiment can produce large swings in equity prices. These sentiments are determined largely by investor expectations regarding future economic conditions and corporate earnings. The P/E ratio is often used as a timing device by assessing reasonable values for stocks at any time in the business cycle, since they tend to increase during rising stock markets and/or during periods of rising earnings or falling interest rates. P/E levels also reflect overall levels of investor confidence.
- It is essential that investors continually monitor their investments and the companies whose shares they purchase, since conditions change quickly and continuously.

INTERPRETING FINANCIAL STATEMENTS

Prior to examining the financial ratios of a company, a good analyst will examine the notes to the financial statements carefully. Some common "warning signs" to look for include

1. changes in accounting practices;
2. long-term commitments; and
3. a series of mergers and takeovers.

Potential problems can also be identified by examining **common-size financial statements**. These statements are constructed by expressing all items on the balance sheet as a percentage of total assets, and by expressing all income statement items as a percentage of net sales. They are useful for highlighting important trends, abnormalities, etc.

- Ratio analysis is one of the most commonly used approaches to examine a company's financial performance. A single ratio has limited value; however, they provide "relative" measures of performance/risk characteristics of firms when they are compared with other ratios. Normally this involves

1. trend analysis; and
2. comparison with similar companies or industry averages.

! Four areas of firm operations that are often analyzed by reference to ratios are

1. **Liquidity**: The firm's ability to generate required cash in a hurry to meet its short-term obligations.
2. **Risk Analysis**: Concerned with the company's ability to deal with its debt, with regard to its ability to repay and its ability to assume more debt.
3. **Operating Performance**: Concerned with the company's ability to make efficient use of its assets to generate profits.
4. **Value**: Relates the market value and returns associated with the company's shares to its accounting values.

- Internal trend lines are constructed by selecting a base period, and setting the ratio for that period as 100, and relating future ratio values to this figure. For example, if the earnings per share (EPS) figures for five successive years are $1.00, $1.20, $1.30, $1.10, and $0.90 and we set the base of 100 equal to the first year's EPS figure, the trend line values will be 100, 120, 130, 110, and 90. The advantages of this approach are that it is simple arithmetically, and it is easy to interpret changes through the years. Two disadvantages of using trend lines arise if the base year does not have a typical value or is negative (e.g., if a loss occurred).
- External comparisons must be careful to compare firms with similar firms and whose ratios have been calculated according to the same basis. For example, it would be incorrect to compare the P/E ratios of two companies if one was calculated based on the year-end price, while the other was determined using the average price over the year. In Canada, the Financial Post Data Group, the Canadian Manufacturers Association, and some banks provide industry ratios for comparison purposes.
- This section presents a large number of ratios. Some are difficult to remember and calculate, while others are more straightforward. As you work your way through the material, there are four main things to remember about the ratios:
    1. what they measure (i.e., what type of information they provide);
    2. if a higher ratio is better (or worse) for the company;
    3. the rules of thumb or industry standards where applicable; and
    4. how to calculate the ratio.

The exam will include a variety of questions covering most of these topics with regard to the ratios included on the exam.

While it is difficult to identify rules of thumb for ratios, improvements in the ratios through time (i.e., positive trends) and a favourable comparison with industry ratios are both positive.

- Ratios will be calculated for the following company throughout the remainder of this section.

XYZ COMPANY
Financial Statements

STATEMENT OF COMPREHENSIVE INCOME

Net Sales	$1,426,000
Cost of Goods Sold	1,238,700
Amortization	40,100
General, Selling, & Admin. Expense	33,100
Earnings before Interest and Taxes	114,100
Interest Expense	5,300
Pre-tax Income	108,800

Income Tax:	
Current	10,900
Future	9,000
Earnings before Extraordinary Items	88,900
Extraordinary Items	0
Income after Extraordinary Items	88,900
Dividends—Preferred Shares	3,500
Income Available to Common Shares	85,400
Other Sources of Comprehensive Income	0
Comprehensive Income	85,400
Earnings/Common Share	0.68
Common Shares—Year-end	125,658
Common Shares—Average	125,536
Preferred Shares—Year-end	3,166
Dividends—Common Shares	14,700
Market Price per Share (Close)	6.69

STATEMENT OF FINANCIAL POSITION

Assets:	
Cash & Equivalents	$150,000
Accounts Receivable	174,000
Inventory	220,200
Total Current Assets	544,200
Capital Assets—Gross	1,372,700
Less: Accumulated Amortization	–766,200
Capital Assets—Net	606,500
Total Assets	1,150,700
Liabilities & Equity:	
Bank Loans & Equivalents	147,800
Accounts Payable	347,200
Current Portion of Long-term Debt	5,400
Total Current Liabilities	500,400
Long-term Debt	83,500
Income Taxes Payable	41,600
Equity: Preferred Stock	158,300
Common Stock	190,600
Retained Earnings	176,300
Total Equity	525,200
Total Liabilities & Equity	1,150,700

Analyzing Liquidity

Commonly used liquidity indicators include the following:

1. Working Capital (or net current assets) = current assets − current liabilities
2. Current (or Working Capital) Ratio = (current assets) ÷ (current liabilities)
3. Quick (or Acid Test) Ratio = (current assets − inventory) ÷ (current liabilities)
4. Operating Cash Flow Ratio = (cash flow from operations) ÷ (current liabilities), where cash flow from operations = net earnings before extraordinary items (BEI) + amortization + future income taxes + non-controlling interest in earnings of subsidiaries − equity income − change in net working capital

The **current ratio** measures a firm's ability to repay current obligations from current assets, while the **quick ratio** is a more conservative estimate of liquidity that reflects the fact that inventories are generally not as "liquid" as other current assets. The **operating cash flow ratio** measures the degree to which the firm would be able to cover its current obligations from operating cash flows. As with most ratios there is no absolute standard for these ratios, but higher values suggest greater firm liquidity. Cash forecasts can provide additional insight into the firm's liquidity situation.

Example 1: For Company XYZ:

Working capital = 544,200 − 500,400 = $43,800

Current ratio = 544,200/500,400 = 1.09

Quick ratio = (544,200 − 220,200)/500,400 = 0.65

Operating cash flow ratio = (88,900 + 40,100 + 9,000 + 0 − 0 − 50,000)/500,400 = 0.1759

(Note: Assume the change in net working capital during the year was $50,000.)

While there are no absolute standards, and standards are industry-specific, generally, current and quick ratios should be greater than 2.0 and 1.0 for both utilities and industrials. Thus, Company XYZ does not satisfy the suggested rules of thumb for the current or quick ratios, and may not have adequate liquidity, according to these guidelines. The operating cash flow ratio of 0.1759 indicates they have only $0.18 of operating cash flow for every $1 of current liabilities, which does not appear great, but should be compared to industry standards and the trend in this ratio for the company.

Risk Analysis

- Commonly used indicators of a firm's debt situation are

  1. asset coverage,
  2. debt/equity ratio,

3. cash flow/total debt, and
4. interest coverage.

All of these ratios are discussed below.

! 1. **Asset Coverage** = **(total assets – goodwill – [current liabilities *less* short-term debt such as bank advances and the current portion of long-term debt]) ÷ (total debt outstanding/$1,000), where total debt = short-term debt + current portion of long-term debt + long-term debt**
   - This measures the protection provided by the firm's tangible assets, after all prior liabilities have been met. Assets well in excess of company debt are required to generate sufficient earnings to meet interest obligations and repay indebtedness. Additionally, asset coverage shows the book value amount of assets backing the debt securities. Higher ratios are better.

! Example 2: For Company XYZ:

Asset coverage = (1,150,700 – 0 – [500,400 – 147,800 – 5,400]) ÷ ([147,800 + 5,400 + 83,500]/$1,000) = (803,500)/(236.7) = $3,394.59

! 2. **Debt/Equity Ratio** = **(total debt outstanding) ÷ (book value of shareholders' equity)**.
   - This ratio pinpoints the relationship of debt to equity and is a direct measure of financial risk. The higher the ratio, the riskier the company.

! Example 3: For Company XYZ:

Debt/equity ratio = (147,800 + 5,400 + 83,500)/525,200 = 0.45

! 3. **Cash Flow/Total Debt** = **(operating cash flow) ÷ (total debt), where operating cash flow = net earnings BEI – equity income + non-controlling interest in earnings of subsidiary companies + future income taxes + amortization + any other deductions not paid out in cash (e.g., depletion, amortization, etc.) – change in net working capital**
   - Cash flow provides a better indicator of a firm's ability to cover interest payments, pay dividends, and finance expansion because of the substantial size of non-cash items on earnings statements. Higher ratios are better.

! Example 4: For Company XYZ:

Cash flow/total debt = ([88,900 – 0 + 0 + 9,000 + 40,100 – 50,000]/[147,800 + 5,400 + 83,500]) × 100% = 37.2%

4. **Interest Coverage** = **EBIT/Interest** = **(net earnings BEI – equity income + non-controlling interest in earnings of subsidiary companies + all income taxes + total interest charges)** ÷ **(total interest charges)**
   - This ratio is generally considered to be the most important quantitative test, since it measures a firm's ability to meet debt obligations, and a stable trend is important. Higher ratios are better.

Example 5: For Company XYZ:

Interest coverage = (88,900 – 0 + 0 + 19,900 + 5,300)/5,300 = 21.53

Operating Performance

- Some commonly used measures of operating performance are
  1. gross profit margin,
  2. net profit margin,
  3. net (or after-tax) return on common equity, and
  4. inventory turnover ratio.

All of these ratios are discussed below.

1. **Gross Profit Margin** = **(net sales – cost of goods sold)** ÷ **(net sales)**
   - This ratio indicates the efficiency of management in turning over the company's goods at a profit. Higher is better.

Example 6: For Company XYZ:

Gross profit margin = ([1,426,000 – 1,238,700]/1,426,000) × 100% = 13.1%

2. **Net Profit Margin** = **(net earnings BEI – equity income + non-controlling interest in earnings of subsidiary companies)** ÷ **(net sales)**
   - This measure accounts for expenses and taxes, and effectively sums up in one figure management's ability to run the business. Adjustments for minority interest and equity income are made to enhance comparability across firms, since not all companies have these items. Higher is better.

Example 7: For Company XYZ:

Net profit margin = ([88,900 – 0 + 0]/1,426,000) × 100% = 6.2%

3. **Net (After-Tax) Return on Common Equity** = **(net earnings BEI – preferred dividend)** ÷ **(total common equity)**
   - This ratio shows how well the capital contributed by common shareholders has been used to generate profits. Higher is better.

Example 8: For Company XYZ:

Net return on common equity = ([88,900 – 3,500]/[190,600 + 176,300]) × 100% = 23.3%

- Some analysts suggest that taxes are an expense of doing business and note that the proportion of equity to capitalization changes from period to period and therefore prefer measure (6) to measures (5) and (7).

4. **Inventory Turnover Ratio** = **(cost of goods sold)** ÷ **(inventory)**

   Note: Sometimes net sales is used to replace cost of goods sold, if this information is unavailable.
   - This ratio varies significantly across industries. Higher ratios suggest that a company is selling existing inventory more quickly than their competitors. As a result it faces less risk of being caught with too much inventory in the event of price declines, or maintaining obsolete or damaged inventory. Low inventory turnover can cause a significant increase in financing charges if inventory accumulates, since it represents a large part of a company's working capital. Low turnover could be due to
     - large portions of unsaleable goods,
     - the firm has too much inventory on hand, or
     - the inventory value is inflated.

Example 9: For Company XYZ:

Using (4) Inventory turnover = 1,238,700/220,200 = 5.62 times

Analyzing Value

- Some commonly used value ratios are
  1. dividend payout (common),

  2a. earnings per share,

  2b. fully diluted earnings per share,

  3. dividend yield,

4. price-earnings ratio, and
5. equity value (book value) per common share.

These ratios are discussed below. They provide a way of relating market value to dividends and earnings.

1. **Dividend Payout (Common)** = **(common dividends)** ÷ **(net earnings BEI – preferred dividends)** !
   - These ratios indicate the percentage of earnings being paid out as dividends and the amount being reinvested for future growth. Since management generally tries to maintain steady dividend payments, an unstable payout ratio is usually associated with unstable earnings.

Example 10: For Company XYZ: !

Dividend payout (common) = ([14,700]/[88,900 – 3,500]) × 100% = 17.2%

2a. **Earnings per Share (EPS)** = **(net earnings BEI – preferred dividends)** ÷ **(number of common shares outstanding)** !
   - It is one of the most widely used and understood of all ratios, provides common shareholders with a measure of earnings available to them after all other obligations have been met, and provides a clue as to the company's ability to maintain or increase dividend payments. Higher is better.

2b. **Fully Diluted EPS** = **(adjusted net earnings BEI)** ÷ **(adjusted common shares outstanding)** !
   - This figure reflects the EPS available to common shareholders if all securities such as convertible preferred stock or debentures, stock options, and warrants were converted into common shares. The adjusted earnings figure would reflect the fact that interest would no longer be payable on convertible debt, and it would not be necessary to subtract the preferred dividends on the convertible preferred shares. The adjusted common shares figure would be increased to reflect the new number of shares outstanding if all securities were converted.

Example 11: For Company XYZ: !

Earnings per share = (88,900 – 3,500)/125,658 = $0.68

There is no mention of convertible securities, warrants, or other dilutive securities for this company; therefore, the fully diluted EPS = basic EPS.

3. **Dividend Yield** = **(annual dividend per share)** ÷ **(current market share price)** !
   - This ratio offers a superficial comparison of the yield offered by different common shares.

! Example 12: For Company XYZ:

Common dividend per share = common dividends/number of common shares outstanding = 14,700/125,658 = $0.117

Dividend yield (common) = (0.117/6.69) × 100% = 1.75%

! 4. **Price-Earnings (P/E) Ratio** = (**current market share price**) ÷ (**EPS**)

   - This is probably the most useful and widely used ratio, because it is, in fact, all the other ratios combined into one figure. It represents the ultimate evaluation of a company and its shares by the investing public, with due consideration for tangible and intangible factors such as quality of management, future growth opportunities, and risks faced by the company. In fact, a major reason for calculating EPS is to enable a comparison with the share's market price. It enables comparisons across firms, provided they are in the same industry. The calculation above uses the most recent 12-month EPS figure; however, in practice, P/E ratios are often calculated based on projected earnings.

! Example 13: For Company XYZ:

Price-earnings ratio = 6.69/0.68 = 9.8 times

5. **Equity Value** (**Book Value**) **per Common Share** = (**total common equity**) ÷ (**number of common shares outstanding**)

   - This ratio measures the amount of assets that shareholders are entitled to if the company was to be liquidated.

! Example 14: For Company XYZ:

Equity value per common share = (525,200 – 158,300)/(125,658) = $2.92

The book value per common share can be calculated by dividing the book value of common equity (525,200 – 158,300) by the number of common shares outstanding (125,658), which equals $2.92, which is less than half of the market value per share of $6.69. This ratio is complicated to interpret, but generally higher ratios mean the market likes the firm more.

ASSESSING PREFERRED SHARE INVESTMENT QUALITY

! The following **four tests** are employed to assess the investment quality of preferred shares:

1. **Preferred Dividend Coverage**: Similar to Interest Coverage but accounts for preferred dividends in the denominator—not required to calculate.

   Rules of thumb are for utilities and industrials to maintain coverage above 2.0 and 3.0 for each of the past five years. The trend is also very important. Before-tax dividend payments may be calculated by multiplying actual payments (which come from after-tax earnings) by (100)/(100 – tax rate).

2. **Record of Continuous Dividend Payments**: This information can be obtained for Canadian companies from *The Dividend Record*, which is published by the Financial Post Data Group.

3. **Adequate Equity Behind Each Preferred Share**: Equity (or book value) per preferred share (as calculated below) should be at least two times the dollar value of assets to which the preferred share is entitled over each of the past five years, and exhibit a stable or rising five-year trend.

   Similar to common equity per common share, but adjusted for preferred number of shares in the denominator, and using "all" equity in the numerators—not required to calculate. A higher number is better.

4. **An Independent Credit Assessment**: In Canada, both DBRS and S&P provide ratings for preferred shares. The DBRS ratings are

   - Pfd1 (superior credit quality—usually debt is AAA or AA rated);
   - Pfd2 (satisfactory quality—usually debt is A rated);
   - Pfd3 (adequate quality—usually debt is BBB high rated);
   - Pfd4 (speculative quality—usually debt is BBB low or BB rated);
   - Pfd5 (highly speculative—usually debt is B rated or lower); and
   - D (in arrears).

   Similarly, DBRS ratings range from Pfd-1 (high) for highest quality to D (in arrears).

- In addition to these four tests, investors should also consider other relevant economic, industry, and financial factors; examine the most recent quarterly results available; and confirm that the shares were underwritten by an established securities firm.
- Top-quality straight preferreds would fit into a conservative investor's portfolio, while medium- to high-quality preferreds would be appropriate for moderately aggressive investors, and low-quality to speculative preferreds would only be appropriate for aggressive, experienced investors and speculators.
- Assuming high-quality preferreds, the following special types would be most appropriate for the following types of individual investment portfolios:
  1. Convertible: aggressive and moderately aggressive
  2. Retractable: conservative

3. Variable dividend: aggressive and sophisticated
4. Warrants attached: aggressive and moderately aggressive
5. Participating: conservative and moderately aggressive
6. Foreign-pay: aggressive and sophisticated

Chapter 14 Review Questions

( ) 1. Comprehensive income statement analysis would examine each of the following EXCEPT:

a) operating costs
b) sales
c) the effect of liquidity
d) cash flow

Refer to the following Statement of Comprehensive Income and Statement of Financial Position for ABC Company to answer Questions 2 to 5:

ABC COMPANY
Financial Statements

STATEMENT OF COMPREHENSIVE INCOME

Net Sales	$150,000
Cost of Goods Sold	105,700
Amortization	6,000
General, Selling, & Admin. Expense	14,000
EBIT	25,000
Interest Expense	10,000
Pre-tax Income	15,000
Income Tax:	
Current	5,000
Future	2,000
Less: Minority Interest in Subsidiaries	2,000
Add: Equity Income	1,000
Earnings before Extraordinary Items	7,000
Extraordinary Items	4,000
Income after Extraordinary Items	3,000
Other Comprehensive Income	0
Comprehensive Income	3,000

Dividends—Preferred Shares	1,500
Common Shares—Year-end	20,000
Dividends—Common Shares	2,000
Market Price per Share (Close)	10.00
STATEMENT OF FINANCIAL POSITION	
Assets:	
Cash & Equivalents	$15,000
Accounts Receivable	20,000
Invontory	30,000
Total Current Assets	65,000
Capital Assets—Net	100,000
Goodwill	5,000
Total Assets	170,000
Liabilities & Equity:	
Bank Loans & Equivalents	10,000
Accounts Payable	15,000
Current Portion of Long-term Debt	5,000
Total Current Liabilities	30,000
Long-term Debt	35,000
Future Income Taxes	5,000
Equity: Preferred Stock	15,000
Common Stock	20,000
Retained Earnings	65,000
Total Equity	100,000
Total Liabilities & Equity	170,000

2. What is ABC's debt-to-equity ratio? ( )
   a) 2.00:1
   b) 0.55:1
   c) 0.50:1
   d) there is insufficient information

3. What is ABC's common equity (book value) per common share? ( )
   a) $1.00
   b) $4.25
   c) $5.00
   d) there is insufficient information

( ) 4. What is ABC's P/E multiple?

a) 20.0 times
b) 28.6 times
c) 36.4 times
d) 66.7 times

( ) 5. What is ABC's interest coverage ratio?

a) 1.95 times
b) 2.50 times
c) 8.95 times
d) there is insufficient information

Refer to the following information to answer Questions 6 to 8:

Firms X and Y are in the same industry and are roughly the same size. Based on the following ratios for the previous year

Ratios	Firm X	Firm Y
current	2.0	1.8
net profit margin	7.00%	6.00%
net return on common equity	12.50%	14.00%
cash flow/total debt	0.32	0.25
quick	1.2	1.1
inventory turnover	20 times	25 times
debt percentage of total capital	30%	40%
interest coverage	3.5 times	2.6 times
preferred dividend coverage	3.5 times	2.4 times
debt/equity	0.5	1.1

( ) 6. Which company appears to be more profitable according to the ratios presented?

a) Firm X, because it has a higher net return on invested capital.
b) Firm Y, because it has a higher net return on common equity.
c) Firm Y, because it has a higher inventory turnover ratio.
d) Cannot say without further analysis.

( ) 7. Which company has a better ability to repay the funds it has borrowed?

a) Firm X, because it has a higher cash flow/total debt ratio.
b) Firm X, because it has a lower debt/equity ratio.
c) Firm Y, because it has a higher interest coverage ratio.
d) Cannot say without further analysis.

8. How many days does Firm Y need to sell current inventory? ( )
   a) 18.25 days
   b) 18 days
   c) 14.6 days
   d) 14.4 days

9. Participating preferred shares would be most appropriate for which of the following types of investors? ( )
   a) speculators
   b) aggressive and sophisticated
   c) conservative and moderately aggressive
   d) none of the above

10. The following suggest that a preferred share of an industrial company is high quality EXCEPT for: ( )
    a) It has a preferred dividend coverage ratio of 2.5.
    b) It has an equity per preferred share ratio that is 2.5 times the par value of the shares.
    c) It is rated P-1 by CBRS.
    d) All of the above suggest that a preferred share of an industrial company is high quality.

11. An unusually high dividend payout ratio may be the result of all of the following, EXCEPT for: ( )
    a) stable earnings
    b) declining earnings
    c) earnings based on resources that are being depleted
    d) peak cyclical earnings

Bonus Questions

12. A low dividend payout ratio may be the result of: ( )
    a) internally financed growth
    b) growing earnings
    c) both (a) and (b)
    d) neither (a) nor (b)

( ) 13. A company is considered leveraged if its capital structure consists of:

a) debt

b) preferred shares

c) both (a) and (b)

d) neither (a) nor (b)

( ) 14. The earnings of a levered company will *increase* ____________ during an economic upswing and *decrease* ____________ during a downswing.

a) faster; slower

b) slower; faster

c) faster; faster

d) slower; slower

( ) 15. The measure of ease in buying or selling stock without significantly impacting the price is referred to as the stock's:

a) liquidity

b) resilience

c) volatility

d) none of the above

( ) 16. The price-earnings ratio is considered to be a:

a) liquidity ratio

b) risk analysis ratio

c) operating performance ratio

d) value ratio

( ) 17. Cash and cash equivalents are NOT included in calculating which of the following?

a) current ratio

b) quick ratio

c) operating cash flow ratio

d) enterprise multiple

( ) 18. The current ratio measures a company's ability to:

a) meet its obligations

b) expand its volume of business

c) take advantage of financial opportunities

d) all of the above

( ) 19. A company's working capital is also known as its:

a) net profit margin

b) net current assets

c) cash flow

d) none of the above

20. Which of the following is NOT an operating cost? ( )

a) costs of goods sold

b) interest charges

c) both (a) and (b)

d) neither (a) nor (b)

21. Company ABC Inc. reported sales (in millions) of $112 in Year 1, $124 in Year 2, and $148 in Year 3. If Year 1 is the base year, what is the sales trend ratio for Year 3? ( )

a) 132

b) 119

c) 84

d) 76

22. The asset coverage ratio is considered a: ( )

a) liquidity ratio

b) risk analysis ratio

c) operating performance ratio

d) value ratio

chapter 15

INTRODUCTION TO THE PORTFOLIO APPROACH

CSC EXAM SUGGESTED GUIDELINES:
12 questions for Chapter 15

INTRODUCTION

The final step of the investment management process (after **security selection**, **asset mix**, and **market timing** decisions) involves **portfolio management**. Portfolio management considers securities based on their contribution to the risks and expected returns of the entire portfolio.

RISK AND RETURN

In an ideal world, investors could obtain high returns, without assuming any risk. Unfortunately, high expected returns usually go hand in hand with high risk. Thus, financial decisions usually entail the classic **risk-return trade-off**: reducing risk tends to reduce expected returns, while increasing expected returns tends to increase risk.

It is common to make the assumption that investors are **risk averse**. This means that investors will require additional expected return in return for assuming additional risk. Given the risk-return trade-off faced by investors, they will attempt to either

- minimize risk for a given level of required return, or
- maximize expected return for a given level of risk.

In other words, if an investor is presented with two equally risky investments, they will choose the one that offers the higher return. Similarly, if presented with two investments with equal expected returns, they will choose the one with the lower risk.

- While all investors are assumed to be risk averse, some are more so than others. More risk-averse investors should pursue investment strategies that are consistent with their low tolerance for risk. They may be attracted to securities such as guaranteed investment certificates (GICs) and Canada Savings Bonds (CSBs), which have low risks, but also relatively low expected rates of return. Less risk-averse investors will be comfortable pursuing riskier investment strategies and may invest more heavily in common shares and other riskier securities.

Returns

The **Total Return (TR)** for any security consists of the sum of two components:

1. cash flow yield, and
2. price change.

Formally, the TR for a given holding period is expressed as a decimal (or percentage) number (Return%) relating all the cash flows received by an investor during a designated time period to the purchase price of the asset:

$$\text{Return\%} = \frac{\text{Cash Flow} + (\text{Ending Value} - \text{Beginning Value})}{\text{Beginning Value}} \times 100$$

Example 1:

Determine the return for each of the following investments:

(a) A common stock is bought for $20 and sold one year later for $21; it did not pay any dividends during the year.

(b) A common stock is bought for $10 and sold one year later for $8; it paid a $1 dividend just before it was sold.

(c) An 8% $1,000 face value bond was bought for $950 and sold after one year for $980.

Solution:

(a) Return% = (0 + 21 – 20)/20 = 1/20 = 0.0500 = 5.00%

(b) Return% = (1 + 8 – 10)/10 = –1/10 = –0.1000 = –10.00%

(c) Return% = (80 + 980 – 950)/950 = 110/950 = 0.1158 = 11.58%, where $80 is the annual amount of coupons received on an 8% $1,000 face value bond.

When we look at past returns (e.g., how well stocks performed over a certain period), we are talking about **ex-post** (or historical) returns. These are important in assessing portfolio performance and also assist in projecting future returns. When we talk about expected (or projected) returns in the future, we are talking about **ex-ante** returns.

Historical returns provide investors with insight into the nature of the risk-return characteristics of different securities. Generally, various asset categories are ranked in the following manner with regard to expected return and risk (as measured by standard deviation, which will be discussed later in this section). Starting from the lowest-risk, lowest-expected return and increasing to the highest-risk, highest-expected return, we have

1. treasury bills,
2. bonds,
3. debentures,
4. preferred shares,
5. common shares, and
6. derivatives.

The **real rate** of return for an investment represents how much its values have increased in real terms, after adjusting for inflation. It may be approximated by subtracting the **inflation rate** from the actual rate of return, referred to as the **nominal rate**. This relationship is depicted in the following equation:

Real Return = Nominal Rate – Inflation Rate

Example 2:

Assume that the rate of inflation over the past year has been 3%.

(a) Determine the real rate of return for an investment that provided a 7% nominal return

(b) Determine the nominal return for an investment that provided a 2% real return.

Solution:

(a) Real Return = 7 – 3 = 4%

(b) Nominal Return = 2 + 3 = 5%

Treasury bill returns usually move together with (and cover) inflation. Since they are guaranteed by the federal government and have a short term to maturity, they are virtually risk-free. Therefore, it is common to refer to the T-bill rate as the **risk-free rate of return**, since it is the return that can be earned without assuming risk. All other investments must provide the risk-free rate of return plus an additional expected return, which is referred to as the risk premium.

Risk

Risk may be defined as the chance that the actual outcome from an investment will differ from the expected outcome. The more variable the possible outcomes that can occur (i.e., the broader the range of possible outcomes), the greater the risk. An investor who purchases a stock for $20 that they expect to sell after one year for $30 faces a great deal of uncertainty (or risk) associated with their expected return. On the other hand, an investor who purchases a one-year federal government T-bill faces very little uncertainty, since the face value of the T-bill will be paid to them after one year, barring default by the federal government.

! Some of the more common types of risks include the following:

1. **Inflation Rate Risk**: A factor affecting all securities is purchasing power risk, or the chance that the purchasing power of invested dollars will decline. With uncertain inflation, the real (inflation-adjusted) return involves risk even if the nominal return is safe (e.g., a T-bill).
2. **Business Risk**: The risk of doing business in a particular industry or environment, as measured by variability in a company's earnings, is called business risk.
3. **Political Risk**: With more investors investing internationally, both directly and indirectly, the political and therefore economic stability and viability of a country's economy need to be considered.
4. **Liquidity Risk**: Liquidity risk is the risk associated with the particular secondary market in which a security trades. An investment that can be bought or sold quickly and without significant price concession is considered liquid. The more uncertainty about the time element and the price concession, the greater the liquidity risk. A T-bill has little or no liquidity risk, whereas a small OTC stock may have substantial liquidity risk.
5. **Interest Rate Risk**: This refers to the variability in a security's return resulting from changes in the level of interest rates. Such changes generally affect securities inversely; that is, all things being equal, security prices move inversely to interest rates. Some securities, such as bonds, are more sensitive to interest rates than others.
6. **Foreign Exchange Risk**: Those who invest globally face the prospect of uncertainty in the returns after they convert the foreign gains back to their own currency. Foreign exchange risk may be defined as the variability in returns on securities caused by currency fluctuations.
7. **Default Risk**: This is the risk associated with a company not being able to pay its debt obligations as they come due. It is a large concern for investors in corporate or foreign securities, and less of a concern for federal government debt issues.

An investor can construct a diversified portfolio and eliminate part of the total risk—the diversifiable or non-market part. What is left is the non-diversifiable portion or the market risk. Variability in a security's total returns that is directly associated with overall movements in the general market or economy is called **systematic** (**market**) **risk**. The investor cannot escape this part of the risk because no matter how well he or she diversifies, the risk of the overall market cannot be avoided. If the stock market declines sharply, most stocks will be adversely affected; if it rises strongly, most stocks will appreciate in value.

The variability in a security's total returns not related to overall market variability is called the **non-systematic** (**non-market**) **risk**. This risk is unique to a particular security and is associated with such factors as business and financial risk as well as liquidity risk. Although all securities tend to have some non-systematic risk, it is generally connected with common stocks.

Investors must be able to quantify and measure risk. Three commonly used measures of risk are variance, standard deviation, and beta. The first two measure the total risk associated with the expected return, while the last is a measure of systematic or market risk.

The **variance**, or its square root, and **standard deviation** are typically used to measure total variability in outcomes. Variance and standard deviation measure the spread or dispersion in the distribution of possible security returns. The larger this dispersion, the larger the variance or standard deviation.

Market risk is usually measured by a variable called "**beta**." Beta measures the risk of an individual stock relative to the market portfolio of all stocks. The higher the beta, the riskier the security.

PORTFOLIO RISK AND RETURN

- The asset allocation decision is a critical one, which involves deciding how much of an investment portfolio should be invested in each of the three major asset classes (cash, fixed income, and equities). As discussed in Chapter 1, cash and near-cash assets provide safety; fixed-income assets provide income and a reasonable level of safety; while equities provide the greatest growth potential.
- The investor's objectives, along with their risk tolerance, dictate appropriate asset mixes. For example, a mix of 5% cash, 15% fixed income, and 80% equities might be considered appropriate for a young, knowledgeable investor with a long time horizon and high risk tolerance. At the opposite end of the spectrum, a mix of 20% cash, 60% fixed income, and 20% equities might be more appropriate for a retired investor with a short to medium time horizon with low risk tolerance and a need for current income from her investments.

Investment returns are influenced by the following factors:

1. asset mix (asset allocation),
2. market timing decisions,
3. security selection, and
4. chance.

It is estimated that asset allocation accounts for 80% to 90% of investment returns.

- The **expected return** (or **actual return**) **on a portfolio** can be calculated as the *weighted average of the expected (or actual) returns* of the individual assets within the portfolio.

Example 3:

The expected return on a portfolio that has \$10,000 invested in security A (which has an expected return [ER_A] of 8%), \$10,000 in security B (with ER_B = 10%), and \$20,000 in security C (with ER_C = 12%), is determined as follows:

Solution:

Weight in A (W_A) = 10,000/40,000 = 0.25; W_B = 10,000 / 40,000 = 0.25; W_C = 20,000 / 40,000 = 0.50

! Expected portfolio return = $W_A (ER_A) + W_B (ER_B) + W_C (ER_C)$ = 0.25 (8%) + 0.25 (10%) + 0.50 (12%) = 2 + 2.5 + 6 = 10.5%

Research shows that most non-systematic risk can be eliminated by holding as few as 32 securities in a portfolio. Holding a great deal more securities than this provides limited diversification benefits and may entail additional tracking, accounting costs, etc.

- Investment managers often use a number of hedging strategies to limit losses on investments, such as the use of put options on individual equities and/or the use of equity and bond index futures or options.

Combining Securities

! The number one principle of portfolio management is to diversify and hold a portfolio of securities; therefore, the risk of individual securities is relevant only to the extent that they add risk to the total portfolio. As discussed, diversification reduces many of the unique risks associated with a particular security, such as the interest rate risk and default risk associated with a particular debt security, or the business risk associated with a common stock investment.

- Portfolio risk is a unique characteristic and not simply the sum of individual security risks. A security may have a large risk if it is held by itself but much less risk when held in a portfolio of securities. Since the investor is concerned primarily with the risk of their total wealth position, as represented by their overall investment portfolio, individual securities are risky only to the extent that they add risk to the total portfolio.

! The co-movements between securities' returns are often referred to as the correlation between their returns. The correlation measures how security returns move in relation to one another. It is a relative measure of association that is bounded by +1.0 and –1.0, with

  - +1.0 indicating perfect positive correlation;
  - –1.0 indicating perfect negative (inverse) correlation; and
  - 0.0 indicating zero correlation (uncorrelated).

- If stocks A and B display perfect positive correlation, the returns have a perfect direct linear relationship. Knowing what the return on one security will do allows an investor to forecast perfectly what the other will do. When stock A's return goes up, stock B's does also. When stock A's return goes down, stock B's does also. With perfect negative correlation, the securities' returns have a perfect inverse linear relationship to each other. Therefore, knowing the return on one security provides full knowledge about the return on the second security. When one security's return is high, the other is low. With zero correlation, there is no relationship between the returns on the two securities. Knowledge of the return on one security is of no value in predicting the return of the second security. In the real world, these extreme correlations are rare. Rather, securities typically have some positive correlation with each other since all security prices tend to move with changes in the overall market and/or economy.

Obviously, there are few benefits to be had from diversification if the securities have high positive correlations. For example, an investor would not eliminate much risk by diversifying across the stocks of the "Big Six" banks, since their fortunes (and future returns) are linked to the same variables. However, investing in five stocks in five different industries would likely provide an investor with the opportunity to eliminate a substantial amount of unique risk. The lower the correlations between the security returns, the greater the benefits from diversification.

Beta measures the volatility of an individual security relative to that of the entire market. Technically, it is a measure of the correlation between individual security returns and those on a chosen market portfolio.

The higher the beta, the riskier the security. If the security's returns move more (less) than the market's returns as the latter changes, the security's returns have more (less) *volatility* (fluctuations in price) than those of the market. The market portfolio has a beta of 1.0, while a security with a beta of 1.5 indicates that, on average, its returns are 1.5 times as volatile as market returns, both up and down. In other words, its returns rise or fall on average 15% when the market return rises or falls 10%. A security with a beta greater than 1.0 is said to be an aggressive, or volatile, security. If the beta is less than 1.0, it indicates that, on average, the stock's returns have less volatility than the market as a whole. For example, a security with a beta of 0.6 indicates that stock returns move up or down, on average, only 60% as much as the market as a whole.

Betas for individual securities and portfolios tend to change through time.

Alpha represents returns earned by a stock or portfolio above and beyond what would be expected given their beta. Positive alphas indicate superior performance, while negative alphas indicate inferior performance (after adjusting for systematic risk).

THE PORTFOLIO MANAGEMENT PROCESS

A critical feature of portfolio formation is that portfolio returns will be an *average of the returns* on all securities within the portfolio, but the risk will be *lower than the weighted average of risks,* as long as the securities are not perfectly correlated. This implies that risk can actually be eliminated by forming portfolios.

Portfolio management is a continuous *process* consisting of six steps:

1. Determine investment objectives and constraints.
2. Design the investment policy statement.
3. Formulate an asset allocation strategy and select investment styles.
4. Implement the asset mix.
5. Monitor the economy, the markets, the portfolio, and the client.
6. Adjust the portfolio and measure performance.

Determining Objectives and Constraints

INVESTMENT OBJECTIVES

! Primary investment objectives include

1. safety,
2. income, or
3. growth of capital.

   These objectives are primarily mutually exclusive in the sense that one security can't maximize two or more of these primary objectives (i.e., trade-offs exist). For example, if you wish to maximize safety, you must be willing to sacrifice income and growth potential.

- Secondary investment objectives include

4. marketability (or liquidity), and
5. tax minimization.

   They are secondary in the sense that they should never "override" a primary investment objective.

! These objectives can be related to asset allocation decisions, and it is essential to communicate to clients the basis for any conclusions that are reached.

- The following table shows in general how well suited bonds, preferred stocks, and common stocks are to satisfying each of these objectives:

	Safety	Income	Growth
Bonds:			
Short-term	best	very steady	very limited
Long-term	next best	very steady	variable
Preferred	good	steady	variable
Common	often the least	variable	often the most

- Managing investor objectives is critical. This is true because it is not possible to simultaneously maximize safety, income, and growth potential.
  - In order to maximize safety, some growth potential and income must be sacrificed.
  - In order to maximize growth potential, some safety and income must be sacrificed.
  - In order to maximize income, some safety and growth potential must be sacrificed.
- Managing the trade-offs involved in satisfying the various investing objectives requires that balanced portfolios are weighted in asset classes to varying degrees to reflect the importance of each objective. In addition, diversification is important, and one security should generally never exceed 10% of the value of an investment portfolio.

- Conservative investors will prefer investment-grade investments while more aggressive investors may be inclined to have some portion of their wealth tied up in speculative investments, which may hold greater growth potential.

Constraints include

- time horizon,
- liquidity requirements,
- tax requirements, and
- unique circumstances (e.g., divorce, investing restrictions, etc.).

!

The Investment Policy Statement

- The **Investment Policy Statement** is a formal written document that dictates the guidelines and objectives that were agreed upon by the portfolio manager and the investor. It is a legal agreement that dictates the role of the manager. Inputs tend to be complex, but they include investment objectives and constraints, as well as a summary description of the prescribed asset mix and the investing style of the manager.

Chapter 15 Review Questions

1. A client has approached you with the following information: ( )

Security	Expected Return	Market Value
ABC Co.	7%	$20,000
DEF Co.	12%	$25,000
GHI Co.	15%	$45,000

If the client holds the given market values of the above securities in their portfolio, what is the return the investor can expect?

a) 11.33%
b) 11.83%
c) 12.39%
d) 12.41%

2. Refer to the information in Question 1. If the portfolio is strictly growth oriented with the only expectation being capital gains, what will the portfolio be worth in one year if the expected growth translates into capital appreciation? ( )

a) $99,000
b) $100,200
c) $101,151
d) none of the above

( ) 3. You purchase a stock for $18 and hold it for 2 years. The annual dividend for this stock is $1.50. If you sell the stock at the end of the 2 years for $21, what is the percentage return on this stock?

a) 16.6%

b) 25%

c) 28.6%

d) 33.3%

( ) 4. The following represent constraints that should be considered when designing an investment policy EXCEPT:

a) liquidity needs

b) taxes

c) time horizon

d) market timing

( ) 5. Each of the following risks can be reduced through diversification EXCEPT:

a) interest rate risk

b) default risk

c) business risk

d) systematic risk

( ) 6. Diversification will provide the greatest benefits when two securities display:

a) perfect positive correlation

b) perfect negative correlation

c) zero correlation

d) similar characteristics

( ) 7. Standard deviation measures total risk, while ______________ is a measure of market risk.

a) variance

b) beta

c) correlation

d) none of the above

( ) 8. A stock with a beta of 0.6 will have an expected return that is:

a) higher than the risk-free rate and the expected return on the market

b) higher than the risk-free rate and lower than the expected return on the market

c) lower than the risk-free rate

d) cannot say without additional information

9. A fund manager is able to consistently buy securities that outperform others. How do you usually measure such performance? ( )
   a) beta
   b) alpha
   c) gamma
   d) SML

10. Which of the following is NOT considered a form of risk? ( )
    a) potential to lose money
    b) potential to lose purchasing power
    c) potential to not meet return objectives
    d) none of the above

11. What does a rental property's return consist of? ( )
    a) cash flows
    b) capital growth
    c) both (a) and (b)
    d) neither (a) nor (b)

12. If a one-year bond reported a return of 8% and inflation over that same year was 2%, then the bond's nominal return was ____________, and its approximate real return was ____________. ( )
    a) 10%; 6%
    b) 10%; 8%
    c) 8%; 10%
    d) 8%; 6%

Bonus Questions

13. Which of the following would be the best approximation of the risk-free rate? ( )
    a) rate of inflation as measured by the CPI
    b) yield on T-bills
    c) yield on a 30-year government bond
    d) return on the S&P/TSX Composite Index

14. The risk that one's purchasing power will *decrease* is known as: ( )
    a) inflation risk
    b) business risk
    c) interest rate risk
    d) foreign exchange risk

( ) 15. Default risk contributes to what type of risk?

a) systematic risk
b) non-systematic risk
c) both (a) and (b)
d) neither (a) nor (b)

( ) 16. An investor looking for safety and income would be best served by which main asset class?

a) cash or near-cash equivalents
b) fixed-income securities
c) real estate
d) equity securities

( ) 17. Which of the following is the best example of market timing?

a) investing a set amount at regular time intervals over the course of a year
b) making stock purchases only in the morning, and making stock sales only in the afternoon
c) adjusting the asset allocation in response to changes in the economy
d) rebalancing a portfolio at the end of the month

( ) 18. If an investor wishes to further diversify his portfolio as much as possible by purchasing another security, he will want a security that has:

a) perfect positive correlation with his portfolio
b) no correlation with his portfolio
c) perfect negative correlation with his portfolio
d) correlation is irrelevant to diversification

( ) 19. What does the term "risk premium" refer to?

a) a security's alpha
b) a security's expected return
c) the difference between a security's return and the risk-free rate
d) none of the above

( ) 20. Which of the following is NOT a step in the portfolio management process?

a) Implement asset allocation.
b) Determine investment objectives and constraints.
c) Design an investment policy statement.
d) None of the above.

21. Consider two stocks: A and B. Stock A has an expected return of 14% and a standard deviation of 12%, while Stock B has an expected return of 14% and a standard deviation of 8%. Which stock is preferred by a rational investor? ( )

a) Stock A

b) Stock B

c) a rational investor would be indifferent

d) there is insufficient information

22. Company XYZ Inc. is considering investing in a new project. During their evaluation, they determine that this new project has the potential to earn 15% a year for 5 years. What type of return is this? ( )

a) ex-ante return

b) ex-post return

c) holding period return

d) none of the above

23. An investor looking for safety and income would be best served by which main asset class? ( )

a) cash or near-cash equivalents

b) fixed-income securities

c) real estate

d) equity securities

24. With respect to a client's risk tolerance, which of the following is the most important factor? ( )

a) risk of the individual security

b) risk of the portfolio

c) (a) and (b) are equally important

d) (a) and (b) are not important

chapter 16

THE PORTFOLIO MANAGEMENT PROCESS

CSC EXAM SUGGESTED GUIDELINES:
12 questions for Chapter 16

DEVELOPING AN ASSET MIX AND SELECTING INVESTMENT STYLES

- It is important to determine which asset categories (cash, fixed income, and equity securities) will be targeted for investment. Additional asset classes such as international investments and derivatives may warrant inclusion for more sophisticated investors. The portfolio composition should be determined based on the client's individual characteristics and risk tolerance.

The Asset Mix

- **Cash** includes currency, money market securities, CSBs, GICs, and other debt instruments such as bonds with maturities of one year or less. It usually makes up at least 5% of a diversified portfolio; however, this amount may increase for more risk-averse investors. In addition, the levels will vary as a result of changing market conditions or portfolio rebalancings.
- **Fixed-income** assets include medium- to long-term bonds, strip bonds, mortgages, and other debt securities, as well as non-convertible preferred shares. Diversification within this asset class may occur across credit quality, duration or maturity of instruments, and types of fixed-income securities. The amount of the total portfolio allocated to fixed income can vary from 15% to 95%, based on several factors, including
  - desire for current income,
  - basic minimum income required,

- desire for preservation of capital, and
- other considerations such as tax and time horizon.

- **Equity assets** include common shares, but also derivatives such as warrants, rights, options, LEAPs, i60s, convertibles, etc. The amount of the total portfolio allocated to equities can account for anywhere from 15% to 95%. Some portfolio managers consider hedge funds as a separate asset class. They are discussed in Chapter 21.

Setting the Asset Mix

! The **equity cycle** refers to the cyclical movements in stock market prices. The phases include **expansionary**, **peak**, **contraction**, and **trough**. It is important to note that there may be temporary setbacks or corrections within the overall phases. Equity cycles are very similar to the economic (or business) cycles discussed in Chapter 4; however, they tend to lead the latter (which is why stock prices are considered to be leading economic indicators).

- The rationale behind **asset class timing** (or **asset allocation**) is that improved returns can result when investors recognize when to shift from stocks to T-bills and/or bonds. This is logical since more than 80% of portfolio returns may be attributed to asset mix.

! General strategies in relation to the equity cycle include the following:

1. Lengthen terms of bond holdings and avoid stocks during *contraction phase.*
2. Sell long-term bonds, which rally ahead of stocks in response to falling interest rates, during the *trough phase.*
3. Maintain or increase stock position during *expansionary phase,* since stocks tend to do well during sustained economic growth periods.
4. Stop buying stock and invest in short-term instruments as *peak phase* approaches, since interest rates are likely to increase.

The difficulty of implementing these strategies is that variations occur within the cycles and it is difficult to anticipate the arrival and duration of these phases.

The Dividend Discount Model (DDM), which was discussed in Chapter 13, is given below:

$$P_0 = \frac{Div_1}{r - g}$$

where:

P_0 = the intrinsic value of the share price today

Div_1 = the expected dividend at the end of year one

r = the required rate of return by the common shareholders

g = the constant annual growth rate in dividends to infinity

The DDM can be used to interpret changes in equity prices in relation to the equity cycle. In particular, !

1. *r* is rising and *g* is falling during the *contraction phase* (one to two years), which causes prices to fall;
2. *r* is falling faster than *g* is falling during the stock market *trough*, which causes an interest-rate-driven rally in stock prices (5–13 months);
3. *r* briefly rises faster than *g* rises during the *expansionary phase*, which causes a brief decline in stock prices (six to nine months); or
4. *g* rises faster than *r* from the *expansionary to peak phase*, which causes stock prices to rise (one to three years).

- **Industry rotation** can also lead to improved results, if one can successfully predict economic cycles and their impact on the security prices of various industries. This approach can be implemented using several strategies such as shifting into and out of cyclical and defensive industries, or moving into and out of interest-rate-sensitive industries in response to interest rate forecasts.
- The appropriate asset mix for an investor should reflect their objectives, constraints, investment knowledge, and risk tolerance. The following represent some asset mixes that might be considered appropriate for three different investors; although in practice specific circumstances must be known in order to develop appropriate mixes:
    - A young, knowledgeable investor with a long time horizon and high risk tolerance: 5% cash, 20% fixed income, and 75% equities.
    - A retired investor with no other source of income, a medium time horizon, and low risk tolerance: 10% cash, 60% fixed income, and 30% equities.
    - A middle-aged white-collar worker with two children who has reasonable investment knowledge and is concerned with providing for her children's education and her own retirement: 10% cash, 30% fixed income, and 60% equities.
- The asset allocation decision can account for 80% to 90% of a portfolio's total return and is therefore much more critical to an investor than security selection and market timing decisions. For example, the total return of one fund may exceed that of another due to the asset mix, even though it underperformed the other in each asset class. Historical evidence regarding the performance of different asset classes highlights this fact.

Manager style will determine how well the investor's objectives and constraints "fit" with the manager's style. !

Three commonly referred-to styles employed by equity managers are listed below. The first two are "bottom-up" strategies, while the third is a "top-down" strategy: !

1. **Growth Managers**: Invest in growth stock portfolios that tend to be very volatile. The securities are subject to risk from market cycles, and individual securities are sensitive to earnings meeting or exceeding analysts' expectations.

! Their portfolios tend to include securities with low dividend yields, high price-earnings (P/E) ratios, high price/cash flow ratios, and high price/book ratios. Investors should be less risk averse and possess relatively long-term investment horizons.

2. **Value Managers**: Look for "bargains" based on intensive "bottom-up" stock research. The portfolios tend to be less volatile than growth portfolios, with lower standard deviations and betas, which reflects the fact that prices are already low. Value stocks tend to possess low P/E ratios, low price/cash flow ratios, low price/book ratios, and high dividend yields. Investors should be reasonably risk tolerant, with long-term investment horizons.
3. **Sector Rotators**: Focus on particular sectors (e.g., industries) in accordance with a top-down analysis. This approach may result in higher volatility and greater risk (due to lower diversification).

! Fixed-income managers may use several styles, some of which are described below:

1. **Interest Rate Anticipators**: These managers lengthen the term of their bond holdings when they expect interest rates to fall, and shorten the term when they expect rates to increase—this is sometimes referred to as a "duration switching" strategy. They do so in order to attempt to maximize capital gains on the portfolio. This strategy is active and entails more risk than a typical buy-and-hold bond strategy, since future interest rates are difficult to predict accurately.
2. **Term to Maturity**: This approach limits the manager to invest in bonds with specified terms to maturity (e.g., less than 10 years to maturity). This limits the risk of the fund. Short-term managers will hold T-bills and bonds with maturities less than three years, mid-term managers will hold 3- to 10-year bonds, while long-term managers will hold those with more than 10 years to maturity.
3. **Credit Quality**: These managers focus on the credit quality of bonds, relative to their yields. In general, corporate bonds provide higher yields than government bonds, and lower rated corporate bonds provide higher yields than higher rated ones. Bonds rated BBB or above are considered investment-grade bonds, while those rated below BBB are referred to as high-yield securities or junk bonds.
4. **Spread Traders**: Bond managers may engage in spread trading (i.e., trading based on beliefs that yield spreads between different categories of bonds will narrow or widen in the future).

IMPLEMENTING THE ASSET MIX

The desired long-term asset mix of a portfolio is referred to as its **strategic asset allocation**. Maintaining this desired mix involves continual monitoring and rebalancing of the portfolio because the asset mix changes continuously as a result of dividend and interest payments, and as market prices change. For example, consider a portfolio that has a desired (or base) asset mix of 50% bonds and 50% equities. At the beginning of the period, the portfolio had $10,000 invested in bonds and $10,000 invested in stocks. After six months, as a result of interest and dividend payments, as well as changes in bond and stock prices, the value of the bonds is $10,000 and the value of the stocks is $8,000. In order to maintain the desired mix, the portfolio manager must sell $1,000 worth of bonds and purchase $1,000 in stocks.

Several asset allocation techniques may be employed:

1. **Tactical Asset Allocation**: A moderately active approach that allows managers short-term deviations from longer-term asset mixes to take advantage of market timing skills.
2. **Dynamic Asset Allocation**: An active approach that adjusts the asset mix as market conditions change by selling equities when markets fall and buying when they rise.
3. **Integrated Asset Allocation**: This strategy may incorporate any or all of the above approaches.

- Some portfolios are managed in a passive manner based on the belief that markets are relatively efficient. These portfolios strive to match the performance of a market benchmark and attempt to reduce portfolio management costs.

Passive portfolio management may involve the use of

- buy-and-hold strategies;
- indexing; or
- exchange-traded funds, such as i60s.

MONITORING THE ECONOMY, THE MARKETS, THE PORTFOLIO, AND THE CLIENT

- Managing a portfolio is an ongoing process that requires systematic monitoring of
  1. changes in the investor's circumstances and
  2. market conditions.

The objective is to incorporate anticipated changes into portfolio adjustments in a systematic manner.

- Portfolio managers must continually monitor information that has the potential to affect portfolio performance. The planner must monitor client circumstances, including changes in their objectives, preferences, and financial position. In addition, market and economic conditions must be followed. This involves analyzing a number of factors and categorizing their overall impact on the portfolio (or asset class) as positive, neutral, or negative. These factors are used as inputs, when obtaining estimates of expected returns for the various asset classes.

- For equities, factors may include many of the fundamental, technical, economic, and value indicators that were discussed in previous chapters.
- Fixed-income factors generally try to predict future interest rate levels and focus on factors such as monetary policy, fiscal policy, economic indicators, inflation, and foreign exchange factors.
- Returns on cash are generally easy to determine due to their short-term nature and merely involve taking the interest rate forecasts used for analyzing fixed-income securities.
- All of the return expectations can be aggregated to estimate the expected total return on the portfolio.

EVALUATING PORTFOLIO PERFORMANCE

Benchmarks should be specified in the investment policy statement as measures against which to compare portfolio performance. For example, the S&P/TSX Index might be an appropriate benchmark for a Canadian equity portfolio, while a customized benchmark made up of 50% of the S&P/TSX Index and 50% of the DEX Universe Bond Index might be appropriate for a balanced fund.

Portfolio performance is usually evaluated by comparing its total rate of return to the average return of *comparable portfolios* during the same time period. Such comparisons may enable a portfolio's performance to be ranked relative to its peers.

!

- Total return may be determined by dividing the portfolio's total earnings (income plus capital gains or losses) by the initial amount invested in the portfolio. A formula for determining the Pre-Tax Total Return that ignores contributions and withdrawals is

  Total (Pre-Tax) Return = Increase in Market Value/Initial Amount Invested

!

Example 1:

Suppose a growth portfolio had a beginning of period market value of $500,000 and an end-of-period market value of $530,000.

Solution:

Its total return is

Return = (530,000 – 500,000) ÷ (500,000)

= 30,000/500,000 = 6.00%

- Differences in portfolio characteristics make accurate performance comparisons difficult. For example, asset mixes and risk characteristics may differ significantly from one fund to another, even within the same fund category.

- After-tax rates of return "net" out the income taxes payable by the portfolio in determining the return, while the real rate of return is approximated by subtracting the inflation rate for the period from the total return.

The **Sharpe Ratio** is a commonly used risk-adjusted performance measure. It measures performance, after adjusting for risk (as measured by standard deviation). In essence, it measures excess return (above the risk-free rate) per unit of risk assumed. Higher ratios indicate better performance, and it is common to compare the Sharpe Ratio to that of the benchmark. It is calculated as follows:

$Sp = (Rp - Rf)/\sigma p$

Example 2:

Determine the Sharpe Ratio for a portfolio that earned a return of 10% during a period when the risk-free rate of return was 4%, if the portfolio's standard deviation was 20%.

Did the portfolio outperform its benchmark, which had a Sharpe Ratio of 0.25 over the same period?

Solution:

$Sp = (10 - 4)/20 = 0.30$

Since 0.30 > 0.25, the portfolio outperformed its benchmark.

Chapter 16 Review Questions

1. An investment plan is devised with a primary investment objective for growth, with a secondary objective of tax minimization. The asset mix for this plan should include: ( )
   a) mostly value stocks
   b) mostly growth stocks
   c) mostly speculative stocks
   d) cannot say without more information

2. A fixed-income manager who actively rebalances her portfolio weights in government versus corporate bonds in response to beliefs regarding changes in the relative yields on these securities would be referred to as a: ( )
   a) maturity switcher
   b) interest rate anticipator
   c) spread trader
   d) credit quality manager

( ) 3. A "value" manager would invest in stocks with relatively ____________ P/E ratios and ____________ dividend yields.

a) high; high
b) high; low
c) low; low
d) low; high

( ) 4. A ____________ asset allocation strategy results in buying stocks when they fall in price and selling them when they rise in price.

a) constant-weighting
b) strategic
c) tactical
d) dynamic

( ) 5. Which of the following would be the best asset mix for an aggressive young investor with good investment knowledge and a high tolerance for risk?

a) 20% cash; 30% fixed income; 50% equities
b) 10% cash; 35% fixed income; 55% equities
c) 10% cash; 20% fixed income; 70% equities
d) 5% cash; 40% fixed income; 55% equities

( ) 6. Which of the following is NOT a general strategy in relation to the equity cycle?

a) Maintain or increase stock position during expansionary phase.
b) Lengthen terms of bond holdings and avoid stocks during contraction phase.
c) Buy long-term bonds that rally ahead of stocks in response to falling interest rates during the trough phase.
d) All of the above are general strategies.

( ) 7. The following investments would be considered as part of the fixed-income component in an investor's portfolio EXCEPT:

a) two-year bonds
b) preferred shares
c) mortgages
d) Canada Savings Bonds

( ) 8. Equity prices often rise due to the growth rate in earnings (and dividends) rising faster than interest rates during the latter part of the ____________ phase of the equity cycle.

a) expansionary
b) peak

c) contraction

d) trough

9. Suppose a portfolio has a return of 10.5% and a standard deviation of 20%, while the T-bill rate is 3%. What is the Sharpe Ratio? ( )

a) 0.287%

b) 0.375%

c) 0.412%

d) 0.650%

10. What does a negative Sharpe Ratio mean about a portfolio? ( )

a) It underperformed the benchmark.

b) It underperformed other portfolios.

c) It underperformed the risk-free asset.

d) None of the above.

11. Consider the following group of portfolios: Sharpe Ratio of portfolio A is 4.2%; B is 3.89%; C is 5.5%; D is –3.6%; and E is 0%. The benchmark Sharpe Ratio is 3.5%. Which of the following portfolios outperformed the market? ( )

a) A and B

b) A, B, and C

c) D and E

d) A, B, C, and E

12. Which of the following is true with respect to investing styles? ( )

a) conservative—low risk, high capitalization, predictable earnings, high yield, low P/E ratios

b) growth—high risk, low capitalization, limited earnings record, no dividends

c) venture—high risk, average capitalization, low dividend payout, high P/E ratios

d) speculative—maximum risk, longer term, average price volatility, little earnings

Bonus Questions

13. Which of the following is true during a stock market trough? ( )

a) g is falling, and r is falling at a lower rate

b) g is beginning to fall, and r is rising

c) g is falling, and r is falling at a faster rate

d) r is stable, but rising less quickly than g

( ) 14. What factors do portfolio managers consider when they develop forecasts for fixed-income securities markets?

a) fiscal policy
b) inflation
c) exchange rates
d) all of the above

( ) 15. When forecasting, which group's analysis tends to be the least complex in method?

a) equity group analysis
b) fixed-income group analysis
c) cash and cash equivalents analysis
d) they all use the same forecasting method

( ) 16. If a portfolio earned a return of 15% with a standard deviation of 20%, and the average three-month T-bill rate was 5%, what is the portfolio's risk-adjusted rate of return?

a) 32.5%
b) 37.5%
c) 40%
d) 50%

( ) 17. Who is *most* likely to have a higher weighting in equities in a balanced portfolio?

a) young, single professional
b) middle-aged, married blue-collar worker
c) retired senior
d) all the above would have the same weighting

( ) 18. Which of the following mutual funds would be the best example of passive management?

a) emerging markets fund
b) dividend fund
c) value fund
d) global index fund

( ) 19. The monitoring step in the portfolio management process involves monitoring:

a) changes in the investor (goals, financial position, risk tolerance, etc.)
b) expectations regarding markets and/or individual securities
c) both (a) and (b)
d) neither (a) nor (b)

20. Which of the following is NOT monitored during the portfolio monitoring phase of the portfolio management process? ( )

    a) the investor's liquidity needs
    b) the actual asset class weights
    c) market forecasts
    d) none of the above

21. Which of the following securities is NOT considered fixed income from a portfolio management standpoint? ( )

    a) a 30-year bond
    b) a 6-month bond
    c) a mortgage
    d) a preferred share

22. The income from which of the following securities is generally taxed most favourably? ( )

    a) GICs
    b) bonds
    c) preferred shares
    d) all of the above are taxed at the same rate

23. The strategy of holding fixed-income securities of varying maturities is best known as: ( )

    a) hedging
    b) integrated asset allocation
    c) tactical asset allocation
    d) laddering

24. Establishing a target long-term asset mix that will be rebalanced when the actual weights differ from the target weights is referred to as: ( )

    a) strategic asset allocation
    b) tactical asset allocation
    c) integrated asset allocation
    d) none of the above

EVOLUTION OF MANAGED AND STRUCTURED PRODUCTS

chapter 17

CSC EXAM SUGGESTED GUIDELINES:
14 questions combined for Chapters 17, 22–24

MANAGED VERSUS STRUCTURED PRODUCTS

Structured products and some forms of managed products avoid the restrictions imposed on mutual funds (such as those restricting the use of leverage or the use of derivatives for speculative purposes).

! **Managed products** are pools of capital that are invested in securities according to a specific investment mandate. They may be in one of two structures:

1. pooled accounts, or
2. separately managed accounts.

Examples include mutual funds, hedge funds, segregated funds, ETFs, private equity funds, closed-end funds and labour-sponsored venture capital corporations (LSVCCs).

Managed products face more demands and restrictions than structured products, such as specifying types of securities that can be traded; individual security concentration limits; defining investable sectors; and limits on the use of leverage.

! **Structured products** are passive investment vehicles designed to provide certain risk/return characteristics using various underlying assets, such as mortgage loans, other loans, equity indexes, etc. They have more risk than their underlying assets (i.e., by combining them), and generally more risk than traditional investment assets.

!

	Advantages	Disadvantages
Managed products	professional management	lack of transparency
	economies of scale	liquidity constraints
	diversification	some very high fees
	liquidity & flexibility	volatility of returns
	some tax benefits	
	low-cost investment options	
Structured products	professional management	complexity
	economies of scale	high cost
	diversification	illiquid secondary market
	higher yield	
	higher probability of return of principal	

There are numerous types of managed products and structured products—these are discussed in detail in Chapters 18–24.

The following risks are involved in investing in managed and structured products—they can vary greatly from one product to the next.

1. Credit risk
2. Inflation risk
3. Currency risk
4. Prepayment risk
5. Manager risk

The growth of both managed and structured products has been phenomenal. For example, ETF trading on the TSX grew from 500 million shares in 2000 to 16 billion in 2009, while the number of principal protected notes (PPNs) grew from 41 in 2002 to 660 by 2007.

! The contributing factors to this growth include

1. the search for yield,
2. growth in passive investing,
3. demographics,
4. bull market in bonds,
5. product innovations, and
6. cheaper commissions and faster computers.

This growth has also led to changing compensation models—away from commission-based models (e.g., from 36% in 2005 to 46% in 2009), and toward fee-based programs (e.g., from 64% to 56%).

Chapter 17 Review Questions

1. Which of the following are structured products? ( )
   - I. segregated funds
   - II. mortgage-backed securities
   - III. hedge funds
   - IV. principal protected notes (PPNs)
   - a) I and II
   - b) III and IV
   - c) I and III
   - d) II and IV

2. Managed and structured products *both* offer the following advantages, EXCEPT: ( )
   - a) diversification
   - b) economies of scale
   - c) higher yield
   - d) professional management

Bonus Questions

3. Which of the following factors has contributed to the growth of structured products? ( )
   - a) bull stock market
   - b) higher commission fees
   - c) search for yield
   - d) enhanced credit risk

4. What is a significant disadvantage of structured products? ( )
   - a) return volatility
   - b) complexity
   - c) liquidity
   - d) flexibility

chapter 18

MUTUAL FUNDS: STRUCTURE AND REGULATION

CSC EXAM SUGGESTED GUIDELINES:
15 questions combined for Chapters 18 and 19

INTRODUCTION

- There are a wide variety of mutual fund products available to investors. Many funds are part of fund groups, which are responsible for their management and distribution to the public. Distribution may be accomplished using internal sales representatives, through stockbrokers, through independent mutual fund salespeople, or through a combination of these approaches. Proprietary funds are alternative fund groups, whose funds are managed and sold using internal resources only, such as those offered by banks, trust companies, life insurance companies, and credit unions.
- The total asset value of Canadian mutual funds has grown dramatically in recent years, increasing from $146.9 billion in 1995 to $697.3 billion in 2007.
- The fund's investment objectives are stated in its prospectus, which also specifies what represents an acceptable level of risk for the fund.

The **advantages** of mutual funds include

1. low-cost professional management,
2. diversification,
3. variety of types of funds and transferability,
4. variety of purchase and redemption plans,
5. various special options,
6. liquidity,
7. ease of estate planning, and
8. loan collateral and eligibility for margin.

! The **disadvantages** of mutual funds include

1. costs such as sales fees and management fees detract from the investor's returns;
2. unsuitable for short-term investment or emergency reserve (except for money market funds, which are so tailored);
3. professional management is not infallible; and
4. tax complications may arise if the investor's tax preferences are not consistent with the objectives of the fund.

THE STRUCTURE OF MUTUAL FUNDS

! **Investment funds** are companies (or trusts) that sell their shares (or units) to the public and invest the proceeds in a diverse securities portfolio. The funds earn income in the form of interest, dividends, and/or capital gains, and they may be organized as a trust or as a corporation.

! **Open-end funds** (or **mutual funds**) continually issue and redeem their units on demand at a value that is very close to the net asset or "break-up" value per unit of the fund's portfolio. This right of redemption is the most distinguishing feature of open-end funds.

- In Canada, the most common form of mutual fund is in the form of an **open-end trust**, which issues units (usually only one class of units) in the trust to investors. Some of these provide unit holders with voting privileges, but not all of them.
- The trust itself is not taxable: the income earned by the fund, net any fees and expenses, is attributed to the unit holders. The fund is established in the form of a **trust deed**, which describes
    - the fund's investment objectives,
    - the fund's investment policy,
    - any investment restrictions,
    - details regarding the fund manager, distributors, and custodians, and
    - which class of units will be sold to the public.
- Some funds are set up as federal or provincial corporations, and investors in these funds receive shares in the fund rather than units. As corporations, the funds are taxable, although they are generally eligible for special rates. In addition, they can virtually eliminate any taxes by declaring dividends that are equivalent to their net income over a given year, thus passing the tax consequences on to shareholders in the form of the dividends they receive.

Organizational Structure

- Mutual fund organizations consist of four parts:

  1. **Directors or Trustees**: Directors (for corporations) or trustees (for trusts) are ultimately responsible for fund activities, although they often hire independent managers, distributors, and/or custodians to operate the fund on their behalf.
  2. **Fund Managers**: They must observe guidelines in the fund's charter, as well as constraints imposed by securities commissions such as owning less than 10% of one firm's total securities or voting stock, no purchases of other non-related mutual funds, no borrowing for leverage purposes, limitations regarding percentage of illiquid securities such as unlisted stocks, and prohibitions regarding commodity or commodity futures purchases.
  3. **Fund Distributors**: Parties that sell shares or units in the fund.
  4. **Custodians**: Collect and distribute cash for the fund as required (usually they are trust companies).

The Pricing of Mutual Fund Securities

The **offering price** refers to the price an investor pays for a share or unit in a mutual fund. !

The **redemption price** refers to the price investors receive when they sell shares or units back to the fund. !

Mutual funds shares or units can be purchased or redeemed at a price that equals or is very close to the fund's **Net Asset Value Per Share (NAVPS)**, which may be calculated as follows: !

NAVPS = (total assets [including portfolio at market value] – total liabilities) ÷ (total shares or units outstanding)

Example 1: !

Determine the NAVPS for a mutual fund that holds a portfolio of securities worth $200 million, has liabilities of $2 million, and has 20 million units outstanding.

Solution:

NAVPS = (200m – 2m)/20m = $9.90

All funds are required to compute the NAVPS at least once a month (once a week for equity funds and once a year for real estate funds). New rules outlined in National Instrument 81-102 require that "new" funds do so weekly. Most do so on a daily basis (quarterly for real estate funds).

Mutual Fund Charges

Mutual funds are often classified with respect to the type of sales commission, or "load" they charge. **Load funds** charge a commission on the purchase and/or sale of fund units or shares. Those that charge sales commissions when the units are purchased are called **front-end load** funds, while those that charge a redemption fee (or deferred sales charge) when the units are sold are called **back-end load** funds. The amount of redemption fee often declines through time and is often completely eliminated after a holding period of six years. Many load funds give the investor the option of front- or back-end loads.

No-load funds do not charge direct selling charges. However, they typically levy modest administration fees and charge other management fees that may add up. Investors should carefully read the prospectus to determine the net cost of these services. Some funds charge a distribution charge to pay commissioned salespeople, while trailer fees (or service fees) are those paid by a manager to the selling organization.

The **offering** or **purchase price** for a front-end load fund relates the sales charge to the net asset value (NAV). It is calculated in the following manner:

Offering or Purchase Price = (NAV) = (100% less sales charge)

Example 2:

Determine the offering price for a fund that has a NAV of $10 and a 5% up-front sales charge.

Solution:

Offering price = $10/(1.0 –.05) = $10.52

- Notice in Example 2 that $0.52 is 5.2% of the NAV (or net amount invested).

The **redemption** or **selling price** for back-end load funds relates the sales charge to the NAV. It is calculated in the following manner:

Redemption or Selling Price = (NAV) ÷ (100% less sales charge)

Example 3:

Determine the selling price for a fund that has a NAV of $10 and a 5% back-end redemption charge.

Solution:

Selling price = $10 × (1.0 –.05) = $9.50

- Notice in Example 3 that $0.50 is 5.3% (0.50/9.50) of the net amount received.
- **Trailer** (or **service**) **fees** are paid by the fund manager to the distributor of the fund and are usually paid out of the management fee. The rationale for the

payment of trailer fees is that salespeople provide an ongoing service for investors. However, their use is criticized because they provide salespeople with the incentive to keep customers in funds, even when it may not be in their best interests. In addition, the higher management fees detract from the wealth of the investor.

- Some funds charge a set-up fee in addition to any load fees. In addition, some funds charge **early redemption fees**, if the funds are redeemed within a certain period of time. For example, some no-load funds charge a 2% early redemption fee if fund units are sold within 90 days of purchase.
- Some fund companies permit investors an unlimited number of "switches" between funds managed by the same company, at no cost. Other funds charge for every switch or permit a specified number of free switches, with any additional switches being subject to a "**switching fee**." These fees may often be negotiated with the investment advisor, and sometimes they can be waived.
- Management fees represent the amount of compensation paid to mutual fund managers. These vary, depending on the nature of the fund (from 1% for some money market and index funds to 3% for some equity funds). They are typically expressed as a percentage of net fund assets.

In addition to management fees, other fund expenses such as trading costs, audit, legal, informational, and safekeeping and custodial fees are also included in the calculation of a measure called the **Management Expense Ratio (MER)**. These expenses decrease the returns to fund holders. It is calculated in the following manner:

MER = (Aggregate Fees and Expenses Payable During the Year) / (Average Net Asset Value for the Year) × 100%

The expenses are charged directly to the fund and not to the investor and reduce the return to investors. For example, a fund that earned a gross return of 20% and had an MER of 2% would report a compound annual return of 18%. Published rates of return for funds are those resulting after deducting the MER.

- The management fees and management expense ratios must be included in the fund prospectus for the past five years.
- As a result of the increasing number of financial advisors providing fee-based accounts, rather than commission-based ones, several fund companies have begun offering **F-class funds**. These funds charge lower MERs than traditional funds, which reduces the impact of having investors being charged two fees.

LABOUR-SPONSORED VENTURE CAPITAL CORPORATIONS (LSVCCs)

LSVCCs (also called Labour-Sponsored Investment Funds, or LSIFs) are sponsored by labour organizations, and their specific mandate is to invest in small- to medium-sized businesses. They offer investors a tax credit and are usually provincially based, although some federally based LSVCCs do exist.

The **advantages** of LSVCCs are:

1. They provide investors with the potential for long-term capital appreciation, and enable investors to invest in specific industry sectors.
2. They provide investors with tax credits. Provincial tax credits vary, but may be as high as 15% of the investment for most LSVCCs, although some do not offer provincial credits. There is no maximum amount an investor may invest in an LSVCC; however, the federal tax credit applies up to a maximum investment of $5,000, and provincial tax credits are subject to maximum amounts. In addition, some provinces impose lifetime limits. The maximum allowable credit for federal LSVCCs is 15%. The unused portion of the federal credits is not refundable and may not be carried forward or backward to apply to other years.
3. Most LSVCCs are RRSP and RRIF eligible, which implies the potential for a double tax advantage. In addition, the foreign content of RRSPs that include LSVCCs may exceed the allowed maximum.

Example 4:

Determine the net investment for an investor in the 40% marginal tax bracket who purchases $5,000 worth of LSVCCs that qualify for a 15% federal credit and a 15% provincial credit, and contributes them to her RRSP.

Solution:

The investor will receive a federal tax credit of $750 ($5,000 ×.15), and a provincial tax credit of $750 ($5,000 ×.15). In addition, she can deduct $5,000 from her taxable income, which results in tax savings of $2,000 (40% of $5,000). Thus, her net investment is $5,000 – $750 – $750 – $2,000 = $1,500.

The **disadvantages** of LSVCCs include the following:

1. They are **highly speculative** investments, which make them suitable only for investors with a high risk tolerance. This is because they invest primarily in start-up companies, and it is estimated that 80% of these companies do not survive more than five years.
2. The management expense ratios tend to be higher than for mutual funds due to the additional effort that must be devoted to managing these investments.
3. Redeeming LSVCCs is more complicated than for mutual funds and the rules vary across the provinces. Federal tax credits are subject to recapture by tax authorities if they are redeemed before they have been held for certain holding periods (e.g., eight years). Provincial holding period requirements range from zero to other predefined periods. This recapture can be avoided under some circumstances.

LSVCCs are suitable only as long-term investments due to their speculative and illiquid nature, as well as to restrictions regarding the provision of tax credit benefits. They are not suitable for investors looking for short-term or income-generating investments. Investors must be aware of the highly speculative and illiquid nature of these investments, which make them suitable only for investors with a high risk tolerance. The track record of the fund manager may be a particularly important factor to consider.

REGULATION OF MUTUAL FUNDS

Most Canadian mutual funds are regulated by the securities acts of the provinces within which they operate. As discussed in Chapter 3, securities regulations are based on the principles of personal trust, disclosure, and regulation.

The **Code of Ethics** for registered salespeople in the securities industry applies to mutual fund salespeople. The code requires mutual fund salespeople to

1. use proper care and exercise professional judgment;
2. display integrity and trustworthiness, and be fair and honest in dealings with the public, clients, employers, and employees;
3. conduct business in a professional manner and encourage others to do so; act in a competent manner and improve their professional knowledge toward this end;
4. maintain client confidentiality; and
5. act in accordance with the requirements of the appropriate securities acts and self-regulatory organizations (SROs).

!

- While mutual funds are regulated by provincial securities commissions, they also deal with the Canadian SROs such as the stock exchanges and IIROC, which were discussed in Chapter 3. The provincial regulators have more power and have greater latitude in imposing penalties on mutual fund companies.
- As discussed in Chapter 3, the Mutual Fund Dealers Association (MFDA) is a newly created SRO that regulates the distribution of mutual funds, but not their management. The mutual fund industry in Quebec is regulated by the Autorité des marchés financiers and the Chambre de la sécuritié finacière, and there is a co-operative agreement in place with the MFDA to avoid regulatory duplication and ensure investor protection.
- Securities regulators have issued several national and provincial policy statements to govern the activities of mutual funds. The most comprehensive and influential policy statements are National Instrument 81-101 (NI 81-101), which deals with fund prospectus disclosure, and NI 81-102, a companion policy, which deals with distribution and advertising guidelines.

- Since most funds continually issue new shares, they are in a *continuous state of primary distribution* and must annually file a prospectus or simplified prospectus.
- Funds file simplified prospectuses if they comply with the appropriate regulations (i.e., NI 81-102). These regulations concern restrictions on investments, changes that require security holder and/or securities' authority approval, custodianship of a fund's portfolio securities, commingling of money, and calculations of net asset values. The simplified prospectus system also requires funds to file annual information forms (AIFs), annual audited or unaudited financial statements, as well as other information such as material change reports and information circulars.

! The **simplified prospectuses** must contain all material information and must be amended when material changes occur. Fund buyers must receive copies of this document *no later than two business days after an agreement of purchase* has been made. The simplified prospectus consists of two parts. The first part provides general information about the particular fund and other funds managed by the fund company, and about mutual funds in general. The second part contains specific information about the fund.

- The AIF contains most of the information included in the simplified prospectus, plus additional information regarding
  - significant holdings in other issuers;
  - the tax status of the issuer;
  - directors, officers, and trustees;
  - associated persons; and
  - details regarding any material contracts outstanding.
- The financial statements should be provided to investors and should be filed with the appropriate securities commission before the specified deadline. The financial statements for the fund should include the
  - balance sheet;
  - income statement;
  - statement of investment portfolio (i.e., details of the securities the fund is holding);
  - statement of changes in net assets (equivalent to a statement of changes in financial position); and
  - statement of portfolio transactions, which is generally not included in the financial statements, but the statements should inform investors that this statement is available to them upon request.

Registration Requirements

- Mutual fund managers, distributors, and their sales personnel must be registered with the securities commissions in which they do business. Educational requirements include that salespeople must complete the Canadian Funds Course, the CSC, or another qualified education program, such as the Investment Funds Institute of Canada (IFIC) mutual fund course.

- In order to become registered under provincial securities laws, salespeople must file an application electronically with the National Registration Database (NRD Form 33-109F4). Once registered, they must inform the provincial administrators of any changes in the information provided in their original application within five business days (10 days in Quebec), including
    - a change of address;
    - any disciplinary actions by a professional body;
    - a personal bankruptcy (Ontario and Quebec);
    - any criminal charges; and
    - any civil judgments.
- If a registered salesperson no longer works for a registered dealer, their registration is suspended automatically, and the dealer must notify the **provincial administrator**. The salesperson's registration can be reinstated only if they go to work for another registered dealer, who must then provide written notice to the administrator.

Mutual Fund Restrictions

Mutual funds are subject to many restrictions. Some are subject to all of the restrictions below, while others are subject to only some of them. These restrictions do not permit funds to

1. purchase more than 10% of the total securities or 10% of the voting stock of a company;
2. buy shares in their own company;
3. purchase more than 10% of the net assets of one company, or 20% of the net assets of companies in the same industry (except for specialty funds);
4. borrow for the purpose of creating leverage;
5. buy on margin or short sell;
6. purchase commodities or commodity futures;
7. hold beyond certain percentages of illiquid securities, such as those sold through private placements or unlisted stocks; and
8. buy units of other mutual funds (unless management fees are not duplicated).

The use of derivative securities such as options, futures, forwards, rights, warrants, and combination products by mutual funds is permissible for specific purposes only. In particular, derivatives should not be used for speculative purposes, but may be used for the following reasons, provided their permitted use is specified in the fund's simplified prospectus:

- to hedge against risk,
- to facilitate market entry and exit, and
- to create clone funds.

- For example, a manager may use options in an index fund such as put options on i60 units (discussed in Chapter 21) to provide price protection for their portfolio against changes in aggregate stock market values. Alternatively, a fund manager holding foreign securities may use currency futures to hedge themselves against changes in exchange rates.
- NI 81-102 regulates the use of derivatives by mutual funds, specifying restrictions on holdings (no more than 10% of the fund's assets, except for clone funds), acceptable hedge positions, terms to expiry, and regarding which advisors are permitted to trade in these securities.

! **Unacceptable sales practices** for fund salespeople include

1. quoting a future price;
2. offering to repurchase securities;
3. selling without a licence (i.e., not being registered in the appropriate province);
4. advertising the fact that they are registered;
5. promising a future price;
6. selling to an individual in another province (or country) where the salesperson is not registered; and
7. selling unqualified securities.

- Fund managers and distributors also face sales restrictions, including these:
  1. Managers may not provide distributors with "rewards."
  2. Commissions can be changed only through a change in the prospectus.
  3. Managers may not provide funds for general marketing expenses of the distributor.
  4. Managers may not subsidize courses designed to enhance selling skills.
  5. Non-monetary benefits cannot be provided beyond a nominal value for salespeople.
- NI 81-102 (discussed previously) provides specific guidelines regarding sales communications, and it is the salesperson's responsibility to know the relevant guidelines. The overriding concern is that such communications are not misleading in any way. The following items can be included in sales communications:
  - fund characteristics;
  - fund comparisons with similar funds or appropriate indexes;
  - performance details, which are subject to specific guidelines;
  - the fact that a fund is no-load; and
  - any information or comparisons must disclose all relevant facts.

- Financial institutions (FIs) that serve as fund distributors must also comply with several guidelines, including
    1. control of registrant: sales are only permitted through branches or departments of registered dealers;
    2. registration of employees;
    3. dual employment: dual employment is permitted for employees if it is permitted by the laws governing the FI;
    4. conflicts of interest: dealers must have appropriate guidelines in place to prevent and/or deal with such situations;
    5. in-house funds: if an FI wants to sell the funds of a third party, they must obtain the appropriate approvals;
    6. proficiency requirements should be satisfied by officers, directors, and salespeople; and
    7. premises and disclosure: the business must conduct business in a way that makes it clear to clients that the dealer and the FI are distinct, and this point should be disclosed to clients.

Chapter 18 Review Questions

1. The offering price of a fund that has a net asset value (NAV) of $40 per unit and has a 6% sales fee is: ( )
    a) $37.60
    b) $40.60
    c) $42.40
    d) $42.55
2. Advantages of mutual funds include the following EXCEPT: ( )
    a) the variety of types of funds available
    b) the variety of purchase plans available
    c) management fees are tax deductible
    d) liquidity
3. The following are components of a mutual fund organization EXCEPT: ( )
    a) the simplified prospectus
    b) fund managers
    c) distributors
    d) custodians

( ) 4. Mutual funds that charge the investor at redemption are known as ____________.

a) open-ended funds
b) no-load funds
c) deferred sales charge loads
d) funds with trailer fees

( ) 5. Mutual fund companies charge ____________ for running the specific funds.

a) management fees
b) switching fees
c) open-end fees
d) trailer fees

( ) 6. The use of derivative products by mutual fund managers is:

a) strictly prohibited
b) only permitted for market entry and exit
c) permissible for creating clone funds
d) none of the above

( ) 7. Mutual funds face all of the following restrictions EXCEPT:

a) They cannot purchase commodity futures.
b) They are limited in their holdings of illiquid securities.
c) They cannot purchase more than 5% of a company's voting stock.
d) They cannot hold more than 10% of the portfolio's net assets in one security.

( ) 8. In order to sell mutual funds, a salesperson must:

a) have completed the CSC, the CFC, or another qualified program, plus the CPH
b) apply for registration through the NRD
c) both (a) and (b)
d) neither (a) nor (b)

( ) 9. Which of the following statements regarding LSVCCs is FALSE?

a) They may exceed 10% ownership in companies.
b) They are primarily long-term investments.
c) They are not RRSP eligible.
d) They provide significant tax advantages for investors.

Bonus Questions

10. What do mutual funds invest in? ( )
    a) stocks
    b) bonds
    c) money market instruments
    d) all of the above

11. What does a mutual fund's trust deed contain? ( )
    a) the fund's investment policy
    b) the fund's principal investment objectives
    c) restrictions regarding the investments the fund may hold
    d) all of the above

12. Investors in a mutual fund trust receive______________, and investors in a mutual fund corporation receive ______________. ( )
    a) units; units
    b) units; shares
    c) shares; units
    d) shares; shares

13. Which type of gift would a licensed mutual fund salesperson be allowed to accept from a fund manager? ( )
    a) golf balls
    b) vacation package
    c) subsidized airfare to an educational seminar on selling practices
    d) none of the above

14. Who is ultimately responsible for the activities of the mutual fund? ( )
    a) fund manager
    b) custodian
    c) directors and trustees
    d) none of the above

15. Which of the following roles may be served by the mutual fund's custodian? ( )
    a) registrar
    b) transfer agent
    c) both (a) and (b)
    d) neither (a) nor (b)

( ) 16. If a mutual fund had equity securities totalling $15 million, cash of $1 million, liabilities of $5 million, and 2 million units outstanding, what would the fund's NAVPS be?

a) $11 per unit
b) $7.50 per unit
c) $5.50 per unit
d) $5 per unit

( ) 17. If a mutual fund does not charge any sales fees, then the redemption price is equal to the:

a) offering price
b) NAVPS
c) both (a) and (b)
d) neither (a) nor (b)

( ) 18. What is the effective after-tax cost of a $4,000 investment in a LSVCC by an investor in a 30% marginal tax bracket if she contributes it to her RRSP? Assume the LSVCC qualifies for the maximum federal tax credit, and an equal provincial tax credit.

a) $1,200
b) $1,600
c) $2,800
d) none of the above

chapter 19

MUTUAL FUNDS: TYPES AND FEATURES

CSC EXAM SUGGESTED GUIDELINES:
15 questions combined for Chapters 18 and 19

TYPES OF MUTUAL FUNDS

- The objectives of investment funds vary significantly, which is reflected in their portfolio composition. The objectives are covered in the fund's offering prospectus and generally cover the degree of safety or risk that is acceptable, whether income or capital gain is the prime objective, and the main types of securities in the fund's investment portfolio. The Investment Funds Standards Committee (IFSC) breaks them into four broad groups (Cash and Equivalent; Fixed Income; Balanced; and Equity) and 34 categories within these groups.
- **1. Cash and Equivalent** or **Money Market Funds**: Their objectives focus on income and liquidity. They invest in short-term money market instruments such as T-bills, commercial paper, and short-term government bonds. These funds will be attractive to investors seeking low risk and high liquidity. Interest distributions are fully taxable. Include Canadian money market and U.S. money market funds.
- **2. Fixed-Income Funds**: These focus on providing a steady stream of income, rather than on capital appreciation. Examples include Canadian and foreign bond funds, income trust funds, high-yield bond funds, and Canadian short-term and mortgage funds. Mortgage and bond funds are discussed below.
- **2a. Mortgage Funds**: Riskier than money market funds since terms of investments may be five years or greater, so there is more interest rate risk (although it's less than most bond funds, which have longer maturities). Distributions are usually in the form of interest.
- **2b. Bond Funds**: Primary investing objectives are income and safety; however, they are still subject to capital gains and losses due to inherent interest rate risk.
- **2c. Canadian Income Trust Funds**: Invest primarily in income trusts.

- **3. Balanced Funds**: Strive to provide a mixture of safety, income, and capital appreciation. Usually, the fund must adhere to minimum and maximum percentages that can be invested in each asset class. Include Canadian balanced, Canadian income balanced, global balanced and asset allocation, and Canadian tactical asset allocation.
- **Asset Allocation Funds**: Similar objectives to balanced funds, but they are typically not restricted to hold specified minimum percentages in any class of investment.
- **4. Equity** or **Common Stock Funds**: Primary objective is capital gains. The bulk of assets are in common shares, although they maintain limited amounts of other assets for liquidity, income, and diversification purposes. Equity funds may vary greatly in degree of risk and growth objectives. Distributions are in the form of capital gains and dividends.

Equity funds are the most popular and diverse type of fund and include several classifications, including the following: Canadian and U.S. equity; Canadian dividends; Canadian and U.S. small- and mid-cap equity; international equity; European equity; emerging markets equity; Asia/Pacific Rim equity; and Japanese equity.

- **Small-Cap and Mid-Cap Equity Funds**: These funds tend to invest in small capitalization (small-cap) stocks. These companies are smaller and are believed to have greater prospects for growth. Many are young, and most do not pay dividends. As a result, these funds tend to be riskier than traditional equity funds.

Dividend Funds: Their objective is to take advantage of the tax advantage afforded by dividends; therefore, they are not that appropriate for RRSPs or RRIFs, where the credit cannot be applied. Price changes tend to be driven by changes in interest rates and general market trends.

- **5. Specialty and Sector Funds**: They attempt to obtain superior capital gains and are less diversified than traditional funds in the hopes of achieving these results. They typically concentrate on companies in one industry, one segment of the capital market, or in one geographical location. Include science and technology, natural resources and precious metals, real estate and financial services, health care, socially responsible funds.

International or **Global Funds**: They represent a type of specialty fund that invests in foreign securities. They carry the additional risk of foreign exchange exposure.

- **6. Index Funds**: Their objective is to mirror the performance of a market index such as the S&P/TSX Composite Index or Scotia McLeod Bond Index. The management fees are generally much lower than for actively managed funds.

! The fund types above have different risk-return characteristics. Generally higher returns entail higher risk. The following list provides the CSI rankings of most of the fund categories above, from lowest-risk, lowest return to highest-risk, highest return:

  - money market
  - mortgage

- bond
- balanced
- dividend
- equity
- specialty

!

FUND MANAGEMENT STYLES

Equity Management Styles

- Fund management styles tend to be **active** or **passive** in nature. Active managers try to outperform benchmarks, while passive managers try to match the benchmark performance, usually by using some manner of indexing. Most equity funds are managed using an active approach, with index funds being an obvious exception. Some of the possible strategies that are pursued by equity fund managers were described in Chapter 16.
- **Indexing and Closet Indexing**: Indexing is a passive strategy that involves the purchase of securities that comprise a market benchmark such as the S&P/TSX Index or the S&P 500 Index. There is no need to perform in-depth security analysis, and the costs of this long-term, buy-and-hold strategy are very low, which corresponds to low management expense ratios. This approach is consistent with the belief that markets are efficient, which means it will be difficult to outperform the market. Therefore, it makes sense to "match" the market performance and reduce expenses.
- **Multi-Manager**: Multi-manager funds are divided into two or more portfolios that are managed separately. Since these funds may be managed using a combination of styles, they tend to be lower risk than those that adhere to one style only. The downside is that the superior performance of one manager may be offset by the weak performance of another.

REDEEMING MUTUAL FUND UNITS OR SHARES

- Mutual fund shares or units can be redeemed at a price that equals or is very close to the fund's NAVPS less any applicable redemption fees.
- Canadian tax regulations generally treat mutual funds as conduits that pass income flows to its holders. Fund holders receive T3 (or T5) forms that report all income earned through the year including interest, dividends, capital gains, and foreign income.

! When fund units are redeemed, this action is considered a disposition for tax purposes, and the proceeds are subject to capital gains or losses. A complication arises due to the reinvestment of interest and dividends. This implies that investors (or their investment advisors) must keep track of the actual purchase prices of all shares (or units) in a fund, and make appropriate adjustments to the **Adjusted Cost Base (ACB)**. The ACB is the value used to estimate the cost of purchasing fund units and is compared to the selling price (less any selling costs) in order to determine the amounts of any resulting capital gains (or losses).

- During the year funds make capital gains and losses when they sell securities. These gains are taxable in the hands of the investor; therefore, investors should determine if a capital gains distribution is pending before purchasing a fund.
- When common stocks pay dividends, the value of the stocks declines by roughly the amount of the dividend on the ex-dividend date. However, most funds automatically reinvest dividends to purchase new shares in the fund at the NAVPS. This policy leaves investors with more units in the fund, but the units are worth less (as a result of the decline in the value of the underlying common shares that paid the dividend). The net effect is that the fund holder's wealth is relatively unaffected by the dividend payments.

! **Systematic withdrawal plans** may be arranged to meet investors' cash flow requirements and can be set up for monthly, quarterly, or other intervals. There are four general types of withdrawal plans:

1. **Ratio Withdrawal Plan**: A specified percentage of fund shares (usually between 4% and 10%) are redeemed at fixed intervals (amounts will vary according to prevailing market values).
2. **Fixed-Dollar Withdrawal Plan**: A specified dollar amount is withdrawn at regular intervals.
3. **Fixed-Period Withdrawal Plan**: A specified amount is withdrawn over a predetermined period of time, with the amount determined in a manner such that all the funds should be used up by the end of the time period. For example, if the time period was established as four years, the investor would withdraw one-quarter in the first year, one-third in the second year, one-half in the third year, and the remaining balance in year four.
4. **Life Expectancy Adjusted Withdrawal Plan**: A variation of (3) that is designed to provide as high an income as possible during the holder's expected life, with the amounts withdrawn being adjusted in relation to the amount of capital remaining in the plan and the plan holder's revised life expectancy.

Most funds have reserved the right to suspend redemptions under extreme circumstances—if, for example, there was a suspension in trading for over half of the fund's holdings. This clause was invoked by many funds after September 11, 2001, when North American markets halted trading for several days.

COMPARING MUTUAL FUND PERFORMANCE

- Mutual fund performance characteristics are published regularly in the financial media. Items of interest include
    - the NAVPS (High, Low, Close);
    - the change in NAVPS;
    - simple rates of return (e.g., for one month or one year);
    - the volatility (as measured by standard deviation, beta, or usually a simple 1–10 rating); and
    - compound rates of return for longer periods (e.g., 3 years, 5 years, and 10 years);

The quotes sometimes include information such as

- the expense ratio;
- how it is distributed;
- how it is (or isn't) loaded; and
- whether it is RRSP eligible.

Rates of return include management fees and expenses, but not sales charges.

- Money market funds are reported differently to reflect the fact that earnings are distributed to shareholders, so the NAVPS remains constant and is not reported. Typically for these funds we observe a current yield (which is the rate of return on the fund over the most recent seven-day period expressed as an annual rate), and an effective yield that is the compound return that would arise if the current yield is compounded over a year.
- In order to gain meaningful information about a fund's performance, it must be compared to something (e.g., its peer group, or an appropriate market benchmark, such as the S&P/TSX Index [for Canadian equity funds]).

The recommended return measure for portfolios is to report a **Time-Weighted Rate of Return (TWRR)** as determined using the Modified Dietz method (discussed below). !

- TWRRs are estimated by finding an average return over some interval. The average returns do not include the effect of cash flows such as deposits, withdrawals, and reinvestments.
- It is recommended that the TWRR is calculated every day to obtain the most accurate estimate, although this may be difficult for funds that hold less liquid securities whose value is difficult to estimate on a daily basis (such as real estate or mortgage-backed securities portfolios).

- The **Modified Dietz method** approximates the TWRR, reducing the extensive calculations required for determining the TWRR on a daily basis.
- For advertising purposes, funds are required to report 1-year, 3-year, 5-year, 10-year, and total returns since inception, after deduction of management expenses, when available. Advisors should focus on returns beyond the one-year horizon, although there is no guarantee that history will repeat itself with respect to fund performance.
- ! While return data are useful in evaluating fund performance, there must be some standard against which to compare this performance. For example, a return of 5% over a three-year period might not seem very impressive for a Canadian equity fund, but if the S&P/TSX Index lost 5% and the average Canadian equity fund lost 4% over the same period, this could be viewed as excellent performance. Accordingly, fund performance is usually compared to a benchmark that is appropriate for the type of fund (e.g., the S&P/TSX Index, the S&P 500 Composite Index, the Scotia Capital Universe Bond Index, etc.). Morningstar Canada provides a series of mutual fund benchmarks for various fund categories. It is also common to compare a fund's performance against that of its peers (i.e., funds with similar investment objectives). Funds are usually compared to the average or median from their group and are often categorized into four quartiles.
- One must be careful not to compare apples with oranges when assessing mutual fund performance. In other words, fund performance should be compared to that of funds with similar stated objectives. In addition, one must be aware that the name or class of the fund may not accurately reflect the asset base. For example, one Canadian equity fund may have 90% invested in Canadian equities, and 10% in cash, while another might hold 30% in cash, 20% in foreign equities, 10% in bonds, and only 40% in Canadian equities. Finally, segregated funds may report their performance before the deduction of any expenses charged to the fund.
- Another complication that arises is that there is often no attempt to account for the relative risk of the fund versus similar funds. In order to obtain a true picture of fund performance, the risk of funds should be measured according to measures such as
  - standard deviation of fund returns, which measures the total volatility of the fund's returns;
  - beta, which measures the volatility of the fund's returns relative to those in the market portfolio (higher betas imply higher risk);
  - the number of years the fund lost money;
  - the fund's best and worst 12-month periods; and
  - the fund's worst annual, quarterly, or monthly losses.

! There are several dangers to be avoided when evaluating a mutual fund's performance:

1. The fund's record is history and there is no guarantee that it will be repeated.
2. The past record of a fund can be misleading if the fund makes fundamental changes in its investment objectives and/or changes the fund manager.

3. The performance of peer group averages will be higher than the appropriate universe because they are "survivorship biased" (i.e., they include the returns of only the funds that survive the period).
4. Funds should be compared against only those with similar objectives.
5. Comparisons should attempt to account for the relative risk of the fund versus similar funds using measures such as beta and/or standard deviation.
6. Avoid short-term comparisons. A minimum of three years is an acceptable comparison period.
7. Avoid selecting comparison periods where there are no comparable figures for peer groups and/or market benchmarks.

!

Chapter 19 Review Questions

1. Which of the following is NOT a type of withdrawal plan available to mutual fund investors? ( )
   a) ratio withdrawal plan
   b) fixed-dollar withdrawal plan
   c) life expectancy adjusted withdrawal plan
   d) none of the above

2. _____________ investment funds are riskier than _____________ funds, but are generally less risky than _____________ funds. ( )
   a) Money market; bond; dividend
   b) Mortgage; money market; bond
   c) Bond; balanced; mortgage
   d) Balanced; equity; dividend

3. The _____________ method provides a good approximation method for estimating mutual fund returns by assuming a constant rate through the period. ( )
   a) apples and oranges
   b) Modified Dietz
   c) time-weighted rate of return
   d) daily valuation method

4. _____________ fund managers' objective is to match the performance of the market as represented by a specific benchmark portfolio. ( )
   a) Equity
   b) Index
   c) Growth
   d) Asset allocation

( ) 5. Which of the following funds would most likely offer the LEAST degree of diversification, assuming they all held the same number of securities?

a) high-yield bond fund
b) global balanced fund
c) North American equity
d) international equity

( ) 6. Which of the four main groups of mutual funds, as classified by the Investment Funds Standards Committee, is considered to be the LOWEST risk?

a) balanced funds
b) cash and cash equivalents funds
c) equity funds
d) fixed-income funds

Bonus Questions

( ) 7. A Canadian tactical asset allocation fund is an example of which class of funds?

a) cash and cash equivalents funds
b) fixed-income funds
c) balanced funds
d) equity funds

( ) 8. A mutual fund that adds to the liquidity of your portfolio while providing a moderate level of income is most likely a(n):

a) cash and cash equivalents fund
b) fixed-income fund
c) balanced fund
d) equity fund

( ) 9. Which of the following is FALSE regarding cash and cash equivalents mutual funds?

a) They maintain a constant net asset value per share.
b) They provide a guaranteed rate of return.
c) All their distributions are taxed as income.
d) None of the above.

10. The returns of fixed-income funds consist of: ( )
    a) interest income
    b) capital gains
    c) both (a) and (b)
    d) neither (a) nor (b)

11. The mutual fund redemption plan whereby the payments made to the fund holder are calculated based on periods of time that are continually adjusted, and which in turn are based on information from mortality tables, is better known as: ( )
    a) ratio withdrawal plan
    b) fixed-dollar withdrawal plan
    c) fixed-period withdrawal plan
    d) none of the above

12. What is a limitation of using absolute return performance measures to evaluate a fund manager's performance? ( )
    a) It does not take into account the overall performance of the market or that of his/her peers.
    b) Realized returns cannot be calculated for periods shorter than a year, as NAVPS is only reported annually.
    c) Both (a) and (b).
    d) Neither (a) nor (b).

SEGREGATED FUNDS AND OTHER INSURANCE PRODUCTS

chapter 20

CSC EXAM SUGGESTED GUIDELINES:
9 questions combined for Chapters 20 and 21

KEY FEATURES OF SEGREGATED FUNDS

- Segregated fund contracts, or **segregated funds** (hereafter seg funds), combine investments with certain insurance aspects. They are sold as insurance contracts known as **Individual Variable Insurance Contracts (IVICs)**.

Seg funds have many similarities to investment funds, which were discussed in Chapters 18 and 19; however, they also have several important differences. Unlike investment funds, they are exempt from provincial securities laws. In addition, the contract holders of a seg fund do not own the underlying assets in the fund but are protected by provisions in the contract.

Seg fund contracts involve three parties:

1. the **contract holder**: the purchaser;
2. the **annuitant**: the person whose life is insured; and
3. the **beneficiary** (or beneficiaries): the person or entity that receives the benefits payable.

- The contract holder may be someone different than the annuitant as long as it is held outside an RRSP.
- More than one beneficiary may be named, and eligible beneficiaries include the estate of the contract holder and charitable organizations.
- Beneficiaries should be designated at the time the contract is established, and they may be either revocable or irrevocable. In the latter case, any changes require the consent of the named beneficiary. An irrevocable beneficiary may be established to control the timing of transferring assets to children. For example, an irrevocable beneficiary could be designated, with the provision that the contract is reassigned to the child when they turn 21.

! One of the most distinguishing features of seg funds is that they must guarantee that a minimum percentage (required is 75%, but most funds offer 100%) of the investor's payments into the fund will be returned at the end of 10 years. These maturity guarantees provide insurance against capital losses, which will appeal to risk-averse investors.

! Some other important features of seg funds include the following:

1. They provide death benefits, and if the holder dies, the fund holdings are not subject to the delays or fees associated with probate hearings (i.e., Probate Bypass).
2. They provide business owners with a way to protect assets from being seized by creditors or lawyers (i.e., Creditor Protection).
3. Contract holders generally pay for these additional benefits in the form of higher management fees, and investment advisors should help investors determine if the benefits justify the additional expense.

MATURITY GUARANTEES AND BENEFITS

! **Maturity guarantees** alter the normal risk-return relationship for investors by allowing them to participate in potential market gains, while at the same time protecting the value of their investment. The OSFI (Office of the Superintendent of Financial Institutions) requires a minimum term of 10 years for these guarantees.

! The minimum guarantee amount under provincial legislation is 75%; however, most companies offer a 100% guarantee. This reflects the fact that it is unlikely that investments will lose money over a 10-year holding period, based on historical evidence. Some companies do provide the minimum 75% guarantee, and these funds tend to have lower management expenses to reflect the lower risk associated with the guarantee.

! Maturity guarantees are generally set up in one of three forms:

1. **Deposit-Based Guarantees**: These provide guarantees for each deposit made, with the term being based upon the date of the deposit.
2. **Yearly Policy-Based Guarantees**: These simplify record-keeping by grouping all contributions made within a 12-month period together, and giving them the same maturity date. Insurers also have the option of grouping together payments within a given calendar year.
3. **Policy-Based Guarantees that Base Guarantees on the Original Policy Issue Date**: These guarantees often restrict the size of subsequent contributions after the initial set-up date.

- The value of maturity guarantees has been subject to debate. Some suggest that the guarantees do not justify the additional expense of ensuring the guarantee, since historical evidence suggests it is very unlikely that investment returns will be negative over a 10-year holding period. For example, the S&P/TSX Composite Index has never had a negative return during a 10-year period. Others suggest that the associated insurance premiums are insufficient to cover the potential cost of such guarantees since the payouts could be very large and widespread, if they ever become necessary. In fact, a 1998 report issued by the Canadian Institute of Actuaries (CIA) characterized the risks associated with seg fund guarantees as "low frequency and high severity."

- There is no maximum age limitation for non-registered seg fund holders; however, many companies enforce their own limits. Those held in RRSPs or locked-in retirement accounts must be terminated before the holder turns 69; while holders of funds in RRIFs or life income funds must be under 90. The minimum age requirement is 16.

Some firms may require that the individual to whom the death benefits apply are 80 years old or younger.

Many seg fund issuers have begun offering investors the option of buying funds with maturity guarantee "**reset dates.**" These permit investors to lock in capital gains, but also extend the maturity date of the guarantee. Some funds provide automatic resets, while others provide investors the option of doing so a certain number of times per year (usually one to four times). Age restrictions may apply. !

- A recent innovation offers holders an automatic daily reset feature. The maturity guarantees for these funds are automatically reset every day, at the higher of the most recently established guaranteed value, or the current market value of the fund. Obviously, there are additional expenses associated with providing such flexible reset provisions.
- If seg funds are purchased primarily due to the maturity guarantees and death benefits, then the investor should consider what proportion of their funds should be held in seg funds. This will depend on several factors including the following:
  - The client's level of risk tolerance: the higher the tolerance, the fewer funds should be contributed to seg funds, due to the costs associated with the maturity guarantee.
  - The proportions of funds held in cash, fixed income, and equity asset classes: the higher the proportion held in cash and fixed income, the lower the need for the guarantee.
  - The investment's time horizon: the shorter the term, the less need for an insured fund.

An alternative strategy would be to invest in seg funds for the long-term investment component, and invest in an annuity product to generate short-term income.

The **death benefits** provided by seg funds are attractive to investors who desire higher returns, but are concerned with insuring the amount they leave to their heirs. The benefits are set up to ensure the beneficiary receives at least the value of contributions to the fund, less associated fees. If the market value of the fund is below this value, the beneficiary would receive the difference in cash. For example, if the guaranteed amount was $50,000 and the market value of the fund was $60,000 at the time of death, there would be no payout. However, if the market value had been $45,000, the beneficiary would receive a payment of $5,000 on top of the fund's value. !

- Age restrictions may apply to death benefits. Beyond a certain age, they may not apply, or the percentage of the guarantee may decline through time.

! Example 1:

The percentage of death benefits for a given seg fund declines from 100% to 90% for contributions made after the annuitant reaches age 80, and then to 80% after they reach age 82. If $10,000 is contributed in each of four years, starting when the annuitant is 79, what is the payout to the beneficiary if the annuitant dies at age 83? At the time of death the market value of the fund was $35,000, assuming no deferred sales charges apply.

Solution:

The contribution when the annuitant is 79 would be 100% guaranteed, the next two would be 90% guaranteed, and the fourth payment would be 80% guaranteed. So,

Death benefit amount = 10,000 + (10,000 × 0.90) + (10,000 × 0.90) + (10,000 × 0.80) = $36,000

Death benefit payment = 36,000 – 35,000 (market value) = $1,000

Death benefits may also be restricted by the length of time the contract has been held, with the percentage often graduating upward and reaching 100% after a certain holding period.

- Insurers are permitted to provide death benefits greater than 100% of the invested amount, and a few have opted to do so. For example, Manulife Financial introduced a series of funds providing death benefits that increased an additional 4% per year. The trade-off for this feature was to eliminate the two optional reset dates per year, and replace this feature with an automatic annual reset date on the anniversary of the contract.

Creditor Protection

Since seg funds are insurance products, they provide protection from creditors, unlike mutual funds. The full value of the fund is payable to the plan's beneficiaries and allows **probate bypass** (i.e., it is not subject to probate fees). In order for "creditor-proofing" to apply, the fund must satisfy one of the following conditions:

- For plans with revocable beneficiary status, the beneficiary must be a spouse, child, or parent of the *contract holder* in Quebec.
- For plans with revocable beneficiary status, the beneficiary must be a spouse, child, or parent of the *annuitant* in other provinces.
- All non-registered plans with irrevocable beneficiaries are eligible, with no restrictions regarding who the *beneficiaries* are.

Once a non-registered plan has been pledged as security for a loan, creditor-proofing may be waived. Registered plans may not be used as loan collateral without triggering tax consequences.

!

Seg funds that qualify for creditor protection are generally exempt from being seized in the event of bankruptcy, although this may be challenged if it can be shown the contributions were made with the intent of evading legal obligations. Creditor protection of these funds may be challenged if

- it can be shown the purpose was to evade debt obligations;
- the contributions were made within one year of the date of bankruptcy; and
- the contributions were made while the client was legally insolvent, which may cover investments made as far as five years in the past.

Since periodic contributions are often made to seg funds, it is possible that some contributions would be protected, while others would not.

- While insurance products are generally not considered a part of the estate of the contract holder, the surrender value of a seg fund is considered matrimonial property. Hence, the cash surrender value is part of the assets to be divided by two spouses who are divorcing in all provinces except Quebec. In Quebec, the spouses will divide the cash surrender value, less the cash surrender value when the marriage began.
- The use of seg funds provides advantages for individuals in the area of estate planning since the proceeds are passed on to beneficiaries without the time delays and financial costs associated with probate. In addition to eliminating probate fees, they also reduce the beneficiary's legal and other related expenses.

FEES AND EXPENSES

- Similar to mutual funds, seg funds incur many expenses that are deducted from the value of the fund assets, including
  - legal, audit, and registration expenses;
  - administration, record-keeping, and accounting expenses;
  - document preparation, mailing, and filing expenses; and
  - taxes (including income taxes, sales taxes, and capital gains taxes).
- Seg funds face expenses above those of mutual funds, primarily related to death benefits and maturity guarantees. The associated costs rise as the term to maturity declines and/or as the percentage value of the guarantee increases. As a result, there has been a recent movement by some funds to reduce the guarantee amount to 75%. While it is difficult to pinpoint the true cost of maturity guarantees, there is no doubt that seg funds display higher management expense ratios (MERs) than mutual funds. The IVIC guidelines require that funds separate the insurance portion of the expenses from the expenses associated with managing the underlying fund.

- The sales charges for seg funds are similar to those for mutual funds. Sales fees are generally front-end or deferred-load charges, although a few offer issuers no-load funds. Trailer fees and switching fees may also apply.

! Some of the most notable differences between mutual funds and seg funds are listed below:

Feature	Seg Funds	Mutual Funds
legal status	insurance contract	security
asset ownership	insurance company	the fund
regulation body	insurance regulators (provincial)	securities regulators
maturity guarantees	minimum 75% after 10 years (usually set at 100%)	usually none
death benefits	yes; may be subject to restrictions	usually none
creditor protection	yes; subject to conditions	none
probate bypass	yes	none

TAX CONSIDERATIONS

! Seg funds are taxed as if they were trusts that are separate from the insurer's other assets. The company that owns the fund is not taxed on its income, which is passed on to the contract holders. Unlike mutual funds, no distributions to contract holders are required, since they do not actually own the fund's assets. Taxes are **allocated** to contract holders based on their percentage share of such income, which is prorated according to the proportion of the year they held the fund. This **time-weighted** allocation of taxes differs from the "distribution" approach used by most mutual funds and avoids having investors pay an undue amount of taxes if they purchase a fund just prior to a distribution. As a result of this practice, seg funds do not experience the seasonal tax distortions experienced by mutual funds.

- When mutual funds make a distribution (usually done once a year, near year-end), the net asset value (NAV) of each unit will fall by this amount; however, most funds purchase units for the holders with the distributions. This process reduces the NAV of each unit, but the investors end up with additional units, leaving the value of their holdings relatively unchanged. However, they must pay taxes on the amount of the distribution, whether they held the funds for the entire year or for only one day.
- In contrast, with seg funds, the income earned on the fund is allocated to contract holders throughout the year and does not reduce the NAV of the fund. This time-weighted approach ensures that investors are taxed only on their portion of the income earned by the fund while they owned the fund. The example below demonstrates the difference in these approaches.

Example 2:

A seg fund and a mutual fund both have a beginning of year NAV of $9, and both earn income of $1.00 per unit during the year.

(a) What will be the year-end NAVs and the total wealth for a shareholder who owned 100 units of each fund at year-end?

(b) How much income will be charged against the investor in part (a) if he bought the units in each fund six months prior to year-end?

Solution:

(a) Mutual Fund:

NAV prior to distribution = 9 + 1 = $10

Investor wealth (prior to distribution) = 100 units × $10 = $1,000

NAV at year-end (after distribution) = 10 – 1 = $9

Investor wealth (year-end) = (100 units + [$100/$9] units) × $9 per unit

= (100 units + 11.11 units) × $9 per unit = $1,000

Seg Fund:

NAV at year-end = 9 + 1 = $10

Investor wealth (year-end) = 100 units × $10 = $1,000

(b) Mutual Fund:

The investor will be charged with (and taxed on) income of $1 × 100 units = $100.

Seg Fund:

The investor will be charged with (and taxed on) income of $1 × 6/12 × 100 units = $50.

- Some general principles to remember regarding seg funds are these:
  1. Seg fund NAVs are the same for all contract holders at a given point in time.
  2. The NAV will vary depending on the time of purchase.
  3. Income allocations do not reduce seg fund NAVs.
  4. Seg fund allocations are paid throughout the year.
- An additional tax advantage of seg funds is that they are able to pass capital losses on to investors, unlike mutual funds, which must save them to offset future capital gains.

The payments associated with maturity guarantees are taxable. While the amount of the payment is usually taxed as a capital gain, some tax experts argue that the entire amount should be fully taxable as regular income. The example below depicts three possible scenarios.

! Example 3:

A client invests in a seg fund with a 100% maturity guarantee. Assume the adjusted cost base (ACB) of her investment is $10,000 (which includes all contributions plus sales commissions paid), and that no redemption fees are payable. Also assume that any maturity guarantees are treated as capital gains. Determine the tax consequences under the following scenarios:

(a) She redeems her deposit after 10 years, when its market value is $12,000.

(b) She redeems her deposit after 10 years, when its market value is $9,000.

(c) She redeems her deposit after 12 years, when its market value is $10,000; however, the maturity guarantee had been reset at $12,000 after she had held the fund two years.

Solution:

(a) She will be taxed on $2,000 in capital gains income (12,000 – 10,000).

(b) No taxes are payable. The $1,000 capital gain associated with the maturity benefit (10,000 – 9,000) will be offset by the $1,000 capital loss on her investment (9,000 – 10,000).

(c) No capital gains are taxable when the maturity guarantee is reset. When the fund is redeemed, a taxable capital gain of $2,000 is triggered (12,000 guaranteed amount – 10,000 ACB).

- Death benefits are also subject to more than one tax treatment. Beneficiaries receive death benefits when the insured person dies. If the contract holder is not the annuitant and the contract holder dies, the contract remains in effect, but the deceased is deemed to have disposed of the contract at fair market value, which may trigger a capital gain or loss. This is the case unless the contract holder named his or her spouse as the successor owner, in which case the contract is transferred to the spouse at its adjusted cost base, thereby deferring the tax liability. If the contract owner and the annuitant are the same person, the gain or loss is charged to their terminal tax return.

A recent interpretation by Canada Revenue Agency has suggested that both maturity guarantees and death benefits should be treated as capital gains.

- The *Income Tax Act* requires seg funds to have a December 31 fiscal year-end. Income allocations are reported annually on a T3 slip, which must be reported by the contract holder. Holders are subject to taxes on capital gains that arise from switches from one fund to another, or when they redeem units.
- Unlike mutual funds, which add any commission fees to the adjusted cost base, commission fees for seg fund transactions are reported separately and may be claimed as capital losses when the contract is redeemed by the contract holder. The amount that may be claimed is in direct proportion to the proportion of the original shares purchased that have been redeemed. For example, if an investor redeemed 30% of fund units that were originally purchased, and the total commission fee was $100, the investor could claim a $30 capital loss.

- If the contract owner is not the annuitant, the policy remains intact after their death. However, the owner's estate would be subject to a resulting capital gain or loss from the disposition of the fund at its fair market value, unless they named a spouse as the successor owner.
- The government has recently announced that it will attempt to capture GST/HST on insurance premiums received by an insurer to cover the death benefits and maturity guarantees associated with seg funds.

When seg funds are held in registered plans the annuitant must be the contract holder, which is not the case for non-registered plans. Registered plans are non-transferable, unless the annuitant dies. As of January 1, 2001, seg fund contracts held within registered plans must comply with foreign content limitations. Seg fund contracts may be registered as locked-in plans in the form of a locked-in RRSP, a locked-in retirement account (LIRA), or a locked-in retirement income fund (LRIF).

- RRSPs must be terminated when the plan holder turns 69. At that time, they may be redeemed or converted into a Registered Retirement Income Fund (RRIF) or annuity. RRIFs may designate spouses, children, or grandchildren as beneficiaries, which allows the fund to be redeemed gradually through time. If not so designated, the sponsor must pay out the entire amount immediately. When these plans are rolled over to a spouse, they become the new annuitant, and the new maturity date will be 10 years hence at that time.

Seg funds may also be contributed to Registered Education Savings Plans (RESPs) in order to provide for post-secondary education for children, which will be discussed in greater detail in Chapter 25. The maturity guarantees may be particularly attractive for these plans since the contributor can attempt to invest the funds aggressively, but have an assured value available when the funds are required.

- Similar funds borrowed for other types of investments, the interest paid on funds borrowed to contribute to non-registered investments, and variable income (e.g., equity or balanced funds) seg funds are tax deductible.

REGULATION

- Issuers must be authorized to conduct life insurance business and must be licensed by provincial insurance regulators. Seg fund laws and regulations are very similar across all provinces and territories, which have all accepted the CLHIA (Canadian Life and Health Insurance Association) guidelines. There are some regulatory differences across the provinces, however. Quebec is distinct in having adopted a more unified approach to regulating the financial services industry than other provinces.
- Before seg funds may be offered to the public, they require approval from the appropriate provincial insurance regulator. Applications must initially be filed with the CLHIA, which conducts an extensive review. Once CLHIA approval has been obtained, the application package is forwarded to the provincial regulators,

which rely heavily on the CLHIA review, and many will not conduct any additional reviews. Most provinces impose a 30-day waiting period from the date of the CLHIA application.

- Compliance reports must be filed annually by the fund, and are reviewed to ensure that the fund's characteristics comply with the CLHIA guidelines.
- The Office of the Superintendent of Financial Institutions (OSFI) requires that federally regulated insurance companies are adequately capitalized, as dictated by the solvency requirements outlines in the federal *Insurance Companies Act.* The main requirements for seg funds include the following:

    1. The amount of the maturity guarantee may not exceed 100% of contributed capital (this also applies to those that permit "reset" guarantee features).
    2. The initial term of the contract cannot be less than 10 years.
    3. No guarantees prior to maturity or death are permissible.

- In addition to the requirements above, the OSFI requires life insurance companies to maintain "minimum continuing capital and surplus requirements," and federally incorporated companies must have at least $10 million in capital when incorporating. If a company does not properly account for its assets, or if its liabilities are not being paid, the OSFI may take temporary control of their assets, including seg funds.
- Seg fund contract holders are protected against the insolvency of its issuer by the very fact that the funds are segregated from the company's general assets. They also receive additional protection through **Assuris** (formerly CompCorp), which was founded in 1990. Assuris is a self-financed industry body that provides customers with protection in the event of insolvency of one of its members.

! **Assuris** provides insurance to seg fund holders in the event of default of any of its members, but this does not apply to fraud. Their guarantee applies to death benefits and maturity guarantees only, not to the fund assets. To qualify for protection, the fund contract has to be written in Canada by a member company; however, the contract holder does not need to be a Canadian resident to qualify.

The coverage is group plans. Thus, an investor who has both an individual and group plan set up with the same company would qualify for total coverage of the higher of 85% of the promised guaranteed amount or $120,000 (i.e., the higher of 85% of guaranteed amounts, or $60,000 coverage for each plan).

- There is no legal requirement for seg fund issuing companies to provide details of their independent credit ratings, as established by agencies such as the Canadian Bond Rating Service (CBRS) or Dominion Bond Rating Service (DBRS). However, these ratings are available for most seg fund providers, and some companies may provide them to customers in promotional materials.

OTHER INSURANCE PRODUCTS

- **Guaranteed Minimum Withdrawal Benefit (GMWB) Plans** are similar to variable annuities. Clients that buy a GMWB plan receive the right to withdraw a certain fixed percentage (typically 7%) of the initial deposit every year, until the entire principle is received. The underlying investment account can be based on a variety of indexes, funds, etc. !

Some plans offer the option to buy the plan years prior to beginning withdrawals and having the guaranteed amount grow by 5% per year.

These plans ensure that the purchaser receives the entire amount of deposits. As such, they will be of interest to those expecting to retire in 5–10 years.

- **Portfolio funds** invest in other seg funds in order to provide investors with the chance to hold diversified portfolios of seg funds. The disadvantage of these funds is that they are less flexible than traditional wrap programs offered by investment dealers. In addition, the management expenses usually exceed those for individual seg funds and Guaranteed Investment Funds (GIFs), since the asset allocation fees are paid on top of the management fees for the individual funds. !
- **Protected funds** are mutual funds that provide the maturity guarantees similar to those offered by seg funds. Since these funds are not insurance products, they can be sold by mutual fund salespeople and may change other features that are required for seg funds. For example, one company has offered a 5-year maturity guarantee instead of a 10-year one. In addition, traditional death benefits do not apply.

Chapter 20 Review Questions

1. In general, segregated funds are: ( )
   a) not protected from creditors
   b) not exempt from bankruptcy protection
   c) normally exempt from being included in the property divided among creditors
   d) none of the above

2. Unlike mutual funds, segregated funds: ( )
   I. may have death benefits
   II. are regulated by provincial securities regulators
   III. must file annual financial statements
   IV. have maturity guarantees

a) I and IV
b) II and III
c) I, III, and IV
d) II, III, and IV

( ) 3. What does Assuris guarantee?
a) the death benefits and maturity guarantees applicable to a segregated fund contract
b) the principal amount should the segregated fund default
c) the principal amount should the segregated fund's insurance company go bankrupt
d) the principal amount should the investor wish to break the segregated fund contract

Refer to the following information to answer Questions 4 and 5:

Assume Bill invested a lump sum of $100,000 in a seg fund on a deferred-sales-charges basis, and the policy was held long enough so there were no redemption fees at the time the policy is surrendered.

( ) 4. What are the tax consequences if Bill wishes to redeem his deposit after 10 years when the market value of his deposit will be $145,000?
a) A capital gain of $45,000 is taxable in the year of redemption.
b) There are no taxes payable.
c) Bill can defer the capital gains payable for seven years.
d) None of the above.

( ) 5. What are the tax consequences if Bill wishes to redeem his $100,000 deposit after 10 years when the market value of his deposit is $78,000?
a) Bill can carry forward the capital loss for seven years.
b) A net capital gain of $22,000 is taxable.
c) There are no taxes payable.
d) None of the above.

Bonus Questions

( ) 6. Which is NOT a benefit of segregated funds?
a) maturity guarantees
b) lower MERs than traditional mutual funds
c) creditor protection
d) none of the above

7. In a segregated fund, the person whose life is insured is known as the: ( )
   a) contract
   b) annuitant
   c) beneficiary
   d) insurer

8. Why might someone be unable to insure their spouse's life in a segregated fund? ( )
   a) They must have an insurable interest in the insured life.
   b) They may be more likely to die before their spouse.
   c) The fund is held in a Registered Education Savings Plan.
   d) One can always insure their spouse in a segregated fund.

9. Which of the following CANNOT be named as a beneficiary in a segregated fund? ( )
   a) grandparent
   b) stepchild
   c) sports team
   d) all of the above can be named

10. What is the consequence of exercising a reset option on a segregated fund? ( )
   a) The current market value becomes the new basis for the maturity guarantee.
   b) The contract's maturity date is extended by seven years.
   c) Both (a) and (b)
   d) Neither (a) nor (b)

HEDGE FUNDS

chapter

21

CSC EXAM SUGGESTED GUIDELINES:

9 questions combined for Chapters 20 and 21

OVERVIEW OF HEDGE FUNDS

Hedge funds are pools of capital that face light regulation and whose managers have significant flexibility in managing their assets. They are permitted to use derivatives for leverage or speculation, assume short positions, and do several other things that are not permitted for traditional mutual fund managers. Hedge funds are often referred to as alternative investment strategies to reflect this investing flexibility, although investments in real estate, private equity, and commodities/managed futures are also considered alternative strategies. !

Hedge funds share some similarities with mutual funds, but they differ in many ways, as shown in the table below: !

Mutual Funds	Hedge Funds
pooled investments with sales charges	same
sold by investment dealers	same
charge management fees	same
very limited short positions	no short position restriction
derivative use limited	no limits on derivative use
usually liquid	may have liquidity restriction

sold through prospectus	sold through offering memorandum to sophisticated or accredited investors only
usually no performance fees	usually performance fees
relative return objective (vs. benchmark)	absolute return objective
most valued daily	most valued monthly
quarterly or annual disclosures	annual disclosures to unit holders
cannot assume concentrated positions in securities	can assume concentrated positions

Eligible hedge fund investors include the following:

1. **High-Net-Worth and Institutional Investors**: Usually funds targeted to this audience are structured as limited partnerships and are sold as private placements through "offering memorandums" rather than through prospectuses. Offering memorandums are legal documents that state the objectives, risks, and terms of investments, but are not required to provide as much information as prospectuses (although some may). Funds sold without prospectuses are sold in the "exempt" market.

   Accredited investor exemption—institutions with significant net assets (e.g., $5 million or more) or individuals with financial assets exceeding $1 million or net income exceeding $200,000 (or $300,000 combined with spouse) in each of last two years.

2. **Retail Investors**: This group can invest in alternative strategies through vehicles other than the typical limited partnership structure, using one of the following structures:

   i. **Commodity pools**—mutual funds that may use leverage and short selling through the use of derivatives;

   ii. **Closed-end funds**—many of which are not subject to the usual mutual fund restrictions; and

   iii. **Principal protected notes (PPNs)**—provide exposure to the returns of one or more hedge funds and have a principal return guaranteed by a bank or highly rated issuer (discussed in Chapter 24).

Alfred Jones pioneered the use of hedge funds in 1949. He created a fund that provided protection from declining equity markets but provided superior returns. His fund was based on the premise that portfolio performance was based more on stock selection than on market conditions. His fund was basically a long/short strategy that was based on going long in stocks expected to outperform the market, while going short on the ones expected to underperform. During increasing or decreasing markets, the long position should outperform, while stocks correctly held in short positions should underperform the market, thereby providing excess returns in either event. Jones also used a small amount of leverage and initiated the use of a performance fee.

The size of the hedge fund market has increased dramatically in recent years. Global estimates for total assets is US$1.6 trillion from $400 billion in 2001, while the number of funds was estimated at over 9,000 compared to only 600 in 1990.

HEDGE FUND INDEXES

While there are many hedge fund indexes tracking various strategies, none of them is exhaustive. This reflects the lack of available information on hedge funds, which makes their decision to report results, or even their existence, optional. One of the best-known indexes is the Credit Suisse First Boston (CSFB)/Tremont Hedge Fund Index. This index is based on the Tremont TASS database, which tracks over 2,600 funds with assets of over $10 million. It has a low correlation with traditional equity indexes such as the DJIA and the S&P 500 Index. This index is also broken down into nine strategy sub-indexes related to strategies such as market-neutral and long/short. In total, CSFB/Tremont claims to track more than 5,500 hedge funds.

BENEFITS AND RISKS OF HEDGE FUNDS

Benefits:

1. **Low Correlations with Traditional Asset Classes**: This implies that hedge funds offer diversification benefits and lower overall portfolio risk.
2. **Risk Minimization**: Many hedge funds minimize risk, which is attested to by summary statistics that suggest a hedge fund index (the CSFB/Tremont Hedge Fund Index) had a lower standard deviation (8.1%) than the MSCI World Index (14.2%) over the 1995 to March 2005 period.
3. **Absolute Returns**: Hedge funds are designed to do well even when general equity markets do poorly, which may lead to higher absolute returns. Over the 1995–2004 period, the CSFB/Tremont Index earned an annual return of 10.8% versus 8.0% for the MSCI World Index.
4. **Potentially Lower Volatility with Higher Returns**: This is evident in items 1 and 2 above. The higher return and lower risk translated into a Sharpe Ratio of 0.86 for the CSFB/Tremont Index versus one of only 0.29 for the MSCI World Index.

! Risks:

1. **Light Regulatory Oversight**: Offering memorandums are not as detailed as prospectuses, and ongoing reporting requirements are less stringent. This implies the need for due diligence by investors.
2. **Manager and Market Risk**: Many hedge funds are not "hedged" at all, and they may involve significant market risks. It all depends on the focus of the manager.
3. **Complex Investment Strategies**: Many strategies are complex, which implies additional effort to try to understand the manager's approach.
4. **Liquidity Constraints**: Hedge funds are often not able to liquidate their portfolios on short notice, and they in turn impose liquidity constraints on investors in the funds. These constraints can be in the form of **"lockups,"** which represent periods of time during which initial investments cannot be removed from the fund. In addition, some funds charge early redemption fees and/or require advanced notice of the intent to redeem units.
5. **Incentive Fees**: Most hedge funds pay their managers an incentive fee, which is above and beyond management and administration fees. Investors should determine if these fees are subject to a "high-water mark" and/or to a stated "hurdle rate." Paying performance fees based on beating previous highs prevents the manager from "double-dipping" on incentive fees, while establishing hurdle rates ensures that managers get rewarded only on the amount by which their return exceeds some predetermined rate of return.
6. **Tax Implications**: Taxation is a complicated and important issue with respect to hedge funds due to the wide variation in their structure, and a tax expert should be consulted for advice. The income from some is fully taxable, while others provide offshore structures that allow tax deferral. Some provide income, while others focus on capital gains that can be deferred.
7. **Short Selling and Leverage**: Many hedge funds employ these techniques, both of which contribute to investment risk.
8. **Business Risk**: Mutual funds are usually part of large, well-established, and well-capitalized organizations. However, many hedge funds are small businesses run by managers whose business savvy may be unknown.

DUE DILIGENCE

Given the complexity of hedge funds and the diversity within this asset class it is critical that IAs perform due diligence before recommending them to any investor. Part of this process involves addressing several questions, such as the ones below, in order to assess the fund's risk profile:

1. **Manager's Investment Process and Strategy**: Consider items such as philosophy, style, leverage use, derivative use, hedging strategies, risk

controls, number of trades, expenses, foreign exchange risks, capacity constraints, stop-loss rules, and best/worst market environments.

2. **Fund Details**: Consider items such as audited financial statement availability, historical returns, lock-up periods, liquidity risks, high-water marks, and subscription/redemption policies.
3. **Investors' Legal and Taxation Issues**: Consider items such as legal/taxation issues for investors, where fund is domiciled, how income is taxed, what regulations apply, legal structures, and potential personal liability.
4. **Business Issues**: Consider items such as long-term track record, personal capital invested by managers, profitability at current asset level, stability, and financial backing.

HEDGE FUND STRATEGIES

Three broad categories of hedge fund strategies (presented in order from lowest risk and expected return to highest) are relative value, event-driven, and directional. Each is discussed below.

Relative Value Strategies: These strategies attempt to exploit market inefficiencies or arbitrage opportunities, while maintaining low exposure to underlying market direction. Three types are discussed below:

1. **Equity Market-Neutral**: Attempt to exploit market inefficiencies by simultaneously creating long and short matched (or market-neutral) equity portfolios. Usually use leverage to magnify returns.
2. **Convertible Arbitrage**: Attempt to exploit mispricings in convertible bonds or preferred shares relative to the price of the underlying common stock. Usually involves buying the convertible and short selling an appropriate amount of the underlying stock, which is less than the number of shares the convertible can be converted into, and is called the "hedge ratio." If the position is properly established, it can provide a steady stream of income (the "static gains") and the potential to earn additional profits whether stock or bond prices go up or down (the "volatility gains").
3. **Fixed-Income Arbitrage**: Attempt to profit from price discrepancies between interest rate securities and other interest rate securities and/or derivative securities based on interest rates. Usually the discrepancies are small, but the funds leverage the capital employed by factors of 10 to 30 times to magnify the gains. One of the most famous hedge fund collapses occurred in 1998 and involved a fund—Long-Term Capital Management—that used this strategy. It was based on extensive computerized models programmed by Nobel laureates. Unfortunately, this debacle highlights the risks associated with this type of strategy.

! **Event-Driven Strategies**: Attempt to exploit unique events such as mergers, acquisitions, stock splits, and buybacks. Possess medium directional risk.

1. **Merger** or **Risk Arbitrage**: Usually involves a long position in the target firm and a short position in the acquiring firm to reflect the fact that the target firm's price usually does not increase by the full amount of the takeover premium.
2. **Distressed Securities**: Attempt to profit from market inefficiencies and/or the inability of institutional investors to purchase the debt or equity securities of distressed companies, which generally sell at deep discounts.
3. **High-Yield Bonds**: Invest in high-yield (or junk) debt securities that the manager feels may be due for a credit upgrade, may be a takeover target, or may be undervalued for some other reason.

Directional Strategies: Take positions based on beliefs about future movements in equity, debt, commodity, and foreign exchange markets. Possess high directional risk.

!

1. **Long/Short Equity**: Most popular form of hedge fund, accounting for more than 75% of Canadian hedge fund activity. These differ from market-neutral funds because they maintain a "net exposure" on either the long or the short side and thus are subject to market risk. Usually they use only moderate leverage, rarely exceeding a factor of three. The net exposure is calculated as follows: (Long exposure – Short exposure)/Capital. For example, if a manager bought $10,000 worth of Royal Bank shares and sold short $7,000 worth of CIBC, the net exposure would be (10,000 – 7,000)/10,000 = 30%. If the market went down by 10%, the fund would lose only about 3% (i.e., .30 x 10%); however, if the market went up 10% the fund would gain only about 3%. Notice that a portion of the market risk is somewhat neutralized (theoretically) by shorting CIBC, but the fund is still subject to stock selection risk. The leverage factor is often estimated by adding the long and short market value and dividing by the net capital invested. For this example, the leverage factor would equal (10,000 + 7,000)/10,000 = 1.7.
2. **Global Macro**: Highly publicized strategies, but represent a small proportion of funds. Participate in all major markets and make bets on global macro events such as currency devaluations and interest rate changes. Usually employ leverage, often through the use of derivatives to accentuate returns. They are very high risk.
3. **Emerging Markets**: Invest in debt and/or equity securities in emerging markets using leverage, derivatives, and/or complex strategies.
4. **Dedicated Short-Bias**: Funds that continually maintain a short-bias net position.
5. **Managed Futures Funds**: Invest in financial and commodity futures markets and currency markets. Managers usually referred to as Commodity Trading Advisors (CTAs). These may be managed using a strict systematic approach or based on a discretionary decision-making approach. In Canada, many of these funds are set up as **commodity pools**, which permits them to be sold to retail investors.

FUNDS OF HEDGE FUNDS

A fund of hedge funds (FoHF) is a portfolio that holds a number of hedge funds. There are two main types: (1) single-strategy multi-manager and (2) multi-strategy multi-manager.

!

Advantages:

1. **Due Diligence**: This function is performed by the FoHF manager.
2. **Reduced Volatility**: Returns should be less volatile.
3. **Professional Management**
4. **Access to Hedge Funds**: Can access funds that might otherwise not be readily available to retail investors.
5. **Ability to Diversify with Smaller Investment**
6. **Manager and Business Risk Control**: Both of these risks are reduced by diversifying across several hedge funds.

Disadvantages:

!

1. **Additional Costs**: Most charge a base fee and an incentive fee in addition to the same fees charged by the underlying hedge funds. For example, a typical FoHF might charge a 1% management fee and a 10% incentive fee.
2. **No Guarantees of Positive Returns**
3. **Low or No Strategy Diversification**: Especially for single-strategy versions.
4. **Insufficient or Excessive Diversification**: Either is possible depending on the type and number of underlying hedge funds held.
5. **Additional Sources of Leverage**: Some FoHFs add more leverage to the mix.

Chapter 21 Review Questions

1. Which of the following characteristics does NOT belong to hedge funds? ( )
   a) They utilize long and short positions.
   b) They use derivatives in any way.
   c) They are sold by prospectuses to the general public.
   d) They apply performance-based fees.

2. Which of the following hedge funds seeks to profit from stock splits? ( )
   a) relative value hedge funds
   b) event-driven hedge funds
   c) directional hedge funds
   d) none of the above

( ) 3. All of the following are advantages of "funds of hedge funds" EXCEPT:

a) consistent returns with lower volatility
b) experienced portfolio manager
c) easier access hedge funds
d) liquidity

( ) 4. When hedge funds are targeted to high-net-worth investors, what is the aggregate realizable value of financial assets the individuals must own in order to qualify?

a) $1 million
b) $2 million
c) $3 million
d) over $3 million

Bonus Questions

( ) 5. Instead of issuing a prospectus, limited partnership hedge funds often substitute by issuing a(n):

a) simplified prospectus
b) offering memorandum
c) annual information form
d) all of the above

( ) 6. All of the following hedge fund structures contribute to the "retailization" of hedge funds or broader access for investors, EXCEPT:

a) principal protected notes
b) commodity pools
c) limited partnerships
d) closed-end funds

( ) 7. Which of the following is a benefit of hedge funds?

a) diversification benefits through low correlations with traditional investment assets
b) seek positive returns in any market condition, even down markets
c) greater risk-adjusted returns
d) all of the above

8. Under which incentive fee scheme would a manager be prevented from earning an incentive fee on the subsequent portfolio value rise after a temporary drop in value? ( )

   a) hurdle rate

   b) high-water mark

   c) both (a) and (b)

   d) neither (a) nor (b)

chapter 22

EXCHANGE-LISTED MANAGED PRODUCTS

CSC EXAM SUGGESTED GUIDELINES:

14 questions combined for Chapters 17, 22–24

CLOSED-END FUNDS

Closed-end funds normally issue shares only at start-up or other infrequent periods. They reinvest proceeds and borrowings in a portfolio to earn income and capital gains. The shares or units of these funds trade on stock exchanges.

Some funds, known as **interval funds** or **closed-end discretionary funds**, have the ability to buy back some of their outstanding shares periodically; these types of funds are more common in the United States.

The market price of these units is typically at a discount from the break-up value of the portfolios to reflect the market's view that the closed-end fund is a going concern, and/or to reflect the lower liquidity that is associated with these funds. In general, the greater the discount, the more attractive these funds are as investments, especially if they are trading below historical discount values.

- The **advantages** of closed-end funds include the following:
    1. They provide diversification potential.
    2. They may be sold short, unlike open-end funds.
    3. They do not require liquid funds to be available for redeeming shares, unlike open-end funds.
    4. Since the number of units is fixed, capital gains, dividends, and interest income may be paid directly to investors, rather than reinvesting in additional units.
    5. They may have lower management expense ratios because they involve the administration of a fixed number of units.

- The possible **disadvantages** of closed-end funds include the following:
  1. They are subject to stock exchange reporting requirements.
  2. Performance comparisons are difficult because there are fewer available, and they are not followed as closely.
  3. Discounts from NAV may increase, resulting in capital losses.
  4. They are less liquid than open-end funds, since they must be bought and sold in the market.
  5. Deferred sales charges are generally not on a declining percentage basis.
  6. They do not generally provide for automatic reinvestment of distributions, so the investor must invest these funds themselves.
  7. If they trade on foreign exchanges, the dividends do not qualify for the dividend tax credit.

INCOME TRUSTS

Income trusts sell a fixed number of units in the trust and the units trade in the over-the-counter market, similar to closed-end funds. The trust holds income-producing assets, and passes the income through to the unit holders. They often provide for tax deferral since the expenses tend to exceed the cash inflows during the early years of the trust. They differ from fixed-income debt instruments such as bonds because their payouts are usually not guaranteed, and the yields are usually higher. Some examples are described below.

! **Real Estate Investment Trusts (REITs)** are pools of funds invested in portfolios of real estate assets (in trust). They usually invest in income-producing properties, and provide investors with a fixed income by paying out a high proportion of their income (usually 95%) to unit holders. As a result, their prices tend to be very sensitive to interest rates—rising when interest rates fall and falling when rates rise. In order to limit the risk of these investments, REITs tend to focus on established, income-generating real estate assets, avoid real estate developments, and limit their leverage ratios to below 50% to 60%. As trusts, they do not provide unit holders with the limited liability feature associated with corporate ownership.

! **Royalty trusts** provide their unit holders with royalties received from the owners of natural resource assets. The income may be eligible for federal or provincial tax credits, and most are eligible for RRSPs, RRIFs, and other registered plans. They provide a hedge against the inflation associated with the underlying assets, since the payments will increase if the value of the underlying commodity increases. They are risky investments due to the volatile nature of commodity prices.

! **Business trusts** represent a wide variety of underlying businesses, ranging from restaurants to propane companies. The underlying companies usually have stable cash flows and relatively limited growth opportunities. In terms of numbers of income trusts, this has been the fastest-growing segment of the market over the past few years.

Miscellaneous income trusts include those that do not fit logically into any of the other classifications. Two examples are trusts that are set up to make extensive use of derivatives, and trusts that invest in other income trusts.

EXCHANGE-TRADED FUNDS

Exchange-traded funds (ETFs) are trusts that hold shares of companies in market indices in proportion to their weights in the underlying index. Units in these trusts trade in secondary markets and most are RRSP- and RRIF-eligible investments.

ETFs differ from traditional mutual funds in several ways:

1. They are traded throughout the day on exchanges.
2. They have lower management fees.
3. They have lower portfolio turnover, which also reduces capital gains income, reducing taxes payable.
4. They permit short selling.
5. They may be purchased on margin, which varies from dealer to dealer for mutual funds.

Several ETFs are presently available to Canadian and global investors, and the growth since the 1990s has been tremendous—for example, in Canada there was only one ETF in 1990, and there were 160 by the fall of 2010. The most popular ETFs in Canada are the **i60s**: These came into existence in March 2000 and represent units in the S&P/TSX 60 Index. They trade on the TSX and dividends are paid every quarter.

While these products started out primarily as products that tracked common equity indexes, today there are main variations such as those that track sector indexes, bond indexes, gold, etc. Newer trends involve the use of actively managed ETFs, leveraged ETFs, inverse leveraged ETFs, and commodity ETFs on commodities such as gold, natural gas, etc.

Private Equity

- A listed private equity company is an investment company that raises capital, which it uses to invest in a wide range of other companies. It may provide this financing in the form of equity or debt, or a combination of the two. Sometimes, it may structure itself as a private equity fund.
- Several types:

  1. leveraged buyouts;
  2. growth capital;
  3. turnaround;
  4. early stage venture capital (VC);

5. late stage VC;
6. distressed debt; and
7. infrastructure.

- Higher risks/higher returns for providers—also lower liquidity than typical investments. Typical providers include pension plans; endowments; foundations; wealthy individuals/families.

! Advantages include

1. access to legitimate inside information; and
2. they exert influence over management and have flexibility in implementation.

! Disadvantages include

1. illiquid investments; and
2. dependence on key personnel.

Chapter 22 Review Questions

( ) 1. Exchange-traded funds (ETFs) provide investors with a:

a) direct stock market investment with low MERs
b) diversified portfolio representing a proportionate interest in the basket of stocks that make up the underlying index
c) liquid investment that trades throughout the day
d) all of the above

( ) 2. Closed-end funds offer the following advantages EXCEPT:

a) They may be sold short.
b) Deferred sales charges usually decline through time.
c) They provide diversification potential.
d) They do not require large amounts of liquid funds.

( ) 3. REITs have which of the following characteristics?

a) Their prices fall when interest rates rise.
b) They generally have leverage ratios above 60%.
c) They provide their unit holders with limited liability.
d) None of the above.

( ) 4. Private equity investments benefit from:

a) high liquidity
b) low leverage

c) flexible implementation

d) none of the above

5. What potential costs do investors incur upon purchasing units in a closed-end fund? ( )

a) transaction commission

b) front-end load

c) back-end load

d) all of the above

Bonus Questions

6. ETFs differ from mutual funds in what important way? ( )

a) active management

b) lower MERs

c) both (a) and (b)

d) neither (a) nor (b)

7. Closed-ends differ from mutual funds in what way? ( )

a) They have a relatively fixed number of shares.

b) They require less liquidity.

c) No automatic reinvestment options.

d) All of the above.

8. In comparing the price of closed-end shares to their underlying net asset value, how do most Canadian closed-end shares trade? ( )

a) at a discount

b) at par

c) at a premium

d) the prices are too disbursed to determine

9. One major advantage that closed-end funds have over their open-ended counterparts is that: ( )

a) They have a maturity guarantee.

b) They have more flexibility in the sense that they do not need to keep funds liquid for redemptions.

c) Since they generally do not issue new shares, the net asset value per share will never decrease.

d) All of the above.

( ) 10. Which of the following is NOT exchange traded?

a) closed-end funds

b) income trusts

c) labour-sponsored venture capital corporations

d) none of the above

FEE-BASED ACCOUNTS

chapter 23

CSC EXAM SUGGESTED GUIDELINES:

14 questions combined for Chapters 17, 22–24

FEE-BASED ACCOUNTS

- **Fee-based accounts** are brokerage accounts that enable the investor to make an unlimited or specified number of trades for a fee, and they usually entitle the investor to professional advice.
- They have grown in popularity in recent years for several reasons (advantages) including:
  1. Under the commission-based models, advisors have focused on "trading," at the expense of focusing on the client's financial planning and wealth management needs.
  2. Surveys show affluent clients prefer to have a portion of fees paid tied to performance.
  3. Clients appreciate the disclosures associated with fee-based accounts.
  4. Under fee-based accounts, advisors have less incentive to invest in "high-commission" products, which may not be in the client's best interests.

  !
- Disadvantages:
  1. Could be more expensive if trading is minimal.
  2. The number of trades may be limited.
  3. Possible neglect by IA.
  4. Extra fees may be charged (i.e., two fees, etc.).
  5. Trading research and time requirements.

  !

Managed accounts are managed on a continuing basis by the member, usually for a management fee. They now represent over 15% of investment firms' sales, having grown six times faster than commission-based assets over the past decade. !

Managed account features:

1. Professional management with discretion.
2. Assets in the account belong exclusively to the client and are not "pooled" with other funds.
3. Include additional services—wealth management and financial planning.
4. An IPS is devised stating how the funds are to be managed.
5. Package of basic services includes trading, rebalancing, custodial assets, portfolio management, reporting, etc.
6. Greater transparency and reporting.

Fee-based non-managed accounts are full-service brokerage accounts that provide financial advice with a fixed or unlimited number of trades. The fees vary based on the dollar size of the account, the number of trades allowed, and by type of investment (equity, bond, money market).

Discretionary accounts are similar but are generally opened as a convenience to clients who are unwilling or unable to attend to their own accounts (for example, if they are seriously ill or are out of the country). Both accounts require written consent of the client, and the authorization must include investment objectives.

There are three types of fee-based managed accounts:

1. single-manager;
2. multi-manager; and
3. private family office.

Single-manager accounts have a single portfolio manager focusing on security selection, asset allocation, and sector allocation—often maintaining a model portfolio. Clients may also receive the benefits of tax-loss selling.

Types include

1. **Advisor** or **Investment Counsellor**: Benefits include
   a. lower costs and
   b. combining client needs with tailored investments.
2. **Propietary Managed Program**: Advisors partner with one or more of their firm's portfolio managers.
3. **ETF Wraps**: These may be managed **passively** (i.e., using a pre-set asset allocation that matches the client's risk tolerances) or **actively** (i.e., by allowing deviations from the long-term strategic mix for "tactical" reasons such as beliefs regarding market conditions, etc.). The active approach has the potential advantages of
   a. lower costs than multi-manager accounts;
   b. more efficient use of the advisor's time; and
   c. firms usually provide marketing support for advisors.

Multi-manager accounts provide clients and advisors access choices regarding professionally managed funds. The overlay manager works with advisors to service clients and is responsible for

1. conducting due diligence of portfolio managers;
2. setting overall optimal asset mix and allocations for each advisor;
3. ongoing monitoring of clients' investments and investment portfolio composition;
4. coordinating efforts of sub-advisors and may conduct rebalancing; and
5. providing market insights to advisors.

Types include

1. **Mutual Fund Wraps**: Benefits include (a) a coordinated investment account in terms of asset allocation and selection of managers; and (b) ongoing oversight management.
2. **Separately Managed Accounts**: If a client has substantial funds to invest (i.e., more than \$150,000–\$500,000), a dedicated account will be set up to hold the investments. These accounts can be tailored to suit the client's needs. Advantages include (a) access to elite portfolio managers via overlay manager; (b) since client directly owns the securities, there is no risk of having to sell long-term positions to meet liquidity requirements and also avoid capital gain distributions; and (c) clients receive account-specific reports.
3. **Multi-Disciplinary Accounts**: Similar to separately managed accounts, except that they hold a mix of securities in the sub-advisors' models and combine them into one portfolio to attempt to achieve higher levels of optimal asset allocation.
4. **Unified Managed Accounts**: An enhancement of multi-disciplinary accounts that include performance reports from sub-advisors that outline distinct models used within the single custody account.

Private family office: A "team" of professionals tends to the client's needs in distinct areas such as investments, trust services, estate planning, estates, etc. Designed for very high-net-worth individuals or estates (e.g., >\$50 million). They allow high-net-worth clients to focus on other issues. Having the services under one roof promotes the appropriate "alignment" of all clients' various needs.

Chapter 23 Review Questions

1. ______________ accounts are opened for clients as a convenience to clients who are unable or unwilling to attend to their own accounts, while ______________ accounts allow investors to tailor portfolios to their individual needs. ( )

   a) Managed; discretionary
   b) Discretionary; managed

c) Wrap; managed
d) Discretionary; wrap

( ) 2. The following have contributed to the growth in popularity in fee-based accounts EXCEPT:
a) They lead to a greater focus on financial planning.
b) They provide advisors with less incentive to invest in high-commission products.
c) They involve lower trading research and time requirements.
d) They provide clients with additional disclosures.

Bonus Questions

( ) 3. Actively managed ETF wraps offer the following advantage:
a) lower costs than passively managed ETF wraps
b) strict adherence to a long-term strategic asset allocation
c) more choices than for multi-manager accounts
d) the ability to react to market beliefs

( ) 4. _____________ are a type of wrap account.
a) Royalty trusts
b) REITs
c) ETF wraps
d) Segregated wraps

STRUCTURED PRODUCTS

chapter 24

CSC EXAM SUGGESTED GUIDELINES:
14 questions combined for Chapters 17, 22–24

PRINCIPAL PROTECTED NOTES (PPNs)

PPNs are similar to debt in that they pay interest, have a principal repayment amount and a maturity date. However, the interest rate is typically tied to some underlying asset such as a portfolio of securities, an index or hedge fund or portfolio of hedge funds. They are not issued through a prospectus and not considered to be securities, and while many are issued by banks, they are not CDIC insured.

The three main types are

1. index-linked notes;
2. mutual fund-linked notes; and
3. hedge fund-linked notes.

PPN structures involve three roles, which may be served by the same entity (i.e., the manager) or by as many as three separate entities:

1. the guarantor or issuer;
2. the manufacturer; and
3. the distributor.

Two popular structures are

1. **Zero-Coupon Bond Plus Call Option**: Issuer invests most of proceeds in zeroes to guarantee the principal, and the remainder in call options on the underlying to enhance potential return.
2. **Constant Proportion Portfolio Insurance (CPPI)**: Shift the portfolio allocation between a risky and riskless asset in response to changing interest rates and risky asset values with the goal of ensuring the promised return, while enhancing the upside.

! Risks:

1. **Performance Risk**: PPNs will likely not match the performance of the underlying assets due to additional expenses (i.e., additional management and incentive fees as well as the costs of providing the principal guarantee).
2. **Liquidity Risk**: Often there is no secondary market for PPNs, which implies the investor will have to sell at big discounts from the net asset value even if they can find a buyer. In addition, there may be risks of the issuer refusing to redeem the units if a "rush" to redemption occurs.
3. **Call Risk**: The issuer may redeem the PPN before maturity.
4. **Credit Risk**: The issuer may not be able to make payments due on time.
5. **Currency Risk**: Occurs when some of the underlying assets are denominated in alternative currencies.

These risks imply they are not appropriate for risk-averse investors that require predictable investment income and/or liquidity.

! The gains on PPNs are treated as interest income and therefore are fully taxable.

INDEX-LINKED GUARANTEED INVESTMENT CERTIFICATES (GICs)

! **Index-linked GICs** link their returns to equity returns based on a particular domestic or global index. They are attractive to conservative investors who desire safety as well as the opportunity to obtain yields above standard deposit instruments.

! While the principal is guaranteed, the total return is unknown; however, it is often limited by a maximum cap or a participation rate. For example if the underlying index grew 50% over a given period, and the participation rate was 70%, the maximum return would be 35% (i.e., 50% × 70%).

! The Canada Deposit Insurance Corporation (CDIC) insures the investors against issuer default. However, they face the risk that the underlying index will not increase in value, producing no returns. GICs are also usually not redeemable prior to maturity. Hence they are illiquid and provide "uncertain" returns, even though the principal is guaranteed. In addition, the income earned on these instruments is treated as interest income.

SPLIT SHARES

! • **Split Shares**: These represent common shares that have been split into two different shares (usually by an investment trust): the ***preferred share*** that receives the dividends and the ***capital share*** that receives the capital gains.

Risks associated with the preferred share include

1. early closing—which means they will need to find other investments with comparable yields;
2. early redemption—be aware of yield-to-call;
3. credit risk;
4. decline in value of underlying portfolio can cause price decline;
5. reinvestment risk—for reinvested dividends;
6. taxation risks—depends on tax rates and existing eligibility for special dividend tax credit (which could change); and
7. dividend cuts.

Risks associated with the capital share include

1. inherent leverage,
2. volatility, and
3. dividend cuts—which can impact gains.

ASSET-BACKED SECURITIES (ABS)

ABSs are formed when financial assets such as mortgages, loans, etc. are transformed into securities through a process referred to as **securitization**.

Basic securitization first pools the underlying assets and transforms them into a separate legal entity called a special purpose vehicle (SPV). Secondly, units in the SPV are sold to investors—these units are marketable securities, referred to as ABS. !

Generally, most SPVs issue more than one "class" of ABS, which are referred to as **tranches**. These tranches differ in terms of risk and potential returns, hence each tranche is likely to be more suitable for different investors, depending on their risk-return profiles. A common hierarchy is to have three tranches (Senior, Mezzanine, Junior), each declining in safety, but increasing in "potential" returns—although there are many variations of this basic structure. !

Asset-Backed Commercial Paper (ABCP) is one type of ABS, where the underlying assets consist of Commercial Paper, and hence the maturity date is less than one year (typically 90–180 days). Repayment depends on the cash flows provided by the underlying CP. !

ABCP products have become very complex in recent years. Unfortunately, there was a huge liquidity crisis in the Canadian ABCP market for the $32 billion in non-bank CP in 2007 that caused an entire cease in trading of these instruments that persisted for many months, causing much hardship.

MORTGAGE-BACKED SECURITIES (MBS)

! **MBSs** are pools of residential mortgages that have been "bundled" or packaged into one big asset pool, with units in the pool sold to investors. They "pass-through" the mortgage payments to unit holders.

In Canada, the most common form of MBS is the NHA MBS, which is guaranteed by the Canada Mortgage and Housing Corporation (CMHC). The most common maturity is five years, although they can vary from 3 to over 10 years in maturity. They can be structured using a closed or open pool. Closed pools include mortgages that cannot be repaid early, whereas open pools may be, and hence are subject to additional **prepayment risk**.

! They usually offer a yield that is higher than that available on government bonds.

Benefits of NHA MBS:

1. Fully guaranteed by the Government of Canada.
2. The CMHC guarantee is unlimited in size.
3. Monthly payments are guaranteed.
4. Yields are higher than G of C bond yields.
5. Very liquid.
6. Low minimum investment (usually $5,000).
7. RRSP and RRIF eligible.

! Risks of NHA MBS:

1. Reinvestment risk due to prepayments.
2. Prepayments reduce future payments received.
3. Mortgage loans may go into default.
4. Mortgage property may be damaged.
5. Capital losses are possible if sold prior to maturity due to interest rate changes, etc.

Chapter 24 Review Questions

( ) 1. The following are risks of NHA MBS, EXCEPT for:

a) Reinvestment risk due to prepayments.
b) Prepayments reduce future payments received.
c) Illiquidity.
d) Mortgage property may be damaged.

2. An ABS investor with a low tolerance for risk would be most likely to invest in which tranche? ( )
   a) Senior
   b) Mezzanine
   c) Junior
   d) Subordinated

3. Which of the following is a risk associated with the capital share of a split share? ( )
   a) early closing
   b) early redemption
   c) taxation risks
   d) volatility

4. Performance risk for PPNs refers to the fact that: ( )
   a) There is no secondary market for PPNs.
   b) They may not match the performance of the underlying assets.
   c) The issuer may redeem the PPN before maturity.
   d) Their performance is not guaranteed.

5. Which of the following has CDIC insurance coverage against default? ( )
   a) PPNs
   b) Index-linked GICs
   c) ABS
   d) NHA MBS

Bonus Questions

6. Which of the following is NOT a benefit of NHA MBSs? ( )
   a) Fully guaranteed by the Government of Canada.
   b) The CMHC guarantee is unlimited in size.
   c) Prepayments are possible.
   d) Yields are higher than G of C bond yields.

7. Which of the following is a risk associated with the preferred share of a split share? ( )
   a) inherent leverage
   b) volatility

c) credit risk
d) a high yield-to-call

( ) 8. An SPV is used or created as part of what process?
a) portfolio insurance
b) securitization
c) splitting shares
d) creating index-linked notes

( ) 9. Liquidity is NOT a huge concern for investors in:
a) PPNs
b) index-linked GICs
c) ABCP
d) NHA MBS

( ) 10. Prepayment risk is of greatest concern for investors in:
a) closed-pool MBS
b) open-pool MBS
c) index-linked GICs
d) capital shares

CANADIAN TAXATION

chapter

25

CSC EXAM SUGGESTED GUIDELINES:

7 questions for Chapter 25

TAXES AND TAXATION ISSUES

Proper tax planning should be incorporated in all financial plans; however, it should not be the overriding objective, as discussed in Chapter 15. It is best to establish the tax plan early and continually reassess it. Legitimate and effective tax avoidance measures include

1. full utilization of allowable deductions;
2. conversion of non-deductible expenses into deductible expenditures;
3. postponing receipt of income;
4. splitting income with other family members; and
5. selecting investments that provide better after-tax yields.

!

- The *Income Tax Act* (ITA) governs federal income taxes, while the provinces have separate laws. The federal government collects taxes for all provinces except Quebec (both individuals and corporations) and Alberta (corporations). Canada imposes taxes on all income (domestic and foreign) earned by its residents (individual or corporate), as well as on foreign companies with management and control in Canada.
- Individuals and corporations must calculate income and pay taxes annually. Individuals must use the calendar year, but corporations can choose any fiscal year-end, as long as it is used consistently.

The following four steps are followed to determine income tax:

1. Determine income from employment, business, or investments.
2. Make allowable deductions to determine taxable income.

3. Determine gross or basic taxes payable based on taxable income.
4. Claim various tax credits to determine the net tax payable.

Income is treated differently, depending on its source:

1. Employment income is taxed on a gross receipt basis, and individuals cannot deduct related costs in earning this income.
2. Income from business requires activity by the firm in earning net income as calculated using GAAP.
3. Income from property is earned passively; however, reasonable expenses such as property taxes, repairs and maintenance, and possibly financing costs for acquisition purposes may be deductible.
4. Capital gains or losses which arise when capital assets are sold at price above (or below) their original acquisition cost.

- Basic federal income tax rates as of 2011 are

1. 15% for taxable income up to $41,544;
2. $6,232 + 22% on the next $41,544 up to $83,088;
3. $15,371 + 26% on the next $45,712 up to $128,800; and
4. $27,256 + 29% on all income above $128,800.

The provinces also charge taxes based on the amount of taxable income. For example, in 2011 a Manitoba taxpayer with $50,000 in taxable income would be in the 22% federal tax bracket and be subject to a 12.75% provincial tax rate, resulting in a combined marginal tax rate of 34.75%.

! Employers must withhold income tax on employee salaries and pay it to the government on behalf of their employees. Most individuals pay income tax on an annual basis unless they earn more than 25% of their income from sources that do not withhold tax. These individuals must make payments quarterly based on the lesser of taxes for the previous year, an average over the previous two years, or an estimate for the current year. Corporations pay income taxes monthly.

TAXATION OF INVESTMENT INCOME

- Interest earned through any investment contract (such as bonds, etc.) is fully taxable as regular income, and the amount of interest is based on an annual accrual basis, rather than on a cash basis.

! **Dividends** (whether they are cash, stock, or reinvested dividends) received from Canadian corporations are taxable in the following manner in all provinces except Quebec:

1. The amount of the dividend is "grossed up" by 45% to obtain the federally taxable amount of dividend that is used in determining net income.

2. The taxpayer is able to claim the **dividend tax credit** (which reduces federal taxes payable) in the amount of 19% of the taxable amount of dividend.
3. The provincial tax is calculated after the tax credit is claimed.

Example 1:

Consider a Canadian investor who receives $80 in dividends; the grossed-up amount of $116 would be added to taxable income. This would produce a federal tax figure of $30.16, if the investor is in the 26% bracket. This amount is then reduced by $22.04 (19% of $116) to arrive at the federal taxes payable figure of $8.12. The marginal tax rates on dividends are lower than on interest and may be lower than those applying to capital gains, depending on the marginal rates and provincial credits. Any shift from interest-bearing securities to dividend-paying ones should enhance after-tax returns.

- Foreign dividends are taxed as regular income and are usually taxed by the source country, and there is an allowable credit that is the lower of the foreign tax paid and the Canadian taxes payable on foreign income.

The following items related to investment income are tax deductible:

1. Carrying charges, including interest on borrowed funds, investment counselling fees, fees paid for administration or safe custody of investments, safety deposit box charges, and accounting fees paid for recording investment income.
2. Interest on borrowed funds is deductible only if the investor had a legal obligation to pay the interest, the purpose of the borrowing was to earn income, and the income earned from the investment is not tax exempt (note: it does not need to be an arm's-length transaction). In addition, the interest charge (a) cannot exceed the amount of interest earned on debt securities unless they are convertible; (b) is disallowed as a deduction if it exceeds the grossed-up amount of preferred dividends; and (c) is for the most part deductible if it is for the purchase of common shares.

Capital Gains and Losses

A **capital gain** occurs when capital assets are sold for more than their cost of acquisition. As of October 2000, only 50% of the capital gain is taxable, provided the transaction involved a taxpayer whose ordinary business does not involve the trading of securities, or that Canada Revenue Agency did not determine the trading to be "speculative" in nature. The general rule is that

Capital gain = (selling proceeds [i.e., selling price − commission costs]) − (the adjusted cost base [which includes commission costs])

The **adjusted cost** base is complicated when shares were purchased at different purchase prices and is based on the **average cost method**.

! Example 2:

(a) If 100 shares were purchased for $5 (including commission) and an additional 300 shares were purchased for $8 (including commission), then the average adjusted cost per share would be ($500 + $2,400)/400 = $7.25 per share.

(b) If 300 shares were later sold for $10 each, with $80 commission costs, the resulting capital gain would be

Capital Gain = ([$10 × 300] – $80) – ($7.25 × 300) = $2,920 – $2,175 = $745

No capital gain or loss arises when *convertible features* are exercised. However, the adjusted cost base of the shares acquired through conversion is based on the cost of the original securities. For example, if 200 preferred shares are purchased for a total cost of $4,000 and each share is convertible into 10 common shares, the adjusted cost base of one common share (after conversion) will be $4,000/(10 × 200) shares = $2 per common share.

Warrants and rights may be acquired through direct purchase by owning the shares associated with a rights offering or by purchasing units with rights or warrants attached. When they are purchased they are treated the same as convertibles. However, if they are the result of owning underlying shares, the adjusted cost base of the original shares is adjusted. When warrants or rights are not exercised, a capital gain or loss may result, unless they were acquired at zero cost.

Taxes on the sale of *debt securities* such as bonds are applied as above. However, the accrued interest portion of a bond purchase price is not included as part of the adjusted cost base and is treated as taxable income in the hands of the bond seller.

Capital losses may be used to offset capital gains income. They cannot be claimed by the security holder unless ownership is transferred in writing to another person. The exception to this rule occurs when the security becomes worthless due to bankruptcy of the underlying company.

Superficial losses occur when the same security is sold but then repurchased within 30 days, and it is still held 30 days after the sale. They are *not* tax deductible; however, the amount of the superficial loss is added to the original cost base of the repurchased shares, which lowers the ultimate capital gain. They do not apply if the losses arise because the investor is leaving Canada or dies, or are due to the expiry of an option.

Investors may consider **tax-loss selling** to produce tax losses that will offset capital gains, if the funds can be more attractively employed elsewhere. The following factors should be considered:

1. Timing must be such as to avoid a superficial loss.
2. The settlement date must be within the current tax period or else the loss is attributed to the following tax year.

Alternative Minimum Tax (ATM) rules can be triggered when taxpayers significantly reduce their tax bill by claiming legitimate deductions or by taking advantage of tax-friendly forms of income such as dividends or capital gains. Under such circumstances, the taxpayer must pay the higher amount as calculated under the usual tax laws or the minimum tax rules. Minimum taxes paid can be recovered in later years if regular taxes exceed the minimum taxes.

TAX DEFERRAL PLANS

Tax deferral plans are designed to reduce taxes during periods of high income (and high tax brackets), by deferring payment until a period such as retirement, when income levels (and tax brackets) are lower. Total contributions to retirement savings plans that provide tax advantages are limited to *18% of earned income* to a maximum dollar amount of *$22,000* for 2010 and rising with inflation thereafter.

The amount contributed to **Registered Pension Plans (RPPs)** and **Deferred Profit Sharing Plans (DPSPs)** is called the **Pension Adjustment (PA)**. When an increase in benefits materializes due to the introduction of a new pension plan, the adjustment to define contributions to the new plan versus the old plan is called the **Past Service Pension Adjustment (PSPA)**. Both the PA and PSPA reduce the allowable contributions to an RRSP by a taxpayer. Carry-forward provisions enable the taxpayer to make up contributions below their maximum amount in subsequent years.

Registered pension plans (RPPs) are established by the employer for the employees' benefit. Both employer and employee make contributions, which are tax deductible.

RPPs may be set up in one of two forms:

1. **Money Purchase Plans** (or **Defined Contribution Plans**): The contributions are defined and benefits vary with the value of the fund (employer/employee contributions are limited by the limits mentioned above).
2. **Defined Benefit Plans (DBPs)**: Benefits are predefined and contributions vary (the current DBP limits are 2% of pre-retirement earnings per year of service with a limit of $2,444 for 2009, and indexed to inflation thereafter.) In addition employee current contributions are restricted to the lesser of
   - 9% of current compensation and
   - $1,000 plus 70% of the employee's PA for the year.

Registered Retirement Savings Plans (RRSPs) allow annual tax-deductible contributions up to predefined limits. The income earned on the plan is not taxed as long as it remains in plans that are registered with Canada Revenue Agency and meet Canadian content requirements.

There are two types of RRSPs:

1. **Single-Vendor RRSPs**: The holder invests in one or more pooled or mutual funds that are managed by fund managers.
2. **Self-Directed RRSPs**: The investor contributes permissible securities into a plan that is administered for a fee; however, the investor directs the investment transactions himself. The foreign content limit has been 30% since 2001.

! RRSPs are trust accounts set up for the investor's benefit upon retirement, and access to funds cannot be gained immediately without paying a withholding tax. In addition, RRSPs are not eligible to provide security for loans.

! RRSP contributions must be made within 60 days of year-end and are limited to 18% of the previous year's earnings or $22,000 in 2010, after which time the contribution limit will be indexed to inflation, less the previous year's PA and PSPA plus the unused RRSP deduction room. A penalty tax of 1% per month is levied on "overcontributions" of $2,000 or more. Investors may contribute securities they already own to the plan (referred to as a "**contribution in kind**"), and they must pay taxes on any capital gains; however, they are unable to claim any capital losses that result.

! Investors may contribute to a **spousal RRSP** provided the contribution does not put them over their own maximum contribution limit. This does not affect the contribution limits of the spouse. For example, if a wife contributes $7,000 of her $20,000 limit in 2008 to her own plan, she may also contribute $13,000 to her husband's plan, without affecting his contribution limits. The proceeds from deregistering a spousal plan is taxable income for the spouse (not the contributor), except for contributions made in the year of deregistration and the two calendar years before the plan is deregistered.

- The following pension income transfers to an RRSP are tax-free and do not affect contribution limits:

  1. direct transfers from RPPs and other RRSPs and
  2. allowances for long service upon retirement for each year of service, subject to specific guidelines.

! RRSPs may be deregistered at any time, but must occur by the time the plan holder is 71. Available options for **deregistering the plan** include

1. withdrawing the full lump sum amount, which is fully taxable;
2. purchasing a life annuity with a guaranteed term;
3. a fixed-term annuity that provides benefits to a specified age;
4. purchasing a **Registered Retirement Income Fund (RRIF)**, which provides annual income;
5. changing it to allow transfer of funds to another RRSP or RPP; or
6. combinations of the above options.

Upon death, remaining benefits on an annuity or RRIF can be transferred to a spouse or child, or else the value is included in the deceased's income in the year of death and is fully taxable.

! Major **advantages** of RRSPs include

1. They reduce taxable income during high taxation years.
2. They shelter income from taxation by transferring it into an RRSP.
3. They allow for tax-exempt accumulation of retirement funds.
4. They allow deferral of some taxes.
5. They provide income-splitting opportunities, which may result in lower total tax payments.

Major **disadvantages** of RRSPs include

1. Any funds withdrawn are fully taxable.
2. The holder cannot take advantage of the Dividend Tax Credit on dividends received within the plan.
3. If the plan holder dies, the estate is taxed against the full amount, unless left to a spouse, or under certain conditions to a child or grandchild.
4. Plan assets cannot be used as collateral for a loan.

RRIF holders must make taxable withdrawals of a certain portion of assets from the fund annually. The minimum withdrawals are designed to provide benefits for a desired term; however, the payout may be accelerated if the owner elects. Individuals may own more than one RRIF and they may be self-directed if desired.

- Payments from **immediate annuities** start right away, while **deferred annuities** start at a later date specified in the contract. Unlike immediate annuities that must be paid in full, deferred annuities can be paid for in monthly installments. While the contributions to a deferred annuity are not tax deductible, they defer the taxes paid on investment income. If the annuities are not purchased using RRSP proceeds, only the interest portion of the payments is taxable; however, the full amount is taxable if received from an RRSP (since the principal has never been taxed). Finally, some deferred annuities are RRSP-eligible investments. They are sold by life insurance companies.

Tax-Free Savings Accounts (TFSAs) came into existence in 2009. The income earned within these plans is not taxable, and there are no restrictions on the timing or withdrawal amounts, or the required use of such withdrawals.

- Since 2009, anyone can contribute $5,000 per year (indexed to inflation to the nearest $500 thereafter)—regardless of whether or not you worked or earned income. The annual amount may be "carried forward" and used any time. Most traditional investments such as bonds, GICS, stocks, etc. are "qualified investments."

Contributions are NOT tax deductible; however, you can "replace" withdrawals in future periods, which provides great flexibility.

Registered Education Savings Plans (RESPs)

RESP contributions are not tax deductible; however, income earned on these plans is not taxable. The beneficiary of the plan will be taxed upon withdrawal of funds, provided they are enrolled in qualifying educational programs.

There is no maximum annual contribution per beneficiary, but a lifetime maximum of $50,000 exists. Contributions can be made for 31 years, but the plan must be collapsed within 35 years of its initiation.

The plans may be individual or self-directed plans, and more than one beneficiary may be named to a plan. In this way, if any children do not attend a qualifying post-secondary institution, any beneficiaries that do qualify will have access to the proceeds of the plan.

! Since 1998, the contributor is permitted to withdraw the invested capital and income from the plan if none of the beneficiaries attends a qualifying institution by age 21, provided the plan is at least 10 years old. Under the same situation, the contributor may also transfer up to $50,000 to an RRSP, provided they have sufficient contribution room. Once the contributor begins to withdraw funds from the plan, it must be terminated by February 28 of the next year.

! **Canada Education Savings Grants (CESGs)** provide an additional attraction for RESPs. The federal government will match 20% of the first $2,500 contributed each year to an RESP (up to $500–$600 per year). These grants do not count toward the contributor's annual or lifetime maximum contributions, and unused grant room can be carried forward up to a maximum of $7,200 per child. If the student does not pursue post-secondary education, the grant must be repaid.

Currently, the CESGs will match up to 40% for the first $500 contributed by families with income under $41,544; up to 30% on the first $500 by families with income between $41,544 and $83,088; and 20% for additional contributions up to the $2,500 contribution limit. Thus, up to $600 matching is possible for those who contribute $2,500 and are in the lowest income bracket.

BASICS OF TAX PLANNING

! **Attribution rules** apply to the transfer of income to family members under many circumstances, and they serve to pass the tax consequences back to the transferor. Exceptions to attribution may occur when

1. the property or assets are transferred at fair market values or through a loan that is established at fair market rates, and where interest is paid within 30 days of year-end;
2. the transfer was a gift, and it can be shown that tax avoidance was not the main purpose of the transaction; or
3. business income is generally not subject to attribution.

- Certain income-splitting opportunities exist, which may result in reduced taxes:

1. Have the higher-income spouse pay the bills, while the lower-income spouse invests more; therefore, the investment income will accrue to the lower-tax-bracket spouse.
2. The higher-income spouse can loan funds for investment opportunities to the lower-income spouse at fair market rates, which results in taxation of only the net investment income over interest paid at the lower tax rates.
3. Direct discharge of a spouse's debts is not subject to attribution.
4. It may pay to have the taxpayer claim dividends as income if the dividend income would reduce the marital tax credit; therefore, a spousal dividend swap may be advantageous.

5. Capital losses may be transferred by selling the asset to a third party, and then having the spouse purchase it within 30 days. This would not represent a capital loss (but rather a superficial one); however, if the spouse then sells it, they can obtain a capital loss.
6. Payment of debts by way of a gift.
7. Splitting CPP income: must split both plans and be agreed to by both parties.
8. Asset swaps at fair market value are allowed, so higher tax bracket may trade income-generating assets for non-income-generating assets at fair market values.
9. Salaries for legitimate services rendered to spouses from proprietorships are deductible.
10. Gifts are not subject to attribution.

Chapter 25 Review Questions

1. An investor buys 300 XYZ preferred shares at a total cost of $7,500. Each preferred share is convertible into two and a half XYZ common shares. If the investor converts into common shares at a later date, what is the adjusted cost base per share? ( )

   a) $10
   b) $15
   c) $25
   d) $62.50

2. The following are examples of a capital loss EXCEPT: ( )

   a) A stock that was originally purchased for $20 is sold for $15 but is repurchased 21 days later.
   b) A stock that was originally purchased for $20 is sold for $15 and is not repurchased.
   c) Common shares that were acquired through the purchase of a warrant for $40 and that had an associated exercise price of $20 were sold for $50.
   d) All of the above represent capital losses.

3. An investor purchases 200 XYZ common shares at $20 and pays $60 in commission, then buys another 300 shares at $25 and pays $100 in commissions. What is the adjusted cost base per share? ( )

   a) $22.50
   b) $23.00
   c) $23.32
   d) none of the above

( ) 4. An investor is in the 29% marginal federal tax bracket and receives $200 in dividends from a Canadian corporation. How much federal tax must they pay on the dividend?

a) $29.00
b) $39.17
c) $58.00
d) none of the above

( ) 5. RRSPs differ from RRIFs because:

a) RRSPs shelter income earned within the plan.
b) RRSPs may hold stocks, bonds, mutual funds, and T-bills.
c) RRSPs do not require minimum annual withdrawals.
d) RRSPs may be self-directed.

( ) 6. Which of the following statements is FALSE?

a) Corporations pay taxes in quarterly installments.
b) Individuals that earn more than 20% of their income from sources that do not deduct taxes must pay taxes quarterly.
c) Neither (a) nor (b) is false.
d) Both (a) and (b) are false.

( ) 7. Which of the following tax avoidance tactics are legitimate?

a) converting a non-deductible expense into a tax-deductible expenditure
b) splitting income among one's family
c) postponing the receipt of income
d) all of the above

Bonus Questions

( ) 8. Canadians are required to pay taxes to the Canadian government on:

a) income earned within Canada
b) income earned outside of Canada
c) both (a) and (b)
d) neither (a) nor (b)

( ) 9. Which companies are considered residents of Canada and are therefore subject to Canadian income tax?

a) companies incorporated in Canada
b) foreign companies with management in Canada
c) both (a) and (b)
d) neither (a) nor (b)

10. Which of the following is NOT taxed on a net-income basis? ( )
    a) employment income
    b) business income
    c) capital property income
    d) none of the above

11. Self-employment income is considered part of which type of income? ( )
    a) employment income
    b) capital property income
    c) both (a) and (b)
    d) neither (a) nor (b)

12. If an individual was subject to a 34% marginal tax rate and a 28% average tax rate, how much would they retain after taxes on an additional dollar earned? ( )
    a) $0.28
    b) $0.34
    c) $0.66
    d) $0.72

13. When is the adjusted cost base for shares acquired through rights or warrants calculated in the same manner as shares acquired through a convertible security? ( )
    a) When the rights or warrants are purchased directly on the market.
    b) When the rights are received from shares already owned.
    c) Both (a) and (b).
    d) Neither (a) nor (b).

14. Which of the following scenarios would result in a superficial loss? ( )
    a) Stock is sold Dec. 15 for a loss, repurchased Jan. 5, and sold again Jan. 10 at a gain.
    b) Stock is sold Dec. 15 for a loss, repurchased Jan. 20, and sold again Jan. 25 at a loss.
    c) Stock is sold Dec. 15 for a gain, repurchased Jan. 10, and sold again Jan. 25 at a gain.
    d) None of the above.

WORKING WITH THE RETAIL CLIENT

chapter
26

CSC EXAM SUGGESTED GUIDELINES:
5 questions for Chapter 26

THE PROCESS OF FINANCIAL PLANNING

- Financial planning requires the consideration of many factors, including the client's age, wealth, career stage, marital status, tax situation, estate considerations, risk tolerance, investment objectives, legal situation, and other matters. This enables the investor and financial planner to obtain a comprehensive picture of the investor's present situation, so that it will be easier to identify future investing objectives. The financial planner's role is to coordinate information and advice from relevant experts in various fields.

Four objectives of a financial plan are that it

1. is doable;
2. accommodates small changes in lifestyle and income level;
3. is not too intimidating; and
4. provides necessities, but has some room built in to allow some luxuries.

The financial planning process involves the following six steps:

1. establishing the client-advisor relationship;
2. collecting data and information;
3. analyzing data and information;
4. recommending strategies to meet goals;
5. implementing recommendations; and
6. conducting a periodic review or follow-up.

1. Establishing the Client-Advisor Relationship

Meet the client, identify potential issues, and learn how a financial plan can work for them. Discuss the financial planning process itself. Establish if a long-term relationship seems viable. Disclose possible conflicts of interest.

2. Collecting Data and Information

! Information gathering is critical for financial advisors. They should be aware of essential details of each of their clients, including an understanding of the client's

- current financial and personal status,
- investment goals and preferences, and
- risk tolerance.

! Advisors also need to be aware of their clients' unique personal needs and goals, including

- their decision-making process,
- their preferred method(s) of communicating with the advisor,
- their psychological profile, and
- the needs, goals, and desires of their family.

- Advisors need to be good listeners since many clients will not communicate their motivation for many decisions directly. Advisors also need to be aware that discussing personal financial matters is an emotional topic for most individuals.
- It is important to maintain regular contact with clients. This reassures clients that the advisor is acting in their best interests, and also enables the advisor to maintain current knowledge of the client's financial and personal situation.
- In order to develop a good working relationship with a client, it is advantageous for the client to be able to understand why certain decisions have been made. This suggests that it will pay to try to educate the client with respect to several matters.

Information collected includes tax information, bank statements, pay slips, and documents such as wills and insurance policies. Personal data such as age, marital status, number of dependents, health, and employment help define an acceptable level of risk for the investor. Information must be gathered regarding the net worth, income, and tax status of clients. It is important that complete client records are maintained and kept up to date.

! 3. Analyzing Data and Information

It is important that the client objectively assesses personal strengths and weaknesses, including their career status and future earnings potential. Personal circumstances such as risk preferences, marital status, and job security can greatly affect the financial plan. **The New Account Application form** includes clearly stated investment objectives that must be used to guide investment actions. These **objectives** can generally be described as in Chapter 15: income, growth, preservation of capital, tax minimization, or liquidity.

It is also important to establish constraints to achieving these objectives. These include many factors including income, risk tolerance, and time horizon, which were discussed in Chapters 15 and 16. The New Client Application form is useful for this purpose.

4. Recommending Strategies to Meet Goals

The strategies should be formalized in a written statement that should include clearly defined goals and a schedule for achieving them. It should be straightforward and easy to put into practice.

5. Implementing Recommendations

The investor must carefully put the plan into practice after reviewing the details of the plan. The advisor should make sure that the investor is aware of the risks and rewards of all of the recommended investments.

6. Conducting a Periodic Review or Follow-up

This is probably the most important step and should be undertaken at regular intervals (at least annually) or if a change in circumstances warrants reconsideration of the plan (e.g., change in employment conditions or marital status).

FINANCIAL PLANNING AIDS

The Life Cycle Theory is a helpful approach that suggests that the typical risk-return preferences or needs change for individuals at different points in their life:

1. Early Earning Years (to age 35): The investor is building a career, family, and net worth; therefore, priorities include savings plans and liquidity for emergencies, while the primary investing objective is growth.
2. Mid-Earning Years (to age 55): Expenses begin to decline, while income and savings generally increase; therefore, objectives tend to focus on growth and tax minimization.
3. Peak Earning Years (to retirement): Preservation of capital becomes very important, and risk reduction measures should be undertaken.
4. Retirement Years: During this period, preservation of capital and income will be the primary objectives.

While this approach is useful as general guideline, many individuals do not fit the typical profile.

- It is important to consider the investor's individual situation, and one useful tool in this regard is the **financial planning pyramid**. It indicates the strength of the base for investor objectives. Levels build one on top of the other:
    1. security: insurance, will;
    2. independence: debt elimination, house, RRSP, emergency fund;
    3. conservative: fixed-income securities and certain mutual funds;
    4. moderate: stocks, mutual funds;
    5. aggressive: tax shelters, commodity derivatives; and
    6. very aggressive: art, IPOs, OTC securities, real estate, precious metals.

ETHICS AND THE FINANCIAL ADVISOR

- **Ethics** may be defined as a set of moral values that guide behaviour and establish standards for judging whether actions are right or wrong.

! All sellers of securities and mutual funds must adhere to the **Code of Ethics** for the securities industry. This code is based upon the following *principles*:

- trust
- integrity
- justice
- fairness
- honesty
- responsibility
- reliability

! The code imposes the following **primary ethical values** on registrants:

1. They must use proper care and exercise independent professional judgment.
2. They must conduct themselves with trustworthiness and integrity, and be honest and fair in all dealings with the public, clients, employers, and colleagues.
3. They must conduct business in a professional manner that will reflect positively on the industry and encourage others to do so. They should also try to maintain and improve their own professional knowledge and encourage others to do so as well.
4. They must comply with the regulations of the appropriate security act(s), as well as the requirements of any self-regulatory organizations (SROs) of which they are members.
5. They must hold client information in strict confidence.

- There is an important distinction between ethical behaviour and complying with rules. While conformance with rules is one component of ethical behaviour, it is not always enough. Ethical behaviour implies making moral judgments and acting accordingly in situations that may not be covered by any specific rules.

Standards of Conduct

The **standards of conduct** for the securities industry expand on the Code of Ethics, establishing behaviour requirements that are based to a large extent on provincial securities acts and SRO rules. !

The following outlines the basic standards of conduct:

A. Duty of Care
  - Know your client
  - Due diligence
  - Unsolicited orders

B. Trustworthiness, Honesty, and Fairness
  - Priority of client interests
  - Protection of client assets
  - Complete and accurate information
  - Disclosure

C. Professionalism
  - Client business
    - Client orders
    - Trades by registered and approved individuals
  - Approved securities
    - Personal business
    - Personal financial dealing with clients
    - Personal trading activity
    - Other personal endeavours
  - Continuous education

D. Conduct in accordance with securities acts
  - Compliance with securities acts and SRO rules
  - Inside information

E. Confidentiality
  - Client information
  - Use of confidential information

Some of the more important standards are discussed below, while the complete description of these standards is included in the Appendix to Chapter 23 of the CSC text.

! **Know Your Client and Suitability**: Advisors must make a concerted effort to *know the client*, including details of their financial and personal situation. This ensures the advisor cannot be faulted for providing the best advice possible, given their knowledge of the client's situation. The client's account should document the information provided, and the information should be updated in order to ensure the suitability of all investment recommendations.

! **Trustworthiness, Honesty, and Fairness**: Clients need to be able to trust their financial advisors. This trust must cover two dimensions: *competency* and *integrity*. A competent advisor with little integrity cannot be trusted to make the best financial decisions for a client; neither can an advisor with integrity who is incompetent. One important aspect of maintaining integrity is the disclosure of all current and potential conflicts of interest. In order to promote competency among advisors, they must satisfy proficiency requirements, as well as participate in continuing education programs.

- **Fiduciary Duty and Professionalism**: The ongoing nature of the advisor-client relationship dictates a **fiduciary relationship** between advisors and their clients. Fiduciary relationships involve two or more parties where there may be an imbalance of knowledge or control, which invokes moral issues. In particular, financial advisors act as agents on the behalf of investors (the principals). Trust is of utmost importance in this principal-agent relationship because the principal's well-being is vulnerable to decisions made by the agent, who is expected to have greater expertise and/or authority. In order to ensure professionalism, the standards require that general business activity as well as attempts to solicit business are conducted in a professional and responsible manner that promotes respect and confidence from the public.

CASE STUDIES

- The following two case studies are similar in nature to those in Appendix B of Chapter 26 in the CSC text. They apply the concepts developed in Chapters 15, 16, 25, and 26 of the CSC text.

Case 1: Brigid

- **Situation**: Brigid is single, is 27 years old, and has been working at the same job for the past five years. She has no plans to leave her job and her current salary is $36,000 per year. It is reasonable to assume this amount will increase approximately 5% per year over the next 30–35 years. She has never invested in RRSPs but has contributed to the CPP and her company pension plan for the past five years. She has recently finished paying off her student loan, and her only remaining debt is a car loan in the amount of $10,000. She rents a modest one-bedroom apartment that costs her $550 per month, and she feels that she can live comfortably on $1,500 a month. Discuss what her primary investment objectives should focus on, and discuss what type of investment mix she should consider.

- **Personal Evaluation**: Brigid has steady employment, with good earnings potential and an employee registered retirement plan. She has good control over her debt situation and likely has room to borrow additional funds if necessary (for investment, housing, or consumption purposes). If we assume she is adequately insured and that she has no immediate plans to purchase a house, it is reasonable to assume that she is in a position to start investing for retirement. Given the fact that she has quickly paid off her student loan and has not borrowed a great deal of additional funds, it may be reasonable to assume she has a fairly conservative attitude toward managing her finances. In addition, the fact that she has not invested in RRSPs at all suggests that she may not be an extremely knowledgeable investor. Alternatively, it may signal that she is extremely conservative and wishes to pay off her debt first, even at the expense of foregoing the tax deduction benefits associated with RRSP contributions.
- **Investment Objectives**: Her primary investment objective should be *growth*, since she should generate more than sufficient income in the coming years to satisfy her cash flow requirements, and since retirement is some years away. Her secondary objectives would be *tax minimization* and *safety* since she is likely to be in the moderate-to-high tax bracket in the coming years, and since she appears to have a fairly conservative attitude toward managing her finances.
- **Investment Strategy**, Brigid's first move should be to take full advantage of her available RRSP contribution limit, which should be substantial due to the carryover amounts available from previous years. This will minimize her tax obligations, and the funds placed in RRSPs should be primarily invested in growth equities to satisfy her primary investment objective of growth. In order to maintain sufficient portfolio diversification, and in light of her apparent conservative disposition, she may want to maintain 5%–10% in money market funds and an additional 10%–20% in fixed-income securities. Once she has exhausted her RRSP contribution limits, she may want to invest additional funds into more aggressive equity funds with long-term growth potential, since capital gains will be realized only when the shares are sold and given the preferential tax treatment associated with any dividends received in the interim.

Case 2: Brennan and Angela

- **Situation:** Brennan and Angela have been married for 25 years and their children, Jason and Siobhan, are grown up and on their own. Angela and Brennan are both 53 years old and both of them have been teaching high school at the same school for the past 30 years. They both earn $62,000 per year and they plan to retire in five years. Each of them has invested $3,000 per year in RRSPs for the past 20 years, allocating approximately 20% to money market funds and the remaining 80% to growth equity funds. They have both also contributed to the CPP and teachers' pension plan for the past 30 years. They recently finished paying off the mortgage on their home, which they plan to live in on retirement, and their only remaining debt is a car loan in the amount of $20,000. They feel they can live comfortably on $2,800 a month after retirement.

- Questions:
  1. Do there appear to be any opportunities for this couple to reduce taxes by using "income-splitting" strategies? Briefly explain.
  2. Identify and briefly discuss what their primary investment objectives should focus on and identify any secondary objectives you feel are relevant.
  3. Prescribe and justify an appropriate investment mix for this couple.
  4. Recommend two options available to them if they decide to deregister their RRSPs immediately upon retirement.
- Suggested Answers:
  1. No, they both earn the same amount now and likely will until retirement; therefore, they are likely in the same tax bracket. In addition, they both have contributed about the same amount to registered plans, hence their income (and tax brackets) will remain virtually identical upon retirement.
  2. They are both in the "peak earnings" stage of their life cycle and preservation of capital should be their primary objective, since they plan on retiring in the near future. Since they are in a high tax bracket, tax minimization should be a secondary objective.
  3. They should begin "adjusting" their asset mix toward safer securities. Many mixes are possible. For example, an appropriate target might be 20% cash (money market instruments), 40% fixed-income securities, and 40% equities (primarily "blue chip" equities).
  4. They could use the proceeds to purchase a life annuity with a guaranteed term or a fixed-term annuity that provides benefits to age 90. Alternatively, or coincidently, they could purchase a Registered Retirement Income Fund (RRIF), which provides annual income to age 90 or life. These strategies avoid paying tax on the full amount, which would occur if the full amounts were withdrawn on deregistration of the plan.

Chapter 26 Review Questions

( ) 1. The following represent desirable objectives for a financial plan EXCEPT:

a) It covers necessities.

b) It is designed primarily to minimize taxes.

c) It accommodates small lifestyle changes.

d) It is not intimidating.

2. According to the life cycle approach to financial planning, investors in the ______________ stage should focus primarily on ______________. ( )

   a) early earning years; growth
   b) peak earning years; tax minimization
   c) mid-earning years; income
   d) retirement years; liquidity

3. Which of the following is a primary ethical value in the Code of Ethics established by the securities industry? ( )

   a) Registrants must not solicit business through channels other than those stipulated in the securities act(s).
   b) Registrants must use proper care and exercise independent professional judgment.
   c) Registrants must act quickly to ensure that all client accounts are settled by the required date.
   d) Registrants must never assure their clients that a particular security price or return will be guaranteed in the future.

4. Which of the following statements best describes a fiduciary relationship? ( )

   a) They are agent-principal relationships where the principal is vulnerable and the agent has greater expertise or authority.
   b) They are agent-principal relationships where the agent is vulnerable and the principal has greater expertise or authority.
   c) They are agent-principal relationships where the principal needs the moral and ethical guidance of the agent.
   d) They are agency-principal relationships where the agent needs the moral and ethical guidance of the principal.

5. Financial advisors are required to know the essential details about each client, which include: ( )

   I. the client's current financial status
   II. the client's current personal status
   III. the client's risk tolerance
   IV. the client's investment goals and preferences

   a) I, II, III, IV
   b) I, II, IV
   c) I, II, III
   d) II, III, IV

Bonus Questions

( ) 6. At a minimum, what client information are advisors required to know?

a) current financial and personal status
b) investment goals
c) risk tolerance
d) all of the above

( ) 7. Analyzing a client's investment knowledge, risk tolerance, and investing time horizon is best described as being part of which step of the financial planning process?

a) establishing the client-advisor relationship
b) collecting data and information
c) analyzing data and information
d) none of the above

( ) 8. Which category is highest on the financial planning pyramid?

a) independence
b) investment
c) security
d) luxury

( ) 9. According to the securities industry's Code of Ethics, it is important that financial advisors comply with the:

a) spirit of the law
b) letter of the law
c) both (a) and (b)
d) neither (a) nor (b)

( ) 10. Which of the following is NOT included in the securities industry standards of conduct?

a) due diligence
b) compliance with securities acts and SRO rules
c) priority of client's interests
d) personal relationships

chapter 27

WORKING WITH THE INSTITUTIONAL CLIENT

CSC EXAM SUGGESTED GUIDELINES:
3 questions for Chapter 27

WHO ARE INSTITUTIONAL CLIENTS?

1. Corporate Treasuries

Responsible for the management of a firm's financial assets. Duties include funding decisions, investing decisions, risk management activities such as foreign currency hedging, etc. They often work with broker dealers, investment bankers, and custodians.

2. Insurance Companies

Accept premiums from policyholders and manage these funds in a manner that ensures payout on policies when necessary. They tend to invest heavily in bonds since income and safety are primary investing objectives. They also invest in equities for growth potential, but they are limited in the exposure to equities.

3. Pension Funds

A pool of assets that is managed to provide beneficiaries with their prescribed payments when they retire. They tend to have very long investment horizons and invest in a mix of equities and fixed-income products, as well as more sophisticated products such as infrastructure.

4. Mutual Funds

As discussed in Chapters 18 and 19, mutual funds have a wide variety of investing objectives and therefore assets they invest in.

5. Hedge Funds

As discussed in Chapter 21, hedge funds have a wide variety of investing objectives and therefore assets they invest in.

6. Endowments

A pool of assets that is managed to provide gifts and donations (such as scholarships). They tend to have very long (i.e., infinite) investment horizons and invest in a mix of equities and fixed-income products.

7. Trusts

Similar to endowments in that they are pools of assets that are managed to provide benefits for designated beneficiaries. Often set up by wealthy individuals and/or as a method of tax planning. They tend to have short to very long horizons, depending on their stated purpose. They tend to invest in a mix of equities and fixed-income products.

SUITABILITY REQUIREMENTS FOR INSTITUTIONAL INVESTORS

! **Suitability requirements** are much more stringent for retail (i.e., Know Your Client) than institutional clients, who by their nature are assumed more sophisticated.

! The "know your client" requirements for retail investors do not apply if the client is a **permitted client**. Permitted clients include the large institutions discussed above, as well individuals (including holding companies and trusts) with more than $5 million in net financial assets, or a person with more than $25 million in net assets.

! IIROC suggests that for such investors, the dealer member need only determine that the investor is sophisticated enough to make their own investment decisions, then they are not responsible for determining the "suitability" of products or services they provide them. They can make this determination by considering the following points:

- examine written or oral agreements with them;
- presence or absence of a pattern of accepting or rejecting the dealer member's advice;
- use of other info by client in making their decisions;
- the use of more than one dealer member;
- their general level of experience in financial markets;
- their experience with the particular product; and
- the complexity of the product involved.

ROLES AND RESPONSIBILITIES IN THE INSTITUTIONAL MARKET

Some key positions in the institutional market include

1. Research Associates (or associate analysts)—provide research reports for/with the analyst. Typically have an MBA, CFA, or CA.
2. Analysts—sell side or research analyst. Often focus on particular sectors and/or products.
3. Institutional Sales—serve as relationship managers with clients. Tend to be more generalists than analysts, although many have MBAs or CFA designation.
4. Institutional Traders—execute orders on behalf of clients and/or their member firms.
5. Investment Bankers—important in three areas: (a) Corporate Finance; (b) Public Finance; and (c) Mergers & Acquisitions. The various positions: (a) Analysts and Associates—analytical work; (b) Vice-Presidents and Associate Directors—day-to-day management; and (c) Managing Directors—strategic direction.

Institutional Salespersons perform the following key tasks:

1. Build and maintain strong client relationships.
2. Work at dealer with good research and/or investment banking services.
3. Have sound knowledge of firm products and capital market factors that affect their products and services.

Accounts are generally divided (1) geographically; (2) by account type; and/or (3) by relationships.

Institutional Traders are generally of two types:

1. Agency Traders—trade only on behalf of "clients," not for the firm. They face formal client responsibilities in their trading decisions.
2. Liability Traders—trade on behalf of the firm. Less in terms of client responsibilities, but are bound by the firm's trading guidelines.

Chapter 27 Review Questions

1. ____________ are pools of assets that are managed to provide benefits for designated beneficiaries, and are often set up by wealthy individuals. ( )

a) Endowments
b) Pensions
c) Trusts
d) Hedge funds

( ) 2. Permitted clients include all of the following EXCEPT:

a) pension funds
b) insurance companies
c) trusts with more than $5 million in net financial assets
d) individuals with more than $5 million in net assets

( ) 3. Traders that trade on behalf of their member firm are referred to as:

a) agency traders
b) liability traders
c) neither (a) nor (b)
d) both (a) and (b)

Bonus Questions

( ) 4. The following institutional investors always have very long time horizons EXCEPT for:

a) pensions
b) endowments
c) trusts
d) foundations

( ) 5. An advisor would be exempt from determining the "suitability" of products or services for an investor if :

a) they never used additional information provided by other investment professional in making their decisions
b) they regularly used more than one dealer member for their financial dealings
c) they had never used this particular product before
d) the level of complexity of the product involved was high

( ) 6. ____________ provide reports for analysts.

a) Institutional salespeople
b) Research associates
c) Liability traders
d) Agency traders

END-OF-CHAPTER REVIEW QUESTIONS

ANSWERS

Answers to End-of-Chapter Review Questions

Question	Answer	Level of Difficulty
CHAPTER 1		
1	B	M
2	A	M
3	C	M
4	C	E
5	B	E
6	B	M
7	C	E
8	C	M
9	C	E
10	C	E
11	D	D
12	A	E
CHAPTER 2		
1	B	D
2	A	E
3	A	D
4	C	E
5	B	E
6	B	M
CHAPTER 3		
1	D	E
2	B	M
3	D	E
4	B	M
5	C	M
6	C	M
7	D	E
8	B	M
9	B	M
10	C	M
11	A	M
12	D	D

Question	Answer	Level of Difficulty
CHAPTER 4		
1	D	M
2	D	E
3	D	M
4	B	M
5	B	M
6	C	D
7	B	M
8	B 7.05% – 3.24% = 3.81%	M
9	D	M
10	C	E
11	C	M
12	A	M
13	D	M
14	A	E
15	C	M
16	B	M
CHAPTER 5		
1	A	M
2	C	M
3	B	D
4	C	D
5	B	M
6	C	E
7	B	E
8	C	E
9	D	M
10	B	D
11	D	M
12	B	M
CHAPTER 6		
1	A	M
2	C	M
3	A	E

Question	Answer	Level of Difficulty
4	A	M
5	B	M
6	D	M
7	C	M
8	B	M
9	C	E
10	D	M
11	A	E
12	B	D
13	C	E
14	B	M
15	C	M
16	A	E
17	B	M
18	B	M
19	D	M
20	A	M
21	D	M
22	B	D
23	D	M

CHAPTER 7

1	C	E
2	C (10 + [100 – 113.4]/10)/([100 + 113.4]/2) = 8.12%	D
3	A (100 – 96)/96 × (365/90) × 100% = 16.9%	M
4	A Price = 50 × ([1 – 1/{1.042}^{28}]/.042) + 1,000 × (1/[1.042]^{28}) = 814.27 + 316.01 = $1,130.28	D
5	C	M
6	C Accrued interest = $1,000 × 0.10 × 39/365 = $10.68	D
7	C	M
8	C	M
9	B	M

Question	Answer	Level of Difficulty
10	B	M
11	D Purchase price = \$1,035 + (31/365 × \$75) = \$1,041.37	D
12	C	E
13	B	D
14	D	D
15	C	M
16	B	M
17	B	M
18	C	M
19	B	M
20	B	E
21	C	D
22	D	M

CHAPTER 8

1	B	E
2	B Premium % = (35 – [3 × 11])/(3 × 11) = 6.1%	M
3	C Common yield = 0.22/\$11 = 2.0%	M
4	D Preferred yield = 2/35 = 5.7 %; payback = 6.1/(5.7 – 2.0) = 1.65 years	D
5	B	E
6	A	M
7	B	M
8	C	M
9	B	M
10	B	M
11	D	M
12	C	E
13	B	D
14	C	M
15	B	E
16	D	M
17	B	M
18	D	E

Question	Answer	Level of Difficulty
19	C	M
20	A	E
21	B	M
22	A	E
23	C	M
24	A	E
25	D	D
26	C	M

CHAPTER 9

1	D	M
2	C Cost = \$1.50 × 500 = \$750; Max. loan = 0.20 × \$750 = \$150; required deposit = \$750 – \$150 = \$600	M
3	D No loan is permissible; therefore, deposit \$150, which when added to the initial deposit of \$600, covers the \$750 purchase price.	M
4	A Require 130% of market value = \$8 × 1,000 × 1.30 = \$10,400; required deposit = \$10,400 – \$8,000 (proceeds) = \$2,400	M
5	D Require 130% of \$7,000 = \$9,100; required deposit = \$9,100 – \$10,400 = –\$1,300 (surplus funds that can be withdrawn)	D
6	A Profit = (\$8 – \$5) × \$1,000 = \$3,000	M
7	D	M
8	B	E
9	C	D
10	D	D
11	A	M
12	D	M
13	C	M
14	B	D

Question	Answer	Level of Difficulty
15	C	D
16	D	M
17	C	M
18	A	E
19	C	M
20	B	M

CHAPTER 10

1	A	E
2	A	M
3	C Call: IV = Max (12 – 15, 0) = 0 Put: IV = Max ($16 – 12, 0) = 4	M
4	A ([$1 × 100] – ($3 × 100]) + (0 – [$4.50 × 100]) Total loss = (–200 – 450) = –$650	D
5	A IV = Max (10 – 12, 0) = 0	M
6	C Time value = 3 – 0 = 3	M
7	C	M
8	D IV = (40 – 35)/(4 + 1) = $1.00	M
9	C IV = (38 – 35)/4 = $0.75	M
10	A	M
11	B	E
12	A	M
13	B	E
14	C	M
15	D	E
16	C	E
17	A	M
18	B	M
19	A	E
20	B	M

CHAPTER 11

1	D	M
2	B	M

Question	Answer	Level of Difficulty
3	B	M
4	C	M
5	D	D
6	B	M
7	D	M
8	A	E
9	B	E
10	C	M
11	C	M
12	B	E
13	C	M
14	C	M

CHAPTER 12

1	C	D
2	A	M
3	A Amortization (year 1) = \$50,000 × 0.10 = \$5,000; amortization (year 2) = \$45,000 × 0.10 = \$4,500	D
4	D	M
5	D	E
6	A	M
7	B	E
8	C	E
9	B	M
10	D	E
11	C	E
12	C	E
13	B	M
14	C	D
15	B	M
16	C	M

CHAPTER 13

1	C	M
2	D	M
3	A	E

Question	Answer	Level of Difficulty
4	A Div^1 = 0.375 × \$4.00 = \$1.50; Intrinsic value = \$1.50/(.11 – 0.5) = \$25.00	D
5	B Payout = 2/5 = 0.40; P/E = 0.40/(.12 – 0.4) = 5.0	D
6	D	M
7	B	M
8	D	M
9	D	M
10	B r = (4.00/50) + .04 = 0.12 or 12%	M
11	A	M
12	C	M
13	C	E
14	D	M
15	A	E
16	D	M
17	A	M
18	C	M
19	D	M
20	D	M
21	B	M
22	C	M
23	B	M
24	B	M

CHAPTER 14

1	C	M
2	C (10,000 + 5,000 + 35,000)/(100,000) = 0.50	M
3	B (85,000)/(20,000) = \$4.25	M
4	C EPS = (7,000 – 1,500)/20,000 = \$0.275, so P/E = (10)/(0.275) = 36.4	D
5	B Coverage = 25,000/10,000 = 2.50	D
6	D	M
7	A	M
8	C (365 days/25 = 14.6 days)	M

Question	Answer	Level of Difficulty
9	C	D
10	A	M
11	D	M
12	C	M
13	C	M
14	C	E
15	A	M
16	D	E
17	C	M
18	D	M
19	B	E
20	B	M
21	A	E
22	B	E

CHAPTER 15

1	C (.07 × [$20,000/90,000]) + (.12 × [$25,000/90,000]) + (.15 × [$45,000/90,000]) = 12.39%	M
2	C (90,000 × 1.1239) = $101,151	D
3	D ([1.5 × 2] + [21 – 18])/18 = 33.3%	D
4	D	E
5	D	E
6	B	M
7	B	E
8	B	M
9	B	M
10	D	M
11	C	E
12	D	M
13	B	M
14	A	E
15	C	M
16	B	E
17	C	M

Question	Answer	Level of Difficulty
18	C	M
19	C	M
20	D	E
21	B	M
22	A	E
23	B	M
24	B	M

CHAPTER 16

1	D All are possible—you would need to know more about risk preferences.	M
2	C	M
3	D	M
4	A	M
5	C	M
6	C	D
7	D	M
8	A	M
9	B	M
10	C	M
11	B	E
12	A	M
13	C	M
14	D	E
15	C	E
16	D	M
17	A	E
18	D	M
19	C	M
20	D	E
21	B	M
22	C	M
23	D	M
24	A	E

Question	Answer	Level of Difficulty
CHAPTER 17		
1	D	M
2	C	M
3	C	M
4	B	M
CHAPTER 18		
1	D Offering price = \$40/ (1 – 0.6) = \$42.55	M
2	C	M
3	A	E
4	C	M
5	A	E
6	C	M
7	C	M
8	B	M
9	C	M
10	D	E
11	D	M
12	B	M
13	A	M
14	C	M
15	C	M
16	C	M
17	C	M
18	B \$4,000 – (.15) (\$4,000) – (.15) (\$4,000) – (.30) (\$4,000) = \$1,600	D
CHAPTER 19		
1	D	M
2	B	M
3	B	M
4	B	E
5	A	M
6	B	E
7	C	M
8	A	M

Question	Answer	Level of Difficulty
9	B	E
10	C	E
11	D	D
12	A	M
CHAPTER 20		
1	C	E
2	A	M
3	A	M
4	A $145,000 – $100,000 = $45,000 taxable capital gain	M
5	C Since the capital gain on the guarantee of $22,000 cancels out the capital loss, no taxes are payable.	D
6	B	M
7	B	M
8	C	D
9	D	M
10	A	M
CHAPTER 21		
1	C	M
2	B	E
3	D	E
4	A	E
5	B	M
6	C	D
7	D	M
8	B	M
CHAPTER 22		
1	D	M
2	B	M
3	A	M
4	C	M
5	A	M

Question	Answer	Level of Difficulty
6	B	M
7	D	M
8	A	E
9	B	M
10	C	M

CHAPTER 23

1	B	M
2	C	M
3	D	M
4	C	E

CHAPTER 24

1	C	M
2	A	E
3	D	M
4	B	E
5	B	M
6	C	M
7	C	M
8	B	M
9	D	M
10	B	M

CHAPTER 25

1	A XYZ = ([$7,500/300]/2.5) = $10 per common share	D
2	A This is a superficial loss.	M
3	C XYZ = {(([$200 × $20] + $60) + ([300 × $25]) + $ 100}/500 = (4,060 + 7,600) /500 = $23.32 per share	D
4	A Taxes payable = ($200 × 1.45 [0.29] – [290 × .19] = $29.00	D
5	C	M
6	D	M
7	D	M
8	C	E

Question	Answer	Level of Difficulty
9	C	D
10	A	M
11	D	M
12	C	M
13	A	D
14	D	D

CHAPTER 26

1	B	E
2	A	E
3	B	M
4	A	M
5	A	M
6	D	M
7	C	M
8	B	M
9	C	M
10	D	D

CHAPTER 27

1	C	M
2	D	M
3	B	E
4	C	M
5	B	M
6	B	E

EXAM #1

CSC PRACTICE EXAMINATION

CHAPTERS 1–12

( ) 1. Primary markets involve ____________, while secondary markets involve ____________.

a) the sale of securities; the sale of derivatives
b) the sale of new securities to investors; trading of previously issued securities among investors
c) the sale of securities of large corporations on stock exchanges; the sale of securities of smaller firms between individual investors
d) trading of securities on stock exchanges; trading of securities between investors using a dealer as an agent

( ) 2. Bearer bonds differ from registered bonds in that bearer bonds:

a) have the name of the owner on the face of the bond, while registered bonds are considered to be owned by the actual holder
b) have no maturity date
c) are considered to be owned by the actual holder of the bond, while registered bonds have the name of the owner on the face of the bonds
d) have no coupon payments

( ) 3. The Canadian Investor Protection Fund (CIPF) covers the personal losses of an investor's position:

a) for securities holdings only
b) for cash holdings only
c) for both securities and cash holdings
d) related to adverse market movements

( ) 4. The minority interest item on a balance sheet arises from the use of the ____________ of accounting.

a) consolidation method
b) cost method
c) FIFO method
d) equity method

( ) 5. ____________ is (are) an example of a leading business cycle indicator.

a) Business investment spending
b) Housing starts
c) Labour costs
d) Inflation levels

( ) 6. The ____________ sits on the board of directors for the Bank of Canada (B of C), but has no voting rights.

a) Governor of the B of C
b) Senior Deputy Governor of the B of C

c) Minister of Finance

d) Deputy Minister of Finance

7. During periods of rising prices, the ____________ method of inventory valuation will lead to the highest profits. ( )

a) LIFO

b) FIFO

c) average cost

d) equity

8. GDP will exceed GNP if: ( )

a) the value of all goods and services produced by the country's nationals exceeds the value of all goods produced within a country in a year

b) the value of all goods and services produced by the country's nationals is less than the value of all goods produced within a country in a year

c) GDP will never exceed GNP

d) none of the above

9. During a period of declining interest rates, which of the following bonds would an investor prefer to hold, assuming they are from the same issuer? ( )

a) 5-year, 10% coupon non-callable bonds

b) 10-year, 10% coupon non-callable bonds

c) 10-year, 10% coupon callable bonds

d) 10-year, non-callable strip bonds

10. The settlement date for Government of Canada treasury bills is the ____________ the transaction. ( )

a) second clearing day after

b) third clearing day after

c) same day as

d) next clearing day after

11. The maximum loan amount by investment dealers to clients for the purchase of shares with a market price of $1.50 per share is: ( )

a) no loans are permissible

b) 20%

c) 40%

d) 50%

12. If a prospectus contains a misrepresentation, security purchasers have the right of: ( )

a) rescission

b) withdrawal

c) limited liability
d) due diligence

( ) 13. When a security offering requires an offering memorandum rather than a full prospectus, it is generally known as a(n) ____________ offering.
a) initial public
b) private
c) final
d) seasoned

( ) 14. Auction markets are characterized as:
a) a market where buyers and sellers of securities converge to trade with one another
b) a network of dealers who trade with each other over the phone or a computer network
c) always having more buyers than sellers
d) a market without a marketplace

( ) 15. You decide to purchase 10 board lots of the common shares of company A on margin. The share is NOT eligible for special margin and is presently trading for $2. How much cash must you deposit with your broker?
a) $800
b) $1,000
c) $1,400
d) $2,000

( ) 16. Refer to the information given in Question 15. If the price of A dropped immediately to $1.80, how much will you be required to deposit into your margin account?
a) $280
b) $720
c) $1,280
d) There is no need to deposit more into the account, but rather you are eligible to withdraw $280.

( ) 17. A friend of yours decides to short sell 1,000 shares of a security that is NOT eligible for special margin and is trading at $5. What amount must she deposit into a margin account?
a) $1,500
b) $2,500
c) $5,000
d) $6,500

18. Refer to the information given in Question 17. What profit (loss) does your friend realize if she closes her short position when the price of the underlying share is $4? ( )

a) profit of $1,000

b) loss of $1,000

c) profit of $2,500

d) loss of $2,500

19. Which one of the following statements concerning the actions of dealers acting as principals in the secondary market is FALSE? ( )

a) They buy and sell from their own inventory.

b) They bear price risk.

c) They tend to reduce the liquidity of the market.

d) Their transactions are conducted principally OTC.

20. The chief difference between a warrant and a right is that: ( )

a) A warrant is generally long term and is issued to enable new funds to be raised immediately, while a right is generally short term and is usually attached to another issue as a sweetener.

b) A warrant is generally long term and is usually attached to another issue as a sweetener, while a right is generally short term and is issued to enable new funds to be raised immediately.

c) A warrant is generally short term and is usually attached to another issue as a sweetener, while a right is generally long term and is issued to enable new funds to be raised immediately.

d) A warrant is generally short term and is issued to enable new funds to be raised immediately, while a right is generally long term and is usually attached to another issue as a sweetener.

21. Unemployment that rises when the economy softens and drops when the economy strengthens again is known as: ( )

a) structural unemployment

b) cyclical unemployment

c) natural unemployment

d) accelerating unemployment

22. ____________ options are primarily European style. ( )

a) Equity

b) Currency

c) Stock index

d) Bond

( ) 23. The Liquidity Preference Theory states that:

a) Investors prefer longer-term bonds to shorter-term bonds because they exhibit less interest rate risk.

b) Investors must be compensated for investing in shorter-term bonds.

c) Investors prefer shorter-term bonds to longer-term bonds because they exhibit less interest rate risk.

d) Investors prefer to invest in stocks instead of bonds.

( ) 24. ____________ orders are executed only if a specific price or better can be obtained.

a) Limit

b) Market

c) Stop-buy

d) Stop-loss

( ) 25. ____________ orders are used to limit losses on short positions.

a) Limit

b) Stop-buy

c) Good Till Cancelled

d) Stop-boss

( ) 26. Medium-sized banks are:

a) owned wholly by residents

b) owned wholly by non-residents

c) owned *only* partially by either residents or non-residents

d) both (a) and (b)

( ) 27. Which of the following is NOT a major use of investment capital?

a) direct investment in land

b) direct investment in equipment

c) indirect investment in financial assets

d) none of the above

( ) 28. The following are all major capital account components EXCEPT for:

a) direct investment

b) international reserves transactions

c) transfers

d) portfolio investment

Refer to the following information to answer Questions 29 to 32:

A firm presently has $100 million (face value) in non-callable bonds outstanding. They pay annual coupons at a rate of 7% and the bonds will mature six years from today.

29. What is the present market price of the bonds if the yield to maturity on identical bonds is 8%? ( )

a) $88.91 million
b) $95.38 million
c) $96.89 million
d) $102.42 million

30. Under which of the following cases would the price of the bond be lower? ( )

a) if the bond was callable
b) if the bond was extendible
c) if the bond was convertible
d) if the bond was retractable

31. What would be an investor's one-year pre-tax percentage return on these bonds if they were purchased at a 5% premium over face value and resold after one year, when the yield on the bonds was 7%? ( )

a) –1.3%
b) 1.9%
c) 7.9%
d) not enough information to answer this question

32. What is the accrued interest on these bonds 120 days after the last coupon date? ( )

a) $2.301 million
b) $2.129 million
c) $1.899 million
d) not enough information to answer this question

Refer to the following information to answer Questions 33 to 35:

A convertible preferred share is presently selling for $40 and is convertible into two common shares that are presently selling for $18.50 each. The annual dividends are $2.00 for the preferred shares, and $0.45 for the common shares.

33. What is the conversion premium percentage? ( )

a) 7.85%
b) 7.90%
c) 8.11%
d) 8.25%

34. What is the dividend yield on the preferred shares? ( )

a) 1.1%
b) 2.4%

c) 5.0%
d) 10.8%

( ) 35. What is the payback for these convertibles?

a) 1.62 years
b) 3.16 years
c) 3.33 years
d) not enough information to answer this question

( ) 36. What is the main difference between collateral trust bonds and equipment trust certificates?

a) Equipment trust certificates are secured by a pledge of financial assets, while collateral trust bonds are secured by rolling stock.
b) Collateral trust bonds are long term, while equipment trust certificates are for less than one year.
c) Collateral trust bonds are short term, while equipment trust certificates are long term.
d) Equipment trust certificates are secured by rolling stock, while collateral trust bonds are secured by a pledge of financial assets.

( ) 37. The following protective provisions place restrictions on additional borrowings by a corporation EXCEPT the ____________.

a) after-acquired clause
b) closed-end mortgage
c) open-end mortgage with restrictive provisions
d) the sinking fund clause

Refer to the following information to answer Questions 38 and 39:

You decide to purchase common shares of two companies on margin. The first share (X) is eligible for special margin and is presently trading for $12, while the second share (Y) is trading at $1.80.

( ) 38. What is your total margin requirement if you purchase 1,000 shares of X and 1,000 shares of Y?

a) $2,340
b) $4,500
c) $4,680
d) $5,900

( ) 39. If the price of X increases immediately to $12.75 and the price of Y falls rapidly to $1.40, how much (if any) will you be required to deposit in your margin account?

a) $0
b) $195

c) $1,800

d) able to withdraw $205

40. What is the difference between direct obligation and guaranteed obligation debt securities? ( )

a) Direct obligation bonds are issued in the name of a Crown corporation, while guaranteed obligation bonds are issued by the government.

b) Direct obligation bonds are issued by the federal government, while guaranteed bonds are issued by provincial governments.

c) Direct obligation bonds are issued by the provincial government, while guaranteed bonds are issued by the federal government.

d) Direct obligation bonds are issued by the government, while guaranteed bonds are issued in the name of a Crown corporation but backed by the provincial government.

41. The following are all advantages to issuing preferred shares EXCEPT for: ( )

a) does not affect debt-equity ratio adversely

b) greater financing flexibility

c) dividends are paid from after-tax earnings

d) none of the above

42. What is the yield on a 190-day Government of Canada treasury bill that is priced at 99.45? ( )

a) 1.06%

b) 2.19%

c) 66.37%

d) not enough information to answer this question

43. What is the yield to maturity on a 10% bond that pays out coupons semi-annually and has 10 years to maturity if the bond is selling at par? ( )

a) 8.31%

b) 10.0%

c) 13.4%

d) not enough information to answer this question

44. The following is an example of a Eurobond: ( )

a) A Canadian corporation issues bonds denominated in Euros in the German market.

b) The U.S. government issues bonds denominated in Swiss francs in the Swiss market.

c) A Japanese firm issues bonds denominated in euros in the Italian market.

d) An Australian company issues bonds denominated in Canadian dollars in the Belgian market.

( ) 45. The primary difference between a futures contract and a forward contract is that:

a) Forward contracts are not standardized.

b) Futures contracts are not standardized.

c) Futures contracts are the OTC equivalent of forward contracts.

d) There is no difference between the two.

( ) 46. Which of the following statements is true of non-competitive bids?

a) Non-competitive bids must be in multiples of $5,000, with a minimum of $250,000 per bid, no maximum amount per bid.

b) Non-competitive bids must be in multiples of $50,000, with a minimum of $250,000 per bid, no maximum amount per bid.

c) Non-competitive bids must be in multiples of $50,000, with a minimum of $100,000 per bid, and a maximum of $500,000 per bid.

d) Non-competitive bids must be in multiples of $1,000, with a minimum of $25,000 per bid, and a maximum of $3 million per bidder.

( ) 47. The difference between an AON buy order and an any part buy order is

a) An any part order is usually at a specific price and remains on the dealer's books until the order is executed or cancelled, while an AON order is one that is good for a specified number of days and then is automatically cancelled if it hasn't been filled.

b) An AON order is usually at a specific price and remains on the dealer's books until the order is executed or cancelled, while an any part order is one that is good for a specified number of days and then is automatically cancelled if it hasn't been filled.

c) An any part order is an order in which the client will accept all stock in odd, broken, or board lots up to the full amount of the order, while an AON order is one in which the total number of shares as specified in the order must be purchased before the client will accept the fill.

d) An AON order is an order in which the client will accept all stock in odd, broken, or board lots up to the full amount of the order, while an any part order is one in which the total number of shares as specified in the order must be purchased before the client will accept the fill.

( ) 48. When is it appropriate to use the consolidated accounting method?

a) when the parent company owns less than 20% of a subsidiary

b) when the parent company owns between 20% and 50% of a subsidiary

c) when the parent company owns more than 50% of the voting shares of a subsidiary

d) none of the above

49. What are the major functions of the Bank of Canada? ( )
 I. act as the government's fiscal agent
 II. regulate credit and currency in the best interests of the country
 III. conduct monetary policy
 IV. control and protect the external value of the national monetary unit
 V. act for the government in the issuance and removal of bank notes
 a) I, II, III
 b) II, IV
 c) I, III, V
 d) I, II, III, IV, V

50. Which of the following is NOT a characteristic of capital? ( )
 a) It is sensitive to its environment.
 b) It is in short supply.
 c) It is mobile.
 d) It is insensitive to risk-adjusted returns.

51. Which of the following statements concerning dividends is FALSE? ( )
 a) The last day that a stock trades cum dividend is the third business day prior to the dividend record date.
 b) Automatically reinvesting dividends into additional shares is referred to as a dividend reinvestment plan.
 c) Dividend reinvestment plans allow shareholders to invest small sums of money and avoid high commissions.
 d) Stock dividends are taxed as capital gains in Canada and therefore investors prefer them to cash dividends.

52. Three advantages of incorporation are: ( )
 a) ease of ownership transfer, professional management, and double taxation
 b) loss of flexibility, the possibility of double taxation, and additional administrative costs
 c) limited liability of shareholders, continuity of existence, and ease of ownership transfer
 d) management flexibility, complications involving withdrawal of capital, and possible tax benefits

Use the following information to answer Questions 53 and 54.

A company has issued warrants which are presently outstanding. One warrant is required to purchase one common share. The common share price is presently $20, the warrant price is $3, and the exercise price of the warrant is $22.

( ) 53. The intrinsic value and time value of one warrant is:

a) $3 and $0, respectively
b) $2 and $19, respectively
c) $2 and $3, respectively
d) $0 and $3, respectively

( ) 54. The leverage potential of the warrant is:

a) 0.67
b) 1.1
c) 6.67
d) 7.33

( ) 55. A dealer market ____________, while an auction market is ____________.

a) is designed for the primary markets; where securities in the secondary markets are traded
b) is where all transactions converge to one location; a network of dealers who trade by phone or computer network
c) is where institutions trade; designed for individual investors
d) consists of a network of dealers who trade with each other over the phone or over a computer network; where all transactions converge to one location

( ) 56. Restricted shares differ from common shares in that they:

a) are entitled to earnings only after common dividends have been paid
b) rank behind common shares in liquidation
c) have little or no voting power in corporate matters
d) all of the above are differences between restricted and common shares

( ) 57. The ____________ refers to the price at which an investor can buy a stock and the ____________ refers to the price at which an investor can sell a stock.

a) bid; ask
b) ask; bid
c) open; close
d) low; high

( ) 58. What factors below influence interest rates?

a) political stability, unemployment rate, demand and supply of capital, inflation, and economy's performance
b) unemployment rate, current account, inflation differentials, default risk, central bank creditability, and the exchange rate

c) inflation, demand and supply of capital, default risk, central bank creditability, central bank operations, and the exchange rate
d) inflation, the exchange rate, political stability, default risk, interest rate differentials, and unemployment rate

59. If a nation is running a fiscal deficit, it is: ( )
a) worse off as the result of its trade with foreign countries
b) encountering a balance of payments disequilibrium
c) spending more on goods and services than it is raising in tax revenues
d) importing more goods and services than it is exporting

60. Which member of IIROC is a joint venture between Canada's six largest investment dealers? ( )
a) CBID
b) CanDeal
c) CanPX
d) none of the above

61. What are the five phases of the business cycle in the correct order? ( )
a) recession, peak, contraction, recovery, expansion
b) peak, recession, recovery, trough, expansion
c) expansion, trough, recession, recovery, peak
d) expansion, peak, recession, trough, recovery

62. Higher interest rates affect the economy in all of the following ways EXCEPT: ( )
a) They raise the cost of borrowing for investment purposes.
b) They discourage consumers from spending capital on items such as durable goods.
c) They reduce available household income because of the higher proportion of income that is needed to service debt.
d) All of the above are effects of higher interest rates.

63. Which of the following statements about investment funds is FALSE? ( )
a) Closed-end funds issue shares at start-up and other infrequent periods.
b) Closed-end funds always trade at large discounts to their net asset value.
c) Open-end funds issue shares regularly throughout their life.
d) Redemption of open-end funds is done on demand and at the net asset value.

Refer to the following bond quote to answer Questions 64 and 65:

XYZ Company	6.00%	1 July 19/24	100.50	101.20	5.94

( ) 64. Which of the following statements regarding this bond is FALSE?

a) It is a retractable bond.
b) It is an extendable bond.
c) It pays coupons on July 1 and January 1 every year.
d) None of the above.

( ) 65. If you were to sell this bond on the date this quote was available, and the date was February 9, how much would you receive from the buyer of the bond?

a) $1,005
b) $1,011.58
c) $1,012
d) $1,018.58

( ) 66. The underwriting expenses associated with a debt issue are usually ______________ those associated with common equity issues.

a) similar to
b) lower than
c) greater than
d) unrelated to

( ) 67. Governments issue debt for the following reasons EXCEPT:

a) to fund deficits
b) to develop income-producing services
c) to increase working capital
d) to fund infrastructure projects

( ) 68. ______________ is an example of a coincident business cycle indicator.

a) Business investment spending
b) Housing starts
c) Retail sales
d) Inflation levels

( ) 69. The bank rate is set at which of the following levels?

a) the yield on three-month T-bills plus 0.25%
b) the upper limit of the Bank's operating band for the overnight rate

c) the lower limit of the Bank's operating band for the overnight rate

d) none of the above

70. A $1,000, 7%, semi-annual coupon bond was issued last year. Today the yield on the bond is 5%. Which of the following statements is FALSE? ( )

a) The bond makes twice-yearly interest payments of $35.

b) The par value of the bond is $1,000.

c) The average annual return on the bond, if held to maturity, is approximately 5%.

d) The bond is trading at a discount.

71. A convertible bond with a 4% annual coupon has a price of $990. It can be converted into 20 common shares, currently valued at $35 each. Which of the following statements is FALSE? ( )

a) The conversion price is $49.50.

b) The conversion value is $700.

c) The price of the bond can be influenced by, among other things, the price of the common shares.

d) The bond can only sell at a premium if the market interest rate is lower than 4%.

72. Which of the following individuals would be considered corporate insiders? ( )

a) an individual owning 5.5% of the company's voting shares

b) a director of a parent company

c) both (a) and (b)

d) neither (a) nor (b)

73. Which of the following activities by investment advisors is NOT prohibited? ( )

a) telephoning residences

b) calling at residences

c) bucketing

d) maintaining confidential numbered accounts

74. Which of the following was established to provide a simple regulatory body for all federally regulated financial institutions? ( )

a) CDIC

b) CSA

c) CIPF
d) OSFI

( ) 75. Safeguards in a bond contract designed to protect investors are referred to as:

a) covenants
b) protection against dilution
c) negotiable bonds
d) negative pledge

( ) 76. According to the Phillips Curve, what will happen to the unemployment rate when inflation increases at a faster rate?

a) decrease in the long run
b) increase in the long run
c) decrease in the short run
d) no change

( ) 77. A capital asset is purchased for $80,000. The amortization expense in year three, if it is amortized on a declining balance method at a rate of 10%, will be:

a) $6,480
b) $7,280
c) $8,000
d) $9,720

( ) 78. Refer to Question 77. If that asset has a useful life of seven years and an expected salvage value of $10,000, what is the amortization charge in year three if the straight line method is used?

a) $8,000
b) $10,000
c) $11,430
d) $12,857

( ) 79. Which of the following theories says that the economy will automatically move to the natural rate of unemployment on its own?

A) monetarist
B) Keynesian
C) supply-side
D) rational expectations

80. A company has 800,000 shares outstanding before it undergoes a one-for-four consolidation. After the consolidation, the number of shares outstanding will be: ( )

a) unchanged
b) 3.2 million
c) 1.6 million
d) 0.2 million

81. Which of the following statements about treasury bonds is FALSE? ( )

a) Treasury bonds may be used to create zero-coupon bonds.
b) The interest earned on treasury bonds is taxed as a capital gain.
c) Treasury bonds come in denominations as small as $1,000.
d) Treasury bonds are sold every two weeks through the Bank of Canada.

82. A company declares a dividend that is payable on March 19 to holders of record on February 1. In order to be entitled to receive this dividend, you must buy the shares prior to: ( )

a) March 19
b) February 1
c) January 31
d) January 30

83. During the process of issuing shares a ____________ is prepared, which is an information circular for in-house use only. ( )

a) preliminary prospectus
b) red herring
c) green-sheet
d) primary prospectus

84. Which of the following statements about issuers under the SFPD system is FALSE? ( )

a) Issuers have been filing annual and interim statements for 24 months prior to the issue.
b) Issuers are not in default of any requirements under the relevant securities legislation.
c) Issuers have a large public float.
d) All of the above are true.

( ) 85. A ____________ preferred share would suit an aggressive and sophisticated investment portfolio.

a) convertible
b) retractable
c) variable dividend
d) participating

( ) 86. Assume that the Government of Canada issues a real return bond priced at 100, with a par value of $1,000, and a coupon of 5%. Which of the following statements is true?

a) If inflation over the first year is 2%, the bond will make an interest payment of $70 (7% of the par value of $1,000) in the second year.
b) If inflation over the first year is 2%, the bond will make an interest payment of $51 (5% of $1,020) in the second year.
c) If inflation is 2% in the first year and 3% in the second year, the bond will make an interest payment of $51.25 (5% of $1,025) in the third year.
d) RRB bonds are not impacted by the level of inflation.

( ) 87. In sales that occur on ____________ dates, buyers are entitled to the next and future dividends of the shares, whereas in sales that occur on and after the ____________ date, buyers are not entitled to the next dividend payment.

a) cum-dividend; dividend record
b) ex-dividend; cum-dividend
c) ex-dividend; dividend record
d) cum-dividend; ex-dividend

( ) 88. All else being equal, a ____________ bond will always sell for more than an otherwise similar ____________ bond.

a) retractable; callable
b) callable; retractable
c) callable; extendible
d) floating rate; fixed-rate

( ) 89. Which of the following statements concerning bonds and debentures is FALSE?

a) Both bonds and debentures are secured by physical assets.
b) Corporations issue both bonds and debentures.
c) Debentures are typically unsecured investments, with the exception of residual claims on assets.
d) A firm can default on a bond or on a debenture.

Refer to the following information to answer Questions 90 to 92.

A company presently has 500,000 shares outstanding that are trading at $50 per share. The shares are presently trading cum rights, and five rights are required to purchase one share at the subscription price of $45.

90. What is the intrinsic value of one right before the ex-rights date? ( )
    a) $0
    b) $0.83
    c) $1.00
    d) $5.00

91. What is the theoretical intrinsic value of one right two days after the ex-rights date if the shares are trading for $49.50? ( )
    a) $0.50
    b) $0.83
    c) $0.90
    d) $4.50

92. How much money will the firm raise if the rights offering is fully subscribed? ( )
    a) $2.5 million
    b) $4.5 million
    c) $4.9 million
    d) $5 million

93. A client may request arbitration from an SRO in which of the following situations? ( )
    a) The claim amount is $150,000 and the events in dispute originated in Ontario in January 1998.
    b) The claim amount is $150,000 and the events in dispute originated in Quebec in January 1998.
    c) The claim amount is $100,000 and the events in dispute originated in Ontario in January 1998.
    d) The claim amount is $100,000 and the events in dispute originated in Quebec in January 1998.

94. What would be the market price of 6% preferred shares with a par value of $20 that have a required rate of return of 8%? ( )
    a) $15
    b) $20
    c) $26.67
    d) none of the above

( ) 95. The Miscellaneous Assets category on the balance sheet would include all of the following EXCEPT:

a) cash surrender value of life insurance
b) amounts due from directors
c) copyrights
d) advances to subsidiaries

Refer to the following information to answer Questions 96 and 97.

An investor obtains the following market prices for a call option on ABC Company's common shares that are currently trading at $8.00 per share. The exercise price on the call option is $10 and the call premium is $1.50.

( ) 96. What is the time value premium for ABC Company's call option?

a) $0
b) $1.50
c) $2.00
d) $8.00

( ) 97. What is the net profit (ignoring transactions costs) for an investor who purchases one contract if they hold the option to the expiration date, at which time the share price is $12?

a) $400
b) $200
c) $50
d) none of the above

( ) 98. Company A owns 25% of company B. If company B earns $100 million and pays dividends of $12.5 million to company A, what entry will company A make on their earnings statement?

a) $100 million in income from subsidiaries
b) $25 million in equity income
c) $12.5 million in dividend income
d) none of the above

( ) 99. ____________ are more common than ____________ for preferred share issues.

a) Purchase funds; sinking fund provisions
b) Sinking fund provisions; purchase funds
c) Callable features; cumulative features
d) Both (b) and (c) are true

100. Which of the following is a valid concern when considering the purchase of convertible preferred shares? ( )

a) A low premium may indicate that the potential for common share price appreciation is low.

b) A high premium indicates that the convertible preferreds are overpriced as the result of irrational investor optimism.

c) Conversion will trigger a capital gain or capital loss for income tax purposes.

d) The option associated with the convertible preferreds results in them paying a lower yield compared with the underlying common stock.

EXAM #2

CSC PRACTICE EXAMINATION

CHAPTERS 13–27

( ) 1. The structure of a principal protected note involves the following roles EXCEPT:

a) the guarantor or issuer
b) the hedge fund or FoHF manager
c) the distributor
d) the trustee

( ) 2. Which of the following would be likely to exert a positive influence on the general level of stock prices?

I. A majority government is replaced by a minority government.
II. Short-term interest rates rise, while long-term interest rates fall.
III. Unemployment approaches the full-employment unemployment rate.
IV. There is a significant increase in long-term bond prices.
V. The government announces a significant cut in corporate tax rates.
VI. The consumer price index declines unexpectedly.
VII. The federal government deficit is higher than anticipated.

a) I, II, VI, VII
b) II, IV, V, VI
c) II, IV, VI, VII
d) II, III, VI

( ) 3. Consider two stocks: A and B. Stock A has an expected return of 12% and a standard deviation of 10%, while Stock B has an expected return of 13% and a standard deviation of 14%. Which stock is preferred by a rational investor?

a) Stock A
b) Stock B
c) a rational investor would be indifferent
d) insufficient information

( ) 4. The net profit margin ratio is considered a(n):

a) liquidity ratio
b) risk analysis ratio
c) operating performance ratio
d) value ratio

( ) 5. What do growth managers focus on?

a) specific stock selection
b) overall economy analysis
c) current and future earnings of individual companies
d) interest rate anticipation

6. _____________ investment funds invest primarily in short-term instruments such as T-bills and commercial paper. ( )

   a) Money market
   b) Mortgage
   c) Bond
   d) Balanced

7. The net asset value (NAV) of a fund that has a 5% sales charge and an offering price of $60 per unit is: ( )

   a) $65.20
   b) $63.00
   c) $57.00
   d) $56.85

8. Which of the following is NOT a consequence of firms carrying excessive debt? ( )

   a) reduces the margin of safety for debt holders
   b) increases the firm's operating charges
   c) reduces free cash flow available for dividends
   d) none of the above

9. A $20-million investment is made in year 1 and the fund increases by 30%. Based on a 10% incentive fee, how much money would the manager earn? ( )

   a) $0.6 million
   b) $1 million
   c) $2 million
   d) $2.6 million

10. Based on Question 9, if the fund subsequently declines in value to $23 million, what amount of incentive fees would the manager receive? ( )

    a) none
    b) $0.3 million
    c) $0.6 million
    d) $1 million

11. Technical analysis would focus on examining: ( )

    a) company financial statements
    b) industry growth opportunities
    c) moving stock price averages
    d) dividend yields

( ) 12. Equity prices often rise due to interest rates falling faster than the growth rate in earnings (and dividends) during this phase of the equity cycle:

a) expansionary
b) peak
c) contraction
d) trough

( ) 13. Which is true regarding cash flow from operations?

a) Normal deductions such as amortization or future income taxes are not deducted.
b) Non-cash revenues are not included.
c) Both (a) and (b).
d) Neither (a) nor (b).

( ) 14. A(n) ____________ asset allocation strategy adheres to a long-term asset mix by monitoring and rebalancing as necessary.

a) strategic
b) tactical
c) dynamic
d) insured

( ) 15. Which of the following benefits do NOT belong to hedge funds?

a) low correlation to traditional asset classes
b) absolute returns
c) potentially low volatility
d) relative returns

( ) 16. The volatility in returns associated with changes in market conditions is known as what type of risk?

a) unsystematic risk
b) cyclical risk
c) systematic risk
d) natural risk

( ) 17. Which of the following attempts to profit from price anomalies between related interest-rate instruments?

a) long/short equity funds
b) convertible arbitrage
c) fixed-income arbitrage
d) equity market-neutral funds

18. If a wife who earned $70,000 in 2010 has contributed $8,000 to her own RRSP, how much can she contribute to her husband's plan? ( )

a) $4,600

b) $5,000

c) $5,500

d) It depends on how much the husband has already contributed.

19. Jennifer has 1,000 XYZ stocks, and the opening value is $31 per share. Assume no distributions or contributions during the period and the ending portfolio value is $34,000. What is her total return on these shares? ( )

a) 6.35%

b) 6.45%

c) 9.52%

d) 9.67%

20. ABC recently reported net earnings of $600,000 for the year. Interest paid was $150,000 and taxes were $256,000. What is ABC's interest coverage ratio? ( )

a) 6.7

b) 5.7

c) 5.0

d) 4.0

21. Which of the following are types of event-driven funds? ( )

I. merger or risk arbitrage

II. distressed securities funds

III. high-yield funds

IV. global macro funds

V. emerging market funds

VI. managed futures funds

a) I, II, III

b) I, II, III, IV

c) II, IV, V, VI

d) III, IV, V, VI

Refer to the following Comprehensive Income Statement and Statement of Financial Position for XYZ Company to answer Questions 22 to 24:

XYZ COMPANY
Financial Statements

COMPREHENSIVE INCOME STATEMENT

Total Revenue	$1,426,000
Cost of Goods Sold	1,238,700
Amortization	40,100
General, Selling, & Admin. Expense	33,100
Earnings before interest and taxes	114,100
Interest Expense	5,300
Pre-tax Income	108,800
Income Tax:	
Current	10,900
Future	9,000
Earnings before Extraordinary Items	88,900
Extraordinary Items	0
Income after Extraordinary Items	88,900
Dividends—Preferred Shares	3,500
Income Available to Common Shares	85,400
Earnings / Common Share	0.68
Common Shares—Year-end	125,658
Common Shares—Average	125,536
Dividends—Common Shares	14,700
Market Price per Share (Close)	6.69

STATEMENT OF FINANCIAL POSITION

Assets:	
Cash & Equivalents	$150,000
Accounts Receivable	174,000
Inventory	220,200
Total Current Assets	544,200
Fixed Assets—Gross	1,372,700
Less: Accumulated Depreciation	766,200
Fixed Assets—Net	606,500
Total Assets	1,150,700
Liabilities & Equities:	
Bank Loans & Equivalents	147,800

Accounts Payable	347,200
Current Portion of Long-term Debt	5,400
Total Current Liabilities	500,400
Long-term Debt	83,500
Deferred Taxes	41,600
Equity: Preferred Stock	158,300
Common Stock	190,600
Retained Earnings	176,300
Total Equity	525,200
Total Liabilities & Equity	1,150,700

22. What is the value of XYZ's quick ratio? ( )

a) 0.65
b) 0.94
c) 1.03
d) 1.09

23. What is XYZ's cash flow to debt ratio? ( )

a) 53.0%
b) 58.3%
c) 62.9%
d) not enough information available

24. What is XYZ's book value per common share at year-end? ( )

a) $2.92
b) $2.78
c) $2.66
d) not enough information available

25. The primary difference between discretionary accounts and managed accounts is that: ( )

a) Managed accounts are client portfolios that are managed by a member, usually for a fee, while discretionary accounts are opened for clients as a convenience to clients who are unable or unwilling to attend to their own accounts.
b) Discretionary accounts are client portfolios that are managed by a member, usually for a fee, while managed accounts are opened for clients as a convenience to clients who are unable or unwilling to attend to their own accounts.

c) Managed accounts are managed by the client, while a discretionary account is managed by a person appointed by the client.

d) Discretionary accounts are managed by the client, while a managed account is managed by a person appointed by the client.

( ) 26. The primary difference between diversifiable and non-diversifiable risk is that:

a) Market risk refers to volatility in returns associated with changes in market conditions, while non-market risk is company specific.

b) Non-market risk refers to volatility in returns associated with changes in market conditions, while market risk is company specific.

c) Diversifiable risk refers to volatility in returns associated with changes in market conditions, while non-diversifiable risk is company specific.

d) Diversifiable risk is market specific, while non-diversifiable is firm specific.

( ) 27. Only ____________ of a capital gain is taxable since October 2000.

a) one quarter

b) one half

c) two thirds

d) three quarters

( ) 28. If a portfolio earned a return of 15% with a standard deviation of 25% and the average three-month T-bill rate was 5%, what is the portfolio's risk-adjusted rate of return?

a) 20%

b) 30%

c) 40%

d) 60%

( ) 29. What is the intrinsic value of a common share that is expected to pay an annual year-end dividend of $1.25, which is expected to grow indefinitely at an annual rate of 5.5% per year, if the required return on the shares is 12%?

a) $10.41

b) $19.23

c) $20.29

d) $21.54

( ) 30. What is the implied P/E ratio for a stock that has an expected EPS of $2.25 and an expected year-end dividend of $0.75, if the appropriate discount rate is 15% and the expected annual growth rate in dividends is 3%?

a) 22 times

b) 2.78 times

c) 6.25 times
d) 11.1 times

31. Which of the following is NOT a competitive force that affects the attractiveness of an industry and its prospects for growth? ( )
a) ease of entry or exit
b) degree of competition
c) availability of complements
d) ability to exert pressure over selling price of products

32. What does beta measure? ( )
a) business risk
b) non-market risk
c) unsystematic risk
d) sensitivity of returns on a security to changes in market returns

33. Why might a company be suffering from a low inventory turnover ratio? ( )
a) purchased too much inventory
b) inventory contains a large portion of unsaleable goods
c.) inventory's value has been overstated
d) all of the above

34. Which type of mutual fund provides the lowest tax advantages? ( )
a) money market funds
b) dividend funds
c) growth equity funds
d) international equity funds

35. Which of the following is NOT one of the four key tests used to assess preferred share quality? ( )
a) preferred dividend yield
b) equity per preferred share
c) record of continuous dividend payments
d) an independent credit assessment

36. An investor purchases 400 ABC common shares at $22.40 on January 31, 2004, then buys another 300 ABC common shares at $24.60 on June 30, 2005. What is the adjusted cost base per share? ( )
a) $23.20
b) $23.34
c) $23.46
d) $23.50

( ) 37. An investor purchases 100 shares for $8 on March 1, 2005, then sells the shares for $6.50 on March 21, 2005. If the investor repurchases the shares on April 10, 2005, for $6.50 and holds them until May, what is the loss incurred?

a) capital loss of $150
b) superficial loss of $150
c) capital loss of $1.50
d) there is no loss

( ) 38. Which of the following is NOT a part of the portfolio management process?

a) designing an investment policy
b) determining investment objectives and constraints
c) soliciting funds when necessary
d) implementing the asset allocation

( ) 39. What is a "spread trader"?

a) an investment manager who looks to profit from differences in bid-ask prices
b) an investment manager who looks to profit by anticipating the direction of interest rates and structuring their portfolios accordingly
c) an investment manager who looks to profit from the differences in rates between federal, provincial, and/or corporate bonds
d) an investor who looks to find the investment manager with the lowest rates and chooses their manager based on who has the lowest rate

( ) 40. What is the difference between a defensive and a speculative industry?

a) Speculative industries have a great deal of risk and uncertainty, while defensive industries are relatively stable.
b) Speculative industries are those whose earnings are affected by a larger than average amount of downturns in the business cycle, while defensive industries are relatively stable.
c) Defensive industries have a great deal of risk and uncertainty, while speculative industries are relatively stable.
d) There is no real difference between the two.

( ) 41. What is the five-week moving average of a stock that has the following end-of-week closing prices: week one—$22, week two—$21, week three—$22, week four—$20, week five—$22?

a) $22.50
b) $21.40
c) $21.20
d) $21.00

42. Refer to Question 41. If the closing price at the end of week six were $20, what is the five-week moving average now? ( )

a) $20.75
b) $21.00
c) $21.16
d) $22.30

43. The portfolio management technique that adjusts the mix between risk-free assets and risky assets as the markets rise and fall is known as: ( )

a) insured asset allocation
b) tactical asset allocation
c) constant-weighting asset allocation
d) dynamic asset allocation

44. When forecasting interest rates, an IA should consider: ( )

a) monetary policy changes
b) fiscal policy changes
c) inflation
d) all of the above

45. Which of the following situations does NOT represent a bull signal? ( )

a) a decrease in the advance-decline line
b) new highs are increasing
c) stock prices break through their moving average line from below
d) a head-and-shoulders bottom formation

46. A young, healthy, single individual professional with medium investment knowledge, high risk tolerance, a moderate tax rate, and a long-term horizon should have the following type of asset mix: ( )

a) little amount of cash, large amount of fixed income, moderate amount of equities
b) moderate amount of cash, large amount of fixed income, little amount of equities
c) little amount of cash, moderate amount of fixed income, large amount of equities
d) large amount of cash, moderate amount of fixed income, little amount of equities

47. If you own $4,500 of XYZ Inc., which has an expected return of 15%, and $2,500 of ABC Ltd., which has an expected return of 7%, what is the expected return on your portfolio? ( )

a) 20%
b) 12%

c) 10%
d) A portfolio requires more than two securities.

( ) 48. The key disclosure forms for a segregated fund include:

a) simple prospectuses, client statements, information folders, and financial statements
b) application forms, contracts, information folders, financial statements, and client statements
c) application forms, contracts, information folders, financial statements, client statements, and summary fact statements
d) application forms, contracts, and financial statements

Refer to the following information to answer Questions 49 and 50:

Assume Helen invested a lump sum of $200,000 in a front-end-load segregated fund with a 100% maturity guarantee after 10 years. Treat the value of any maturity guarantees as capital gains income.

( ) 49. What are the tax consequences if Helen wishes to redeem her $200,000 deposit after 10 years, when the market value of her holdings is $195,000?

a) She can claim a capital loss of $5,000 against any income earned.
b) A capital gain of $5,000 is taxable in the year of redemption.
c) There are no taxes payable on the transaction.
d) None of the above.

( ) 50. What are the tax consequences if Helen resets her deposit after five years, locking in the gain in market value to $220,000, and at the end of the additional 10 years, she liquidates her holdings, which have a market value of $210,000?

a) She can defer the capital gains payable for five years to the end of her initial 10-year contract.
b) A capital gain of $20,000 is taxable in the year the contract is reset.
c) No capital gain liability is triggered at the time of redemption.
d) A capital gain of $20,000 is taxable in the year of redemption.

( ) 51. The combination of securities in a portfolio is determined using the following guideline:

a) The investor's primary objectives determine the asset allocation strategy; the investor's secondary objectives determine specific securities that are selected.
b) The investor's primary objectives determine the specific securities that are selected; the investor's secondary objectives determine the asset allocation strategy.
c) Neither (a) nor (b).
d) Both (a) and (b), depending on the investor's level of risk tolerance.

52. The securities industry's Code of Ethics is based upon the principles of: ( )
    a) fairness and trust
    b) integrity, justice, honesty, responsibility, and reliability
    c) the financial advisor's Code of Ethics
    d) both (a) and (b)

53. Which of the following is a structured product? ( )
    a) segregated funds
    b) mutual funds
    c) hedge funds
    d) principal protected notes (PPNs)

54. Which of the following practices would be deemed acceptable according to mutual fund regulators? ( )
    a) filling an unsolicited mutual fund order from a client in another province
    b) displaying your registration with the securities authority on your business card
    c) offering to buy back units at the purchase price should the fund NAVPS drop
    d) none of the above

55. Permitted clients include all of the following EXCEPT: ( )
    a) endowments
    b) insurance companies
    c) trusts with more than $2 million in net financial assets
    d) individuals with more than $25 million in net assets

56. What is the main danger in comparing mutual fund performance? ( )
    a) The funds may have two different investment objectives.
    b) Historical returns provide no guarantee of future returns.
    c) A fund's asset allocation may not be taken into consideration.
    d) Comparisons with stock market indices may not account for dividend reinvestment.

57. What are two reasons why mutual fund managers would use derivative securities in managing their portfolios? ( )
    a) to reduce risk and assist in market entry and exit
    b) to speculate and reduce the amount of money leaving the fund
    c) to provide greater diversification and reduce risk
    d) to take advantage of volatile securities and assist in entry and exit of the market

( ) 58. The composite P/E ratio represents which of the following types of indicators?

a) fundamental indicator
b) technical indicator
c) economic indicator
d) value indicator

( ) 59. A knowledgeable financial advisor recommends that you stop buying common stocks and invest in short-term interest-bearing paper. What is the most likely point in the equity cycle at that point in time?

a) contraction phase
b) stock market trough
c) expansion phase
d) equity cycle peak

( ) 60. Exchange-traded funds (ETFs) can be used in part of which trading strategy?

a) active strategy
b) passive strategy
c) both (a) and (b)
d) neither (a) nor (b)

Refer to the following information to answer Questions 61 and 62:

Atlantic Fund Company is offering a new mutual fund to investors. The new fund's net asset value per unit is $12 plus a 3.5% up-front sales charge.

( ) 61. What is the offering price for Atlantic Fund Company's new mutual fund?

a) $11.58
b) $12.42
c) $12.44
d) none of the above

( ) 62. What is the sales charge as a percentage of the net amount invested by purchasers?

a) 3.50%
b) 3.67%
c) 3.84%
d) none of the above

( ) 63. The main disadvantages of mutual funds include:

a) lack of liquidity, they are unsuitable for short-term investments, and there are few types of funds available
b) they are not suitable for both short-term investments and emergency reserves, plus professional management is not perfect in building mutual fund portfolios

c) they are not eligible for margin accounts, few purchase plans are available, and they are not accepted as loan collateral

d) high management fees, they are not suitable for emergency reserves, and are not eligible for margin accounts

64. What is the fully diluted EPS for a company that has net earnings of $10 million, and has 1 million shares outstanding, if the company has 200,000 convertible preferred shares outstanding, each of which is convertible into one common share? The preferred shares receive an annual dividend of $5. ( )

a) $10.00

b) $9.00

c) $8.33

d) none of the above

65. A fixed-dollar withdrawal plan withdraws a specified: ( )

a) percentage of the investor's mutual fund portfolio each year

b) amount of the investor's mutual fund portfolio over a predetermined time period

c) dollar amount determined by the mutual fund investor on a monthly or quarterly basis

d) dollar amount determined by the mutual fund holder each year

66. You purchase a stock for $26 and hold it for five years. The annual dividend per share for this stock is $2.50. If you sell the stock at the end of the fifth year for $24, what is your return on this stock? ( )

a) –7.7%

b) 8.1%

c) 40.4%

d) none of the above

67. A "growth" manager would invest in stocks with relatively ____________ P/E ratios and ____________ dividend yields. ( )

a) high; high

b) high; low

c) low; low

d) low; high

68. ETFs provide which of the following advantages over mutual funds? ( )

a) They trade throughout the day.

b) They are diversified.

c) They can track an underlying index.

d) They can be redeemed with the issuer.

( ) 69. According to the Life Cycle Theory, a person aged 52 years would focus on:

a) preserving capital and income
b) growth and tax minimization
c) income and liquidity
d) safety and liquidity

( ) 70. Which of the following is not a style related to fixed-income managers?

a) credit quality
b) spread traders
c) exchange rate anticipators
d) all of the above are fixed income manager styles

( ) 71. RRIFs differ from RRSPs because:

a) RRIFs shelter income earned within the plan.
b) RRIFs may hold stocks, bonds, mutual funds, and T-bills.
c) RRIFs require minimum annual withdrawals.
d) RRIFs may be self-directed.

( ) 72. What is the main objective(s) of equity mutual funds?

a) to search for capital gains and be willing to forego broad diversification benefits in hope of achieving above-average returns
b) capital gains
c) to provide diversification with a combination of income, safety, and capital appreciation
d) income and safety of principal

( ) 73. The following factors should be considered when establishing investment objectives EXCEPT:

a) a stock's volatility
b) time horizon
c) risk
d) liquidity

( ) 74. When there is falling inflation, P/E levels will ____________ as the discount rate ____________.

a) increase; decreases
b) decrease; increases
c) remain unchanged; remains unchanged
d) none of the above

75. The Elliot Wave Theory suggests that the stock market moves up in a series of ______________ waves and down in a series of ______________ waves. ( )

a) three; three
b) five; five
c) three; five
d) five; three

76. Which of the following has contributed to the growth in popularity in fee-based accounts? ( )

a) They lead to a greater focus on trading.
b) Clients prefer to have a portion of fees paid tied to performance.
c) Both (a) and (b).
d) Neither (a) nor (b).

77. A client has approached you with the following information: ( )

Security	**Expected Return**	**Market Value**
ABC Co.	9%	$200,000
DEF Co.	10%	$220,000
GHI Co.	12%	$430,000

If the client holds the given market values of the above securities in their portfolio, what is the return the investor can expect?

a) 10.33%
b) 10.78%
c) 11%
d) none of the above

78. Full-service brokerage accounts that provide financial advice with a fixed or unlimited number of trades are called: ( )

a) mutual fund wraps
b) separately managed accounts
c) fee-based non-managed accounts
d) unified managed accounts

79. The following are risks of NHA MBS, EXCEPT for: ( )

a) reinvestment risk
b) prepayments reduce future payments received
c) potential capital losses
d) mortgage property may increase

( ) 80. An investor is in the 15% federal tax bracket and receives $140 in dividends from a Canadian corporation. How much federal tax must be paid on the dividend?

a) $22.40
b) $28.00
c) $30.00
d) none of the above

81. An ABS investor with a high tolerance for risk would be most likely to invest in which tranche?

a) Senior A
b) Mezzanine
c) Junior
d) Senior B

( ) 82. Which of the following is a risk associated with the capital share of a split share?

a) credit risk
b) reinvestment risk
c) inherent leverage
d) taxation risks

( ) 83. The following are major risks of PPNs, EXCEPT for:

a) There is often no secondary market for PPNs.
b) They may not match the performance of the underlying assets.
c) The issuer may redeem the PPN before maturity.
d) The principal repayment is not guaranteed.

( ) 84. ____________ investment funds usually provide higher returns than ____________ funds, but lower returns than ____________ funds.

a) Money market; mortgage; dividend
b) Balanced; equity; specialty
c) Balanced; bond; dividend
d) Balanced; real estate; specialty

( ) 85. What is the effective after-tax cost of a $6,000 investment in an LSVCC by an investor in a 40% marginal tax bracket, if she contributes it to her RRSP? Assume the LSVCC qualifies for the maximum federal tax credit and an equal provincial tax credit.

a) $1,800
b) $2,100

c) $4,500

d) none of the above

86. The following restrictions apply to most mutual funds: ( )

a) cannot own more than 10% of a company's total securities

b) cannot own more than 10% of a company's voting stock

c) both (a) and (b)

d) neither (a) nor (b)

87. A change in the capital gains tax rate is of greatest concern for investors in: ( )

a) PPNs

b) index-linked GICs

c) preferred shares

d) capital shares

88. What are some of the advantages to an RRSP? ( )

a) defer reporting some income during high taxation years until potentially lower taxation years

b) retirement fund returns compound tax-free

c) retirement income splitting option (at retirement)

d) all of the above

89. Which of the following statements regarding mutual fund regulation is (are) true? ( )

I. The distribution of mutual funds is regulated by the MFDA.

II. The funds themselves are regulated by the IDA.

III. Both the distribution of mutual funds as well as the funds themselves are regulated by the provincial securities commissions.

IV. The MFDA and the IDA are both SROs.

a) I, II

b) I, IV

c) II, IV

d) III

90. Closed-end funds have the following disadvantages EXCEPT: ( )

a) They may be sold short.

b) They are subject to stock exchange requirements.

c) Deferred sales charges do not usually decline through time.

d) They often do not provide for automatic reinvestment of distributions.

( ) 91. REITs and business trusts are examples of ____________.

a) unit investment trusts
b) income trusts
c) MBSs
d) none of the above

( ) 92. Segregated funds must satisfy the following requirements EXCEPT:

a) The initial term of the segregated fund must be at least 10 years.
b) The amount of the maturity guarantee payable at the end of the term must be at least 75%.
c) There can be no guarantee of any amounts payable on redemption of the contract before death or the maturity date.
d) None of the above.

( ) 93. Segregated funds provide investors with the following advantage(s) EXCEPT:

a) protection from creditors
b) maturity guarantees
c) probate bypass
d) CDIC protection

( ) 94. Which ratio shows how well liabilities to be paid within one year are covered by the cash generated by the operating activities?

a) current ratio
b) interest coverage ratio
c) operating cash flow ratio
d) asset coverage

( ) 95. The following are primary ethical values in the Code of Ethics established by the securities industry, EXCEPT for:

a) Registrants must hold client information in strict confidence.
b) Registrants must use proper care and exercise independent professional judgment.
c) Registrants must act quickly to ensure that all client accounts are settled by the required date.
d) Registrants must act in accordance with applicable securities act(s).

( ) 96. Advisors are exempt from determining the "suitability" of products or services for investors they believe to be "permitted" based upon consideration of several factors including all of the following EXCEPT:

a) The client regularly uses other sources of information in making their decisions.
b) They use more than one dealer member on a regular basis.

c) Their relationship with the client.

d) Their general level of experience in financial markets.

97. A fund that is established to make annual scholarship payments would most likely be set up in the form of a(n): ( )

a) endowment

b) pension

c) trust

d) foundation

98. Michael is a conservative investor and Linda is his financial consultant. Which type of preferred shares should Linda recommend that Michael include in his portfolio? ( )

a) medium to high quality

b) convertible

c) preferreds with warrants

d) retractable

Refer to the following information to answer Questions 99 and 100:

Margaret is a 25-year-old dot-com entrepreneur. She just sold her business and "netted" $5 million after all tax considerations. She has no plans to re-enter the workforce in the near future and would like to enjoy life and live off her windfall, indefinitely if possible. She has never contributed to an RRSP or a company pension plan.

99. Margaret's primary investment objective(s) should focus on ____________, while relevant secondary objectives should include ____________. ( )

a) growth and income; tax minimization

b) tax minimization; growth

c) preservation of capital and income; tax minimization

d) liquidity; growth

100. The most appropriate investment mix for Margaret from the following would be ( )

a) 20% cash, 50% fixed income, 30% equities

b) 10% cash, 30% fixed income, 60% equities

c) 40% cash, 50% fixed income, 10% equities

d) 30% cash, 50% fixed income, 20% equities

EXAM #1

CSC PRACTICE EXAMINATION

ANSWERS

Answers to CSC Practice Examination #1

Question	Answer	Level of Difficulty	Chapter
1	B	E	2
2	C	E	7
3	C	E	3
4	A	E	12
5	B	M	4
6	D	D	5
7	B	M	12
8	B	M	4
9	D	D	7
10	C	M	7
11	B	M	9
12	A	E	3
13	B	M	11
14	A	E	1
15	B 50% margin = 0.50 × \$2 × 100 × 10 = \$1,000		
16	A Max. loan = 0.40 × \$1,800 = \$720 Deposit = \$1,000 – \$720 = \$280	D	9
17	B Deposit = 0.50 × \$5 × 1,000 = \$2,500	D	9
18	A Profit = (\$5 – \$4) × 1,000 = \$1,000	M	9
19	C	M	2
20	B	E	10
21	B	E	4
22	C	M	10
23	C	M	7
24	A	M	9
25	B	M	9
26	C	M	2

Question	Answer	Level of Difficulty	Chapter
27	D	M	1
28	C	M	4
29	B $7M × ({1 – [1/1.08]5.5)/0.08} + $100M × (1/[1.08]5.5) = $95.38M	D	7
30	A	D	7
31	B Price at year 1 = $100 since yield = coupon rate/return = (100 – 105 +7) /105 =1.9%	D	7
32	A $7M × (120/365) = $2.301M	D	7
33	C (40 – 18.5 – 2)/(18.5 × 2) = 8.11%	D	8
34	C 2/40 = 5.0%	D	8
35	B Common share yield = (0.4 5/18.5) = 2.43%; payback = 8.1/(5 – 2.43) = 3.16 years	D	8
36	D	M	6
37	D	M	6
38	C (1,000 × $12 × 0.30) + (1,000 × 1.8 × 0.6) = $4,680	D	9
39	B Stock X: Max. loan = 0.70 × $12,750 = $8,925; previous loan: $12,000 – $3,600 = $8,400; excess: $8,925 – $8,400 = $525 Stock Y: Max. loan = 0; repay previous loan $1,800 – $1,080 = $720 (deposit required); total deposit = $720 – $525 = $195	D	9
40	D	M	6
41	C	M	8
42	A ([100 – 99.45]/99.45) × (365/190) = 1.06%	D	7
43	B Bond sells at face value so YTM = coupon rate	M	7

Question	Answer	Level of Difficulty	Chapter
44	D	M	6
45	A	M	10
46	D	D	11
47	C	M	9
48	C	E	12
49	C	D	5
50	D	M	1
51	D	M	9
52	C	M	11
53	D IV = Max ($20 – $22, $0) = $0 TV = $3 – $0 = $3	M	10
54	C 20/3 = 6.67	M	10
55	D	M	1
56	C	M	9
57	B	M	9
58	C	M	4
59	C	M	4
60	B	M	3
61	D	M	4
62	D	M	4
63	B	M	2
64	A	M	6
65	B Purchase price = $1,005 + (40/365 × $60) = $1,011.58	D	7
66	B	M	11
67	C	M	11
68	C	M	4

Question	Answer	Level of Difficulty	Chapter
69	B	M	5
70	D	M	7
71	D	M	7
72	B	M	3
73	B	M	3
74	D	M	3
75	A	E	7
76	C	M	4
77	A ($80,000 – [$80,000 × 0.1 0] – [72,000 × 0.10]) x 0.10 = $6,480	D	12
78	B (800,000 – 10,000)/7 = $10,000	M	12
79	A	M	5
80	D 80,000/4 = 0.20 m	E	12
81	B	E	7
82	D	M	8
83	C	M	11
84	A	D	11
85	C	D	8
86	B	M	7
87	D	M	7
88	A	M	6
89	A	M	6
90	B ($50 – $45)/(5 + 1) = $0.83	M	10
91	C ($49.5 – $45)/5 = $0.90	M	10
92	B (500,000/5) × $45 = $4.5M	D	10
93	D	D	3
94	A Price = (0.06 × $20)/0.08 = $15	D	6

Question	Answer	Level of Difficulty	Chapter
95	C	M	12
96	B TV = \$1.50 – 0 = \$1.50	M	10
97	C Profit = (12 – 10) × 100 – 150 = \$50	D	10
98	B	M	12
99	A	M	8
100	A	D	9

EXAM #2

CSC PRACTICE EXAMINATION

ANSWERS

Answers to CSC Practice Examination #2

Question	Answer	Level of Difficulty	Chapter
1	D	M	24
2	B	D	13
3	D	M	15
4	C	E	14
5	C	M	16
6	A	E	19
7	C $60 = NAV/(1 – .05), so NAV = $60 × 0.95 = $57.00	M	18
8	B	M	14
9	A	M	21
10	A	M	21
11	C	E	13
12	D	D	16
13	C	M	14
14	A	M	16
15	D	E	21
16	C	E	15
17	C	M	16
18	A Maximum is the lower of $22,000 or 0.18 × $70,000 = $12,600 So, $12,600 – $8,000 = $4,600	M	25
19	D Return = ($34,000 – $31,000)/(31,000) = .0967 = 9.67%	M	15
20	A ($600,000 + $150,000 + $256,000)/$150,000 = 6.7	M	14
21	A	M	21
22	A ($544,200 – $220,200)/$500,400 = 0.65	M	14

Question	Answer	Level of Difficulty	Chapter
23	B ($88,900 + $9,000 + 40,100)/($147,800 + 5,400 + 83,500) × 100 = 58.3%	D	14
24	A ($525,000 – $158,300)/125,658 = $2.92	D	14
25	A	M	23
26	A	M	15
27	B	M	25
28	C Sharpe Ratio: (15% – 5%)/25% = 40%	M	16
29	B $1.25/(.12 – 0.055) = $19.23	M	13
30	B (0.75/$2.25)/(.15 – 0.3) = 2.78 times	D	13
31	C	M	13
32	D	E	15
33	D	M	14
34	A	E	19
35	A	M	14
36	B ([$22.40 × 400] + [$24.60 × 300])/700 = $23.34	M	25
37	B (100 × $8) – (100 × $6.5) = $150 Superficial loss	M	25
38	C	E	15
39	C	E	16
40	A	E	13
41	B ($22 + $21 + $22 + $20 + $22)/5 = $21.40	M	13
42	B ($21 + $22 + $20 + $22 + $20)/5 = $21.00	M	13
43	D	M	16
44	D	M	16
45	A	M	13
46	C	M	15

Question	Answer	Level of Difficulty	Chapter
47	B Expected return = .15 x ($4,500/ [$4,500 + $2,500]) + .07 x ($2,500/ [$4,500 + $2,500]) = 12%	M	15
48	C	M	20
49	C The capital gain of $5,000 on the maturity guarantee is offset by the capital loss of $5,000.	M	20
50	D	D	20
51	A	M	15
52	D	M	26
53	D	M	17
54	D	D	18
55	C	M	27
56	B	M	19
57	A	M	18
58	C	E	13
59	D	M	16
60	C	M	22
61	C $12/(1 – .035) = $12.44	M	18
62	B 0.44/$12 = 3.67%	M	18
63	B	M	18
64	C Basic EPS = (10M – 1M)/1M = $9.00; fully diluted EPS = 10M/(1M + 0.2M) = $8.33	D	14
65	C	M	19
66	C (24 + [5 × $2.50] – $26)/$26 = 40.4%	D	15
67	B	M	16
68	A	M	22
69	B	M	26
70	C	E	16

Question	Answer	Level of Difficulty	Chapter
71	C	M	25
72	B	M	19
73	A	M	15
74	A	M	13
75	D	M	13
76	B	M	23
77	B (.09 × \$200,000/850,000) + (.10 × \$220,000/850,000) + (.12 × \$430,000/850,000) = 10.78%	M	15
78	C	M	23
79	D	M	24
80	D (\$140 × 1.45 × 0.15) – (\$140 × 1.45 × 0.19)= \$ –8.12, or \$0	D	25
81	C	E	24
82	C	M	24
83	D	M	24
84	B	M	19
85	B The maximum federal credit = 0.15 × \$5,000 (limit for credit) = \$750 provincial credit = \$750; net after-tax contribution to RRSP = \$6,000 – \$750 – \$750 – (\$6,000 × 0.40) = \$2,100	D	18
86	C	M	18
87	D	M	24
88	D	M	25
89	B	M	18
90	A	M	22
91	B	M	22
92	D	M	20
93	D	M	20

Question	Answer	Level of Difficulty	Chapter
94	C	E	14
95	C	M	26
96	C	M	27
97	A	M	27
98	D	M	16
99	A	M	26
100	B Options A, C, and D are overly conservative and also entail higher taxes on interest income.	M	26